After Raymond Williams

Writing Wales in English

CREW series of Critical and Scholarly Studies
General Editor: Professor M. Wynn Thomas (CREW, Swansea University)

This *CREW* series is dedicated to Emyr Humphreys, a major figure in the literary culture of modern Wales, a founding patron of the *Centre for Research into the English Literature and Language of Wales*, and, along with Gillian Clarke and Seamus Heaney, one of *CREW*'s Honorary Associates. Grateful thanks are extended to Richard Dynevor for making this series possible.

Other titles in the series
Stephen Knight, *A Hundred Years of Fiction* (978-0-7083-1846-1)
Barbara Prys-Williams, *Twentieth-century Autobiography* (978-0-7083-1891-1)
Kirsti Bohata, *Postcolonialism Revisted* (978-0-7083-1892-8)
Chris Wigginton, *Modernism from the Margins* (978-0-7083-1927-7)
Linden Peach, *Contemporary Irish and Welsh Women's Fiction* (978-0-7083-1998-7)
Sarah Prescott, *Eighteenth-Century Writing from Wales: Bards and Britons* (978-0-7083-2053-2)

After Raymond Williams:

Cultural Materialism and the Break-Up of Britain

Writing Wales in English

HYWEL ROWLAND DIX

UNIVERSITY OF WALES PRESS
CARDIFF
2008

British Library Cataloguing-in-Publication Data
A catalogue record for this book is available from the British Library.

ISBN   978-0-7083-26640
e.ISBN 978-0-7083-26657

THE *A*SSOCIATION FOR
*W*ELSH *W*RITING IN *E*NGLISH
*C*YMDEITHAS *L*ÊN *S*AESNEG *C*YMRU

Recommended text

Typeset in Wales by Eira Fenn Gaunt, Cardiff
Printed by CPI Antony Rowe, Chippenham, Wiltshire

CONTENTS

General Editor's Preface

The aim of this series is to produce a body of scholarly and critical work that reflects the richness and variety of the English-language literature of modern Wales. Drawing upon the expertise both of established specialists and of younger scholars, it will seek to take advantage of the concepts, models and discourses current in the best contemporary studies to promote a better understanding of the literature's significance, viewed not only as an expression of Welsh culture but also as an instance of modern literatures in English world-wide. In addition, it will seek to make available the scholarly materials (such as bibliographies) necessary for this kind of advanced, informed study.

M. Wynn Thomas,
Director, CREW (*Centre for Research into the English Language and Literature of Wales*)
Swansea University

ACKNOWLEDGEMENTS

This book began life as a doctoral thesis at the University of Glamorgan. I would like to thank Jane Aaron and Jeff Wallace for giving me the opportunity to undertake the research which led to its writing. Both of them have been extremely generous in their time and in their criticism of early drafts of the project.

Other friends and colleagues who made the University of Glamorgan a stimulating and supportive environment in which to carry out research were Steve Blandford, Gavin Edwards, Claire Flay, Diana Wallace, Alyn Webley and Martin Willis.

I am grateful to Professor Dai Smith, currently of Swansea University, for giving me the opportunity to view certain Raymond Williams manuscripts first-hand, and for taking the time to comment on early versions of some of this work.

It would have been impossible to produce a study of this kind without engaging explicitly with Tom Nairn's seminal book *The Break-Up of Britain*, as well as with the entire Raymond Williams oeuvre. My debt to both writers is fully acknowledged.

Ever since publication of the first edition of *After Raymond Williams* my most generous and loving reader has been my partner Rosemary Edwards whose willingness to listen to me trying out ideas made it seem worth writing them up. Finally, I would like to thank my family, Lesley Dix, Andrew Dix and Gareth Dix for showing an enthusiastic and encouraging attitude throughout the period of research. In a real sense, my first experiences of crossing the many different internal borders of the United Kingdom were provided by my grandfather Leslie Davies. It saddens me more than I can say that he did not survive to see this project completed.

ABBREVIATIONS

A full bibliographic entry is provided the first time each book by Raymond Williams is referred to in the text. Thereafter, the following abbreviations are used:

BC   *Border Country* (1960)
CC   *The Country and the City* (1973)
CS   *Culture and Society* (1958)
DIB   *Drama from Ibsen to Brecht* (1968)
DIE   *Drama from Ibsen to Eliot* (1952)
EN   *The English Novel from Dickens to Lawrence* (1970)
FM   *The Fight for Manod* (1979)
L   *Loyalties* (1985)
LR   *The Long Revolution* (1961)
ML   *Marxism and Literature* (1977)
PF   *Preface to Film* (1954)
PL   *Politics and Letters* (1979)
PM   *The Politics of Modernism* (1989)
PMC   *Problems in Materialism and Culture* (1980)
RH   *Resources of Hope* (1988)
SG   *Second Generation* (1984)
T   *Television: Technology and Cultural Form* (1974)
T2000   *Towards 2000* (1983)
V   *The Volunteers* (1978)
WCS   *What I Came to Say* (1989)
WS   *Writing in Society* (1984)
WSW   *Who Speaks for Wales?* (2003)

Foreword to the New Edition

Since the first edition of this book was published, there have been a number of important developments in the political process of devolution around the United Kingdom. In Wales, the nationalist political party Plaid Cymru experienced its first period of office in the so-called One Wales Assembly coalition with the Welsh Labour Party between 2007 and 2011. During the same period, the limited legislative powers introduced by the 2006 Government of Wales Act were enhanced after the 2011 referendum on law-making powers, resulting in the Welsh Assembly's status being increased to that of Welsh Government. In Northern Ireland, Martin McGuinness of the Irish Republican political party Sinn Féin retained the position of Deputy First Minister in the province's power-sharing Executive following the 2011 Assembly election, in which the party increased both its share of the popular vote and its number of seats. In Scotland, the Scottish National Party has become a party of government and a timetable has been set for holding a referendum on potential independence from the rest of the United Kingdom. Indeed, it seems likely that of the many different questions being asked of British political life in the second decade of the twenty-first century, one with among the most far-reaching implications will be: what will the people of Scotland vote?

It will be argued here that this question has political and cultural consequences that extend far beyond the Scottish border. It will also be argued, however, that behind the question, 'What will the people of Scotland vote?' lies another question of almost equal contemporary cultural importance. This second question is not *what* will the Scottish people vote, but *how* will they *decide*? To move from the surface question relating to the potential outcome of a proposed referendum to a deeper theoretical question about how the electorate will make their decisions is to open up important further questions of criteria, experience, judgement and evidence: what are the benchmarks by which the Scottish people will measure their sense of nationhood? How will they identify

and articulate those benchmarks? Is Scottish nationalism a phenomenon that can only be extrapolated through political separatism, or does
it have a cultural element that is able to flourish with or without full
independence? What in any case is the relationship between a national
culture and the politics of national independence movements? These are
the questions that the Scottish voters will have to ask themselves when
deciding whether or not to vote for full political independence from the
rest of the United Kingdom. In other words, just as answering the
question, 'What will the Scottish people vote?' has major implications
for the future of the United Kingdom, so too answering the question,
'How will the Scottish people decide?' will be hardly any less significant
in revealing the different definitions and approaches to nationalism in
contemporary Scotland – and other parts of the United Kingdom.

The shift in emphasis from 'What will the Scottish people vote?' to
'How will the Scottish people decide?' reveals that the political question,
like perhaps all political questions, has to be interrogated before it can
be answered, inviting us to wonder not just what decision the Scottish
electorate will make, but what mental process the voters will go through
in order to make their minds up. Two of the arguments presented by
this book are that the Welsh writer Raymond Williams advocated the
extension of participatory democracy through the enfranchisement
of a culturally literate populace, and that this has implications for
the political process known as devolution. The book will explore how
political and cultural judgements inform each other, and how Williams
attempted to theorize the relationship between the two in a complex
manner that he referred to as cultural materialism. It will argue that
the dialectical relationship that exists between culture and politics has
been pivotal in bringing about a gradual increase in cultural confidence in Wales and Scotland, bringing the latter towards its moment
of decision.

In Wales, in the short term at least, a referendum on independence
is not on the cards. This does not mean, however, that the people of
Wales have no decision to make. In a famous summation of Welsh
cultural history, Gwyn Alf Williams concluded that Wales is an 'artefact'
that the Welsh people 'produce' – if they want to.[1] Possibly because
Wales has a longer history of amalgamation to a wider Britain than
Scotland has; perhaps because the culture and people of Wales have
been more thoroughly assimilated than have those of Scotland; and
perhaps because the nationalist political party Plaid Cymru was for a

long time associated exclusively with the claims to cultural nationhood of a Welsh-speaking minority, movements for political separatism
have been more muted in Wales than in Scotland. On the other hand,
the fragile 'yes' vote in the 1997 referendum on devolution in Wales
and the clearer second 'yes' vote on the extending of legislative powers
to the Welsh Government in 2011 indicate that the Welsh people feel
a certain appetite for continuing the cultural work that is also the
political work of creating the artefact of the Welsh nation.

In other words, although there is not currently a timetable for further
electoral devolution in Wales – as there is in Scotland – it nevertheless
remains true that the people of Wales have also to ask themselves
what kind of nation they wish to inhabit, and how they can bring such
a nation about. Moreover, just as the increasing political autonomy of
the devolved nations of Britain requires that the people in those
nations make this decision for themselves, so too is it true of the people
of England. Indeed, Raymond Williams was aware of the danger of
seeing England as a kind of vacuum, as if it can be defined merely by
what remains of the United Kingdom when the other nations have
either devolved or seceded. Implicit in the increasing autonomy and
self-rule in Northern Ireland, Scotland and Wales is the necessity of redefining and re-articulating a confident English culture. In other words,
the political process of increased self-representation in Northern Ireland,
Scotland and Wales necessitates new forms of representation in England.[2]
Those forms of representation in turn will be both political and cultural.
If they are to have any political efficacy, they must gain assent in the
popular imagination and this is the area in which the domain of the
political intersects with the domain of the cultural for it is in the cultural
imagination that political questions come to be recognized, valorized
or contested.

This relationship between cultural expression and political articulation is perhaps important in any society in the world. What gives it
a distinctively British flavour is the question of whether or not anyone
sees political, economic or cultural benefit in remaining part of a wider
British union; whether some or all four of the nations of Britain would
benefit from seceding; or whether a range of as-yet unimagined forms
of political representation might be brought into existence, capable
of articulating simultaneously the aspirations of a range of different
nationalisms and a form of continued political federation. How individuals answer this question for themselves, around the different nations

of the United Kingdom, is likely to depend at least in part on how they read and interpret the history of the United Kingdom's multinational state, as the two following accounts aim to show.

HISTORICIZING THE UNITED KINGDOM

In a paraphrase of Gwyn Alf Williams's 'When was Wales?', Arthur Aughey has raised the question 'When was Britain?' in order to explore the historical construction of the United Kingdom, and the implications its history has for recent and current political relationships in Britain. Aughey echoes Linda Colley in suggesting that the concepts of *Britain* and of *Britons* came into being as such in the aftermath of the 1707 Act of Union between England and Scotland. Aughey also follows Colley in outlining the construction of *Britain* and *Britishness* as a process that was actively created and cultivated by the political class through recourse to myth making and the popularization of 'national' narratives of all kinds from 1707 up until the accession of Queen Victoria in 1830. In other words, during the period of nascent imperialism, the national identity of a greater Britain was cultivated among the people of England, Scotland, Wales and Ireland through the gradual development of what would later (and retrospectively) come to be known as the discipline of English literature, which provided a coherent vehicle for the imperialism that would be propounded in the name of that Britain. Similarly, the people living in England, Scotland, Wales and Ireland had their Britishness inflicted on them by the political class in the same period in order to drive that vehicle. In Aughey's view, this historical experience of having a greater national identity inflicted on the populace by a minority class gave rise to a particular paradox, the 'paradox of Britishness'.[3] Britishness is a paradox because since the Glorious Revolution of 1688, the people living on the islands of Britain have articulated their relationship to the political order primarily in terms of individual liberty and of freedom from tyranny. This liberty of the free-born individual as such is the very thing that is surrendered in the process of having a greater political identity imposed from above, despite the material and economic benefits offered by participation in empire, so that Aughey's paradox can be expressed in a rhetorical question: how is it possible to obey the laws laid down by a patrician class and retain an individual sense of liberty?

One potential resolution to this paradox was suggested by Tom Nairn in *The Break-Up of Britain*, where Nairn argued that only a radical idea of the people could square individual liberty with systematic politicization, because there should be an ideal bond of continuity or solidarity between the ruling class and the people. In such a situation, members of the ruling class would *be* the people. Unfortunately, however, Nairn also suggested in *The Break-Up of Britain* that unlike in revolutionary France or America, this idea of the people as a popular participatory political class has largely been absent in Britain. For this reason, Nairn argued, no level of accommodation, management or redefinition can transform the British political state into anything other than an imperial state – increasingly lacking in the material prosperity and moral guardianship cultivated by empire; and hence that the British state will inevitably have to be succeeded by a series of different political formations.

Contra Nairn, Aughey argues that there was a strong populist element in the make-up of the British state during the years 1707–1830, and that this was so because the concept of Britishness itself was not only an imperial construct; it also had an important domestic orientation. Aughey therefore does not locate the paradox of Britishness – or its potential resolution – in the peculiar simultaneous presence and absence of the British people in the political imagination, but in a different (and equally paradoxical) idea of the *constitution*. Though unwritten, Aughey suggests, the particular effect of the British constitution is to provide a new 'persona' for the people of and across Britain, capable of envisaging a common sense of belonging while also allowing for a dualism of national difference within a British whole in each of the nations.[4] It is in this constitutional flexibility and duality that Aughey situates a tradition of populist political action and solidarity across national borders within Britain. This constitutional flexibility, Aughey argues, kept alive the potential popular nationalisms of Scotland and England post-1707 by enabling each half of the partnership to gain from it. Similarly, it enabled the Ulster Unionists to remain distinctively Irish while also having access to the wider solidarity, economic benefits and security offered by participation in empire. Moreover, as history has taken away the symbolic affinity with empire, Aughey thinks that a flexible idea of the 'constitutional people' has become more immediately available to members of Britain's ethnic minorities, allowing them to belong both to a sub-culture, and something transcendent, at the same time.[5]

For Aughey, an idea of the constitutional people therefore resolves the paradox of Britishness by combining a political process of entering into contract, with an imaginative bond of solidarity. Political separatists in the different nations of Britain, he argues, tend to overvalue the concept of the contract, because this keeps alive the sense of different nations actively deciding to enter into the union. By contrast, unionists tend to favour the idea of solidarity, seeing in the British whole a transcendent quality with benefits for all along with a commitment to equality. In Aughey's account, the constitution mediates between political structures and individual liberties, and this mediator role held the United Kingdom together as a functioning state for perhaps three centuries. Only when constitutional change occurs does the state of the union as such need to be re-visited.

Aughey argues that this is what happened in 1997, the year of two large events: the 'yes' votes in Scotland and Wales; and the funeral of Princess Diana. He contrasts the relatively narrow margins of each of the 'yes' votes with a large, public and participatory response to the death of Diana, in which he identifies an idea of popular political action that Nairn had struggled to find in British public culture. In *After Britain*, Nairn argued that the United Kingdom's political class has only been able to keep itself afloat since the 1970s by managing a series of discrete, individual crises; that none of these episodes would enable the political class to redeem the British state from its imperial past; and that therefore the state itself should be abandoned.[6] In contrast, Aughey's commitment to a combination of the popular with the political underwrites a belief that the British political state can still function in the manner of an effective democracy and that as such it can give rise to new kinds of civic nationalism capable of continuing the duality of national identities he had argued arose from the constitution.

Aughey's reading of political devolution springs from this position: he sees it primarily as a mechanism for holding the overall union together in a new way – which is precisely how it was envisaged by New Labour. Whether it has been interpreted in the same way in the different nations is a different question. Aughey argues that a dual constitutional nationalism is capable of transforming the terms of contemporary political debates from a logic of 'either/or' to a plurality of different positions, expressed by the word 'and': Scottish *and* British or Welsh *and* British.[7] This logic of 'and' enables Aughey to argue that devolution itself is primarily a political policy aimed at guaranteeing the continuing political sovereignty of the metropolitan centre. The Labour Party that enacted that policy had been committed to state socialism for much of the twentieth century and had needed to change this prerogative in order to achieve mainstream electoral success in an era when the majority of British voters no longer saw themselves as working class. For New Labour, abandoning socialism also entailed abandoning political centralism so that the dispersal of power implicit in devolution could be presented as a constitutional libertarianism. In other words, the imperative for devolution was not national, in the Scottish or Welsh sense. It was based on a new concept of the citizenry across the United Kingdom, where devolution would supply the citizens with political liberty and solidarity equally everywhere.

To put it another way, New Labour was not hugely enthusiastic for self-rule in the different nations of Britain, and devolution was certainly not a case of New Labour simply capitulating to traditional electoral allies in Scotland and Wales. Rather, the party saw devolution as a practical way of protecting Scotland and Wales from the onslaughts of Thatcherism and the assaults on local government powers that occurred throughout the 1980s and of maintaining the union. In order to become electable in England, New Labour had to convince members of the English middle class that it, rather than the Conservatives, would look after their interests best. In other words, the irony of devolution is that the success of New Labour, which delivered it, was dependent on re-building Labour as an electoral entity in the south of England. To do this, it had to present itself as the party of individual liberty – hence the apparatus of devolution, which are designed to provide that liberty against centralization, while at the same time maintaining an overall union of the newly envisaged citizenry – in a new kind of solidarity across the nations.

Aughey believes that the success of New Labour indicates that the idea of the constitutional people continues to hold powerful – perhaps majority – appeal around the nations of the United Kingdom. He suggests this is because it combines a politically underwritten guarantee of individual liberty with an imaginative solidarity wherein the constitutional individual is capable of combining two or more different allegiances.

To Aughey, this constitutional dualism has the advantage that it defines national identity in civic, rather than ethnic, terms. For example, he suggests that British ethnic communities might fear that they will be 'locked out emotionally' if the nationalisms of England, Wales, Scotland and Ireland become too chauvinistic and ethnocentric. By contrast, the pan-British whole provides a transcendent – as opposed to an exclusivist – sense of identity.[8]

In developing his sense of constitutional dualism, Aughey returns to a question Tom Nairn had asked in 1977 at the start of *The Break-Up of Britain*: why did populist political response to the economic crises of the 1970s mainly become manifest in neo-nationalism in the different nations of Britain, as opposed to socialism across it? In answering this, Aughey points out that many socialists had wanted to do away with nationalism altogether, and that in doing so, they failed to acknowledge the 'secondary identification' on which modern nation states were founded.

'Secondary identification' refers to the process, first theorized during the enlightenment by Hegel, whereby the modern nation is born when its people stop identifying with others at a purely local level, and instead identify, on a secondary level, with something bigger, that is, the nation. Aughey refers to 'secondary identification' as a 'nationalization of the ethnic' because it is a process of extrapolating bonded identities and cultures at a very local level onto more and more diverse circles of identification.[9] In the original 'Introduction' to *After Raymond Williams*, which follows this 'Foreword to the New Edition', it is argued that Williams associated the elaboration of national identification in Britain with the growth of the popular press and the expansion of a British railway network because these are the things that enabled secondary identification to occur.

'Secondary elaboration' enables the concept of the modern nation state to take hold in the popular imagination by situating a series of different local relationships in the context of a much broader set of relationships than any of the local levels on which it is operative. In this sense, the national offers to subsume the local in something greater and provide a transcendent structure to a series of otherwise diverse localities. According to Aughey, the renewed confidence of nationalist movements in Scotland and Wales can be seen as the reversal of that whole process of nationalizing the ethnic. By questioning the transcendent quality of the United Kingdom as a whole, those nationalist movements reverse the work of secondary elaboration that had enabled the United Kingdom to be imagined out of those very different ingredients. Aughey concludes that whereas the creation of the United Kingdom was tantamount to a 'nationalization of the ethnic', the questioning or unpicking of the United Kingdom is therefore the exact opposite – a re-articulation of difference at local level, and what he calls an 'ethnicization of the national'.[10]

By 'ethnicization of the national' Aughey refers to the return to or re-discovery of the locally different elements that had been made to cohere into a national whole during the process of secondary identification. In the case of the United Kingdom, this refers to the rediscovery – or at times re-assertion – of the cultural differences between the different people of England, Scotland, Wales and Northern Ireland, as opposed to the transcendent quality that had held them together. Perhaps, though, 'ethnic' is a slightly unfortunate term because the theoretical model of the 'ethnicization of the national' appears relatively closed to a real range of different ethnicities. It starts with one set of ethnicities at a local level – Scottish, English and Welsh – and extrapolates them onto a larger national unit – British – before collapsing them back again as if the end product of the process will neatly mirror the starting material. This relatively closed model of national identity appears to leave little room for the introduction or inclusion of ethnic diversity or multicultural identities. As a result, despite his enthusiasm for the constitutional dualities propounded by his view of devolution, Aughey's account of the prospects for multi-ethnic secondary identification in Britain after devolution seem idealistic, perhaps naive.

DECOUPLING NATION AND ETHNICITY

In many ways, the arguments presented by Aughey in *Nationalism, Devolution and the Challenge to the United Kingdom State* are complementary to those expounded in Michael Gardiner's *Cultural Roots of British Devolution*. Where Aughey identifies resources of hope for the prospects of a civic and inclusive multicultural Britain based on the duality of national identities following a logic of 'British and –', Gardiner provides a materialist reading of the distinction between ethnic and civic nationalisms in the four nations of Britain in order to argue that new kinds of nationalism in each of them have become necessary because no really democratic society can be imagined without the latter, that is civic, kind.

Gardiner started off by noting that modes of cultural analysis in the post-devolution nations of Britain have increasingly been informed by postcolonial approaches. Against a rising current of enthusiasm for such work, he points out that the people of Scotland, Wales and Northern Ireland have all in different ways been deeply implicated – not to mention directly involved – in the process of imperialism, so that any straightforward reading of devolution that claims a postcolonial identity for those nations does not sit well with their material history.[11]

Like Aughey, Gardiner begins his inquiry into the cultural origins of devolution in Britain by asking the question, 'When was Britain?' Like Aughey and Colley, he situates the invention of Britain some time after the 1707 Act of Union – specifically, one generation later. Perhaps the most innovative element of Gardiner's research is his location of the forging of Britishness in the context of eighteenth-century thought, which he claims was primarily experienced in Britain in the form of the Scottish enlightenment, which in turn was also the origin of the concept of a British canon of English literature. Through a reading of Adam Smith and David Hume, Gardiner argues that the first philosophical overtures towards a British empire originated in the Scottish enlightenment idea of free trade and efficient global management of resources. He also demonstrates that the idea of English literature arose at the same time in the work of Smith and Hume in order to drive the ideological vehicle of imperialism. In other words, during the same generation that Scottish intellectuals started to cultivate an imaginative symbolic identity with the British whole during the late eighteenth century, Gardiner argues that they also advocated the expansion of a British empire. The ideological justification of that empire was to be provided through the dissemination of a pan-British Anglophone literature. For Gardiner, a logical deduction to be drawn from this (unlike in Aughey's account) is that *Britain, Britons, Britishness* and *English literature* were all exclusively imperial constructs, with no domestic orientation at all. Accordingly, to enter into a post-imperial phase of history is to enter also a phase when those constructs have become obsolescent and when their historical *raison d'être* no longer obtains.

Gardiner's reading of devolution stems from this position. He reasons that confronting the political realities of post-imperial Britain requires that Scotland, Wales and Northern Ireland come to terms with the fact of their own involvement in empire on the one hand – militating against a straightforward reading of cultural nationalisms based on postcolonial modes of analysis in each case; and that England comes to terms with the fact that it never had an empire, which was rather an effect of *Britain* and *Britishness*, on the other.

Since no democracy can be possible without a commitment to nationalism as such, Gardiner argues that the post-devolution cultural challenge in each of the nations of Britain is to come to terms with these uncomfortable truths of the imperial past and therefore implicitly to catch up with, perhaps create, new forms of cultural and political representation. This has started to occur in Scotland and Wales, but since new political forms do not yet exist in England, Gardiner argues that a civic sense of post-imperial English nationalism has not yet become possible. As a result of having only recently been established in Scotland and Wales, and not at all in England, Gardiner suggests that the political forms capable of generating a civic post-British nationalism in each of the nations of Britain do not yet really exist. Therefore, he suggests that the emerging nationalisms in each case can only be ethnocentric in the first instance, because no other means of expressing such nationalism has yet become available. How rapidly each nation is able to make the transition from an ethnic nationalism to a civic nationalism, he concludes, will be one indicator of the success or otherwise of the new cultural and political forms in the post-union nations of Britain. In the required move beyond an ethnocentric stage of nationalism, for example, he sees the novelist Salman Rushdie as properly belonging to a specifically English tradition of popular cultural activism that can be traced back through William Morris and William Wordsworth, as far back as the middle ages, when arguably England was involved neither in a wider British union or an empire.[12]

Aughey and Gardiner provide complementary readings of the postcolonial phase of British history, and therefore different ways of approaching the question, 'How will the people of Scotland decide?' In Aughey's account, political devolution is a unionist policy aimed at maintaining and guaranteeing overall political sovereignty at the centre. As a result, the devolved nations cannot be considered *post*-colonial. To Gardiner, by contrast, the nations of Britain were more deeply imbricated in the process of imperialism than some recent thinkers and theorists would imply. Therefore, the histories of those nations belong to the history of the colonizer rather than to that of the colonized, and they cannot be considered post-*colonial*.

In Wales, Scotland and Northern Ireland, the established political units have created opportunities for building the civic, participatory and democratic nationalisms that Gardiner advocates – and that in part draw on the increasing confidence in those nations that arises from rich, renewed and re-made cultural resources. Gardiner argues that post-imperial Englishness is a concept that has started to be explored – and re-made – in the popular multicultural forms of some kinds of music, film and literature, but without a corresponding system of post-imperial English political representation. Gardiner's argument is that Britain itself was an imperial construct, and that Britain, not England, was the main player in imperial history. As a result, he refers to the British state not as a 'nation-state' but as an 'empire-state' – and one increasingly without an empire.[13] Gardiner's conclusion is that in superseding this empire state the people of England also have a choice to make: either to hold onto the remaining apparatus of the former empire state; or to supersede it with a new English populist and partici-patory political state. Only, he concludes, if the English political class continue to uphold the machinery of the imperial state will it retro-spectively become possible to suggest that the other nations of Britain have entered postcolonial phases of history.

Like Linda Colley, Aughey and Gardiner both conclude that British-ness was an imperial construct brought into being through conscious political intervention and the propagation of new popular narratives of empire during the century after the 1707 Act of Union. In other words, the British empire and the category of English literature are revealed to have a common origin. In Gardiner's account, *Britain* is exclusively a Scottish and imperial construct of the 'long' eighteenth century. The shifting pre-history of that creation is relatively under-valued in Gardiner's account, as is his unhistorical reference to the history of the relationship between England and Wales, which he takes simply as an a priori object waiting for insertion in the union during the 1700s, rather than a product of conscious intervention and conflict over a much earlier and longer period. As a result, the argument that he presents maps an already established England-and-Wales onto a unionist history that is assumed to have started exclusively during the Scottish enlightenment. This uninterrogated mapping in turn informs the kind of argument he is able to present: that Scottish and Welsh history cannot be considered postcolonial in any simplistic way because of the involvement of those nations in the project of empire. What this fails to account for is the very different nature of the involvement of each nation. Scotland entered the union through the conscious choice of its parliament; its philosophers and political figures took the lead in advocating imperial practices, rather than following where they were led. By contrast, and as Kirsti Bohata convincingly argued in *Postcolonialism Revisited*, Wales entered the union through an experience of military subjugation, legal denial of its status as a nation, and economic and cultural subordination.[14] Its involvement in empire was one of following rather than one of leading.

Perhaps as a corrective to Gardiner's exclusive situating of Britishness in the context of the Scottish enlightenment, therefore, John Kerrigan's *Archipelagic English* analyses the role played by cultural production in bringing about a sense of Britishness across the islands during the century and a half *before* 1707 rather than *after* it.[15] Marc Morris goes further and locates the early stages of the forging of Britain in the reign of Edward I in the 1270s.[16] In many ways, Emyr Humphreys had already gone even further again in his *Taliesin Tradition*, providing a completely different history of the Britishness of Welsh culture from the early Christian era onwards.[17] Indeed, Humphreys's work was praised by Raymond Williams precisely because it provided this oppositional reading of the relationship of Welsh culture to the British whole. Williams, like Humphreys, pointed out that 'the long Welsh experience of a precarious and threatened identity' had 'informed' the kinds of cultural thought operative in Wales.[18]

The important point here is not that the people of Wales saw any less enthusiasm or opportunity in imperialism than did the people of Scotland, and Gardiner is on firm ground when taking to task those who would deny such fervent historical imperial nationalism in Scotland and Wales during the period of British imperialism. It is more that the historical experience and conditions in which the people of each nation cultivated their enthusiasm for imperialism was different in each case.

WILLIAMS, THE RETROSPECTIVE AND THE PRE-EMERGENT

At first glance, Raymond Williams's thinking on imperialism and the extent to which the contemporary nations of the United Kingdom can be considered postcolonial appears to be unequivocal, even perhaps unnuanced. However, deeper examination reveals a fault line in his thinking, a fault line that once identified can be detected in many different areas of his work and which points towards a lack of systematic analysis with

regard to the role of the nations of Britain in colonization and also therefore towards an equally incomplete thinking through of the cultural and
political implications of devolution. In other words, although this book
was written as an attempt to elucidate a strain in Williams's writing about
how culture plays an important part in the making of political decisions
in the area of devolution and vice versa, the fact that this strain required
elucidating rather than having been argued analytically in Williams's
own work in full suggests that many of his ideas on the topic remained
latent rather than fully formed. There is in his work an occasional in-
consistency with regard to the different nationalisms in Britain, and, in
particular, their sometimes common and sometimes divergent histories.[19]

For example, when Williams writes about early postcolonial novelists
such as Achebe, Ngugi and Naipaul in *The Country and the City* (1973),
he evaluates their work positively because in it, 'we can see the history
happening, see it being made, from the base of an England which, within
our own literature, has been so differently described'.[20] Yet the 'we' and
'our' used by Williams to inform the terms of the discussion is under-
conceptualized. Is this a British 'we'? A Welsh 'we'? An English 'we'
even? As is argued in chapter 4 of this book, Williams was working on
The Country and the City at the same time as his novel *The Volunteers*,
in which he juxtaposes authoritarian violence in a then imagined post-
devolution Wales with colonial violence in Kenya in order to imply
some kind of parallel between the two. He seems to hint that there is
a common historical experience between the two nations, possibly in
a common shared experience of having been colonized. However, the
precise nature of that parallel is not grounded historically, leading to
the under-theorization of Williams's speaking 'we'.

Given that elsewhere in his work Williams attempts to develop a
materialist reading of Welsh cultural history orientated towards the
cultivation of an anti-capitalist, anti-imperial national consciousness,
this under-theorization of his speaking 'we' is a significant limitation.
It contrasts strikingly, for example, with the 'we' invoked when Williams
is discussing Welsh literature, as in his discussion of 'The Welsh Industrial
Novel' where he places the development of twentieth-century Welsh
working-class fiction in English in the context of a wider history since
the Industrial Revolution: 'if we have learned to look in this way, it is
no surprise to find at the centre of so many of the Welsh industrial
novels of this period one decisive experience: the General Strike of
1926 in its specifically Welsh form' (*WSW*, p. 104). Williams's Welsh

'we' is uncomplicated and unambiguous, perhaps even over-idealistic, especially in his conclusion about the earlier Welsh industrial writers of the 1930s: 'it is right to look back and to honour . . . that effective generation, that brotherhood of fiction writers; adapting as we can' (*WSW*, p. 110). This single, unquestioned and unproblematic use of 'we' is in contrast to the unselfconscious complexities introduced into Williams's work by the earlier uninterrogated use of a British 'we' fraught with ambiguities, contradictions and unexamined assumptions. It is only when the two are read alongside each other that Williams's inability fully to conceptualize *Britain*, *England* and *Wales* becomes apparent.

Williams himself appears to have been at least partly aware of this inability; indeed, his thinking and writing engaged more explicitly with the areas of Welsh culture, history and politics from the mid 1970s onwards. Yet the problem of clarifying the distinction between *British*, *English* and *Welsh* history does not go away in his work and neither does he fully rise to the challenge of achieving such a distinction.

For Welsh readers, one of the most frustrating moments in Michael Gardiner's (later) study of the cultural roots of devolution in Britain is the moment at which Gardiner suggests that the distinctive education system that exists in Scotland is likely to help the generation of a civic political culture because the system of proportional representation that exists in the Scottish Parliament can allow for a greater plurality of voices than in England and Wales.[21] Not only does Gardiner fail to register the fact that the kind of proportional representation operative in the Scottish Parliament is of the same kind as that operative in the Welsh Government,[22] but he also fails to examine or interrogate the historical construction of the unit 'England and Wales' that he takes for granted.[23] Similarly, and of equal frustration to Welsh readers, is the short-sightedness with which Gardiner suggests that the legacy of Chartism and the foundation of the welfare state should be interpreted primarily as indicators of the resources available to a civic post-British *English* political nationalism.[24] There is no mention at all of the Welsh contribution to those things or to the historical resources that contribution provides for a potential renewal of Welsh populist political culture.

These are precisely the methodological blind spots that a Welsh writer and activist such as Williams might have been expected to avoid. It is, however, quite symptomatic of the incomplete nature of Williams's attempt to theorize the relationship between *Britain*, *England* and *Wales*

that his whole oeuvre includes relatively little reference to the Welsh
contribution to either Chartism or the welfare state – which might if
Williams had got that there have been important cornerstones for a fully
thought through programme of Welsh populist political culture. In a
review of the book *When Was Wales?* in 1985, Williams shows himself
to be aware of the need for a detailed historical reconstruction of the
relationship between England and Wales, but stops short of generating
such analysis himself:

> One of the central advantages of being born and bred among the
> presumed Welsh is the profusion of official identities. Wales and
> Monmouthshire, as it was for me at school, with special force since
> we lived in the appendage. England-and-Wales: that administrative,
> legal and even weather-forecasting area. Wales for rugby but All-
> England for cricket. Welsh Wales and English Wales. Wales and
> Cymru. To anyone looking for an official status it was a nightmare.
> To anyone trying to think about communities and societies a blessing.
> (*WSW*, p. 67)

To a very limited degree, Williams shows himself to be aware of the
historical construction of the amorphous political and cultural unit
'England and Wales'. To the extent that he draws attention to the different,
varying and at times overlapping formations, he also implicitly raises the
question of how that profusion of identities came into being in the first
place – yet without ever answering that question. To Williams in 1985,
the lack of clear, singular identities in favour of a range of complexities
is taken to be a blessing, rather than a nightmare. While the avoidance
of simplicities and banalities is an important part of Williams's critical
thinking however, the inability he reveals to explore the historical construction of 'England and Wales' underlines an ongoing shortfall in his
thinking. The singular is rejected as simplistic in favour of the complex
and the composite. Yet this fails to provide theoretical clarification of the
different elements that make up that composite whole. Arthur Aughey's
more recent clarification of some of the terms involved in the discussion,
and his commitment to a logic beyond 'either/or' embracing a logic of
'both . . . and' seems much more sophisticated by comparison.

   Williams had made one other attempt at trying to clarify the historical relationship between *Britain*, *England* and *Wales* in his essay on
'Welsh Culture' in 1975. Possibly owing to the political context of the

approaching referendum, his thinking here had come closer than anywhere else to carrying out that necessary act of historical and cultural
clarification. Ironically, Williams initially aligns himself and his Wales
with then current trends in postcolonial thinking. Indeed, the essay on
'Welsh Culture' registers one of Williams's few uses of the term 'postcolonial'. Here, though still in latent rather than fully extrapolated
form, he does approach a more nuanced understanding of the history
of Wales with regard to colonization and the history of the colonized:

> What is it that has happened? It is nothing surprising. It is in general
> very well known. To the extent that we are a people, we have been
> defeated, colonized, penetrated, incorporated. Never finally, of
> course. The living resilience, in many forms, has always been there.
> But its forms are distinct . . . There is a drawing back to some of our
> own resources. There is a very skillful kind of accommodation,
> finding a few ways to be recognized as different, which we then
> actively cultivate, while not noticing, beyond them, the profound
> resignation. These are some of the signs of a post-colonial culture,
> conscious all the time of its own real strengths and potentials, longing
> only to be itself, to become its own world but with so much, too
> much, on its back to be able, consistently, to face its real future.
> (*WSW*, p. 9)

The account begins with a straightforward claim for the history of Wales
as a history of the conquered and of the exploited. As it progresses,
however, something else intervenes. In Williams's account of the resilience
of Welsh culture made manifest in a series of cultural and political accommodations, a number of important points are hinted at more strongly
than elsewhere in his thinking, though without quite adding up to a clear
argument. The emphasis he places on the resilience of Welsh culture over
centuries of incorporation is clearly designed to align Williams with a
wider working-class consciousness, and in this sense it is interesting to
go from Gardiner's more recent refusal to see Scottish and Welsh history
as the history of colonized peoples to Williams's earlier insistence on
seeing Welsh history in that way. Yet Williams's reading of Welsh history
is neither as absolute nor as unambiguous in its claim to the history of
the colonized as its opening words proclaim. Behind the abstract reference
to the cultural and political 'accommodations' with imperialism that
Wales was drawn into during the period of empire is an uncomfortable
truth. It is not fully teased out but it is present nevertheless, and it is

tantamount to an acknowledgement that Wales itself, rather than having been the first colony of the British Empire in any simplistic sense, had taken its place as one of the partners within the imperial project. Williams hints, again without explicitly suggesting, that it was the long-term history of having been conquered, incorporated and rendered economically subordinate that had caused the people of Wales to seek compensation in the sense of belonging and relative prosperity offered by forming an accommodation with imperialism – which for several centuries they did. Chapter 2 will explore Williams's concept of the *pre-emergent* as that stage in the 1920s during which a minority of Welsh cultural and political thinkers started to imagine their relationship to the British Empire outside a partnership within the imperial project, and how the development of new forms of cultural and political representation in Wales since 1979, 1997 and 2010 all represent a transition from the *pre-emergent* to an *emergent* stage of Welsh cultural history.

To fully elucidate an account of the relationship between *Britain*, *England* and *Wales* from Williams is to draw out an account that was never fully developed in his own critical thinking. Re-reading the work of Williams in this reconstructive way supplements those more recent thinkers who situate the history of Wales either within the history of the colonizer or within the history of the colonized with a more subtle account of how, in the face of economic, linguistic, political and cultural pressures the people of Wales during the period of imperialism gradually came to see that their best interests were served by entering into the partnership of empire.[25] Which brings us back to the starting point, and the question of how people learn to make value judgements, both political and cultural.

It was suggested at the outset that what happens in the Scottish referendum on independence will have much broader implications for the people of twenty-first-century Britain. It was argued also that not only, 'What will the people of Scotland vote?', but 'How will they vote?' and 'How will they decide?' are the important questions to be asked by anyone interested in the analysis of contemporary British culture. Cultural materialism is the term and the practice Raymond Williams developed for analysing how we all learn to make value judgements historically, and for drawing attention to the fact that those political judgements always have a cultural underpinning – as the following chapters will show.[26]

Notes

[1] Gwyn Alf Williams, *When Was Wales?* (Harmondsworth: Penguin, 1985), p. 304.

[2] Raymond Williams, 'Wales and England' (1983), in *Who Speaks for Wales?: Nation, Culture Identity. Raymond Williams*, ed. Daniel Williams (Cardiff: University of Wales Press, 2003), pp. 15–26.

[3] Arthur Aughey, *Nationalism, Devolution and the Challenge to the United Kingdom State* (London: Pluto Press, 2001), p. 24.

[4] Ibid., p. 27.

[5] Ibid., p. 32.

[6] Tom Nairn, 'Introduction' to *After Britain* (London: Granta, 2000), pp. 1–17.

[7] Aughey, *Nationalism, Devolution and the Challenge to the United Kingdom State*, p. 56.

[8] Ibid., p. 58.

[9] Ibid., p. 113.

[10] Ibid.

[11] Michael Gardiner, *The Cultural Roots of British Devolution* (Edinburgh: Edinburgh University Press, 2004), p. 4.

[12] On the other hand, R. R. Davies suggests that the late middle ages was the period when the union was established precisely as the first stage of English imperialism. See R. R. Davies, *The First English Empire: Power and Identity in the British Isles, 1093–1343* (Oxford: Oxford University Press, 2002).

[13] Gardiner, *The Cultural Roots of British Devolution*, p. 168.

[14] Kirsti Bohata, *Postcolonialism Revisited* (Cardiff: University of Wales Press, 2004).

[15] John Kerrigan, 'Devolutionary Activities', in *Archipelagic English: Literature, History, and Politics, 1603–1707* (Oxford: Oxford University Press, 2008), pp. 79–90.

[16] Marc Morris, 'Uniting the Kingdom?', in *A Great and Terrible King: Edward I and the Forging of Britain* (London: Windmill, 2009), pp. 301–44.

[17] Emyr Humphreys, *The Taliesin Tradition* (Bridgend: Seren, 1989; first published 1983).

[18] Raymond Williams, 'Community', in *Who Speaks for Wales?*, p. 29.

[19] These points have been explored in detail since the publication of the first edition of this book in Dai Smith's biography of Williams, *Raymond Williams: A Warrior's Tale* (Cardigan: Parthian, 2008).

[20] Raymond Williams, *The Country and the City* (1973; London: Hogarth, 1985), p. 285.

[21] Gardiner, *The Cultural Roots of British Devolution*, p. 72.

[22] See Aughey, *Nationalism, Devolution and the Challenge to the United Kingdom State*, p. 150.

[23] Gardiner, *The Cultural Roots of British Devolution*, p. 72.

[24] Ibid., p. 150; p. 174.

[25] See, for example, Bohata, *Postcolonialism Revisited*; Jane Aaron and Chris Williams (eds), *Postcolonial Wales* (Cardiff: University of Wales Press, 2005); Stephen Knight, *A Hundred Years of Fiction: From Colony to Independence* (Cardiff: University of Wales Press, 2004).

[26] That Williams developed the culturalist argument explicitly in contrast to figures such as Perry Anderson and Tom Nairn, who emphasized the importance of the development of new forms of political state, is argued by Daniel Williams in his 'Introduction: the return of the native', in *Who Speaks for Wales?*, xv–liii.

Introduction: Williams and Modernity

Cultural materialism is the name Raymond Williams gave to a series of theoretical and methodological perspectives that he worked out for the critical analysis of culture. He suggested that there is an important relationship between what is happening in a society and the content of the cultural forms produced by it. Moreover, the central proposition of cultural materialism is that this relationship is not merely reflexive or post-dated. Cultural forms and especially literature do not just reflect other social events. The creation of these things is also a material part of the make-up of the society.

The text in which Williams most succinctly propounded the central themes of cultural materialism was *The Country and the City* (1973). As an example of how writing plays an active part in social and historical processes, that study shows us how English literature became involved with a putative national tradition throughout the period of modernization, from about 1550 (the early modern period) to about 1880 (the period of high nationalism and imperialism).

Williams in *The Country and the City* looks at the tradition of country house writing, and probes its role in idealizing the social order of early capitalist Britain. He showed that texts such as Shakespeare's *The Tempest* or *Henry V* or Jonson's 'To Penshurst' are related to the political and social order of the day. By performing certain ideological and symbolic work, they contribute directly to its creation, and play a specific part in the dissemination of a poetics of nationhood.

Williams demonstrated that the relationship between writing and social order was dialectical. Events in the society give rise to their depiction in poetry; at the same time, the idealization that occurs in poetry strengthens and helps to cement the social order. This was true not only of the period in which the unified British nation-state was being created, but also of the period of empire. In other words, *The Country and the City* draws an implicit connection between the processes of nation building at home and of empire building overseas. Implicitly, then, the break-up of empire might be related to an accompanying break-up of the nation-state itself.

Raymond Williams's thinking about nationhood is best understood within the context of a range of theorizing on that subject that took place on the political left during the 1970s. We know that Williams had read Michael Hechter's important study *Internal Colonialism: The Celtic Fringe in British National Development, 1536–1960* (1975) by the end of that decade.[1] Similarly, he had read Tom Nairn's seminal text *The Break-Up of Britain* (1977) by the time of the 1979 referenda in Scotland and Wales.[2] We know moreover that Williams was interested in probing the dialectical relationship that exists between writing and political change. Looking back over the course of Williams's career with these facts in mind, it becomes apparent that examining the relationship between writing and the break-up of Britain was a consistent and important strand in Williams's thinking.

Other strands of course were there from the beginning. As a socialist political activist, Williams was interested in electoral reform; the education system; the relationship between technology and culture; and, above all, the ongoing need to resist the inequalities thrown up by capitalist society. Patrick Brantlinger has described his early work *Culture and Society* (1958), along with Richard Hoggart's *The Uses of Literacy* (1957) and E. P. Thompson's *The Making of the English Working Classes* (1961), as the 'founding texts' of British left-wing cultural analysis.[3] Previous studies such as Andrew Milner's *Cultural Materialism* and Anthony Easthope's *Literary into Cultural Studies* have dealt with these important aspects of Williams's work in detail.[4] The present study is the first to concentrate solely on the relationship between writing and the break-up of Britain as it was implicitly expounded in Williams's work.

Williams began his career with a fascination in the experience of cultural, political and economic modernity. This led him into an examination of the historical process of modernization in general, and the modernization of the nation-state in particular. This involved complex analysis of the interplay between the practices of nation building, capitalism and imperialism. The goal of his historical analysis was to develop a sense of how the nation, and in particular the national interest, can be rethought. Williams emphasised the fact that nationhood had originally been imagined into existence in part through its literature and cultural forms. Accordingly, to produce a different kind of literature is to imagine a different kind of nation.

Late in his career, Williams began advocating political self-rule in Scotland and Wales, and – crucially – in the English regions. He envisaged this to be part of the long revolution towards finding democratic processes. Cultural materialism is a theory capable of explaining the part played by cultural forms in contributing to such historical developments. In order to understand precisely how the theory can be used to shed light on the process of political break-up in Britain, it is necessary to go back to the beginning of Williams's thinking on the subject, and examine the ways in which he understood the history of the British state.

WILLIAMS, NATION-STATE AND MODERNITY

To Williams, the nation-state was fundamentally an organ of cultural and political modernity. He suggested that the development from *nation* to *state* is analogous to the whole history of modernity. This draws in all sorts of related histories, from the development of technologies of transport and communication to the experience of rapid urbanization; and from the development of political and economic institutions to modernist cultural forms such as the newspaper, the novel and the cinema. Modernization is the term by which Williams understands these and a myriad other developments. Their sum total is the modern nation-state.

The term *nation* implies a people, rather than a state. The organization of a nation of people into a political *state* was heavily dependent on two factors: the developing technologies of transport and communication; and an element of consciously willed political association – usually carried out by a ruling or powerful elite. Williams draws attention to this drift when he writes:

A *nation* once was unproblematic, with its strong connections with the fact of birth, the fact that a nation was a group of people who shared a *native* land. This meaning was overridden but never destroyed, by the development of the *nation-state*, in which what really matters is not common birth or the sharing of native land, but a specific independent kind of political organisation.[5]

The process of consciously constructing the institution of the state occurred between the early modern period (around 1550) and the late nineteenth century (the period of high imperialism). Throughout that time, an ever greater number of people were being brought within the domain of the organized nation-state.

The work of mediation between impersonal apparatus and scattered population naturally became more complex as the borders of the nation-state and the empire were expanded. Indeed, the slow emergence of modernity through the development of the nation-state can be understood as the coupling of *nation* and *state*. Initially, the people constituted a national body, separate from any concept of a political *state*. It was only the gradual development of a range of centralized political institutions that led to a marriage between these two concepts, bringing a varied population into the fold of the new *nation-state*.

Raymond Williams draws attention to a further term capable of implying both people and *state*. This term is *society*, and it was a crucial one throughout Williams's career. Williams points out that the word retained the dual meanings of people in general and a specific form of political organization, until the end of the eighteenth century:

> If you look through an eighteenth-century writer . . . and see how he uses the word 'society,' you'll find that in one paragraph he will mean what we would now have to express as 'company' or simply 'being with other people . . .' He will in the next paragraph be likely to use 'society' to mean . . . the systematic set of political and general arrangements by which a given people live: society as a social *system*. And this simultaneous use of the same term for quite different meanings has a piece of history in it which may be crucially relevant in the attempt to think nationalist politics in our own generation. (RH, p. 112)

Until comparatively recently the ideas of a people and of a political organization were coterminous. The term *society* retained these twin implications until well into the eighteenth century. It was only the process of modernization as it was enabled by ever expanding technologies of transport and communication that would bring different peoples into the fold of the nation-state and so separate the immediacy of control that had previously existed between individuals or small-scale groups of people and their leaders. The change in meaning of the term *nation*, from a local group of people to a large-scale political organization, was a recent change. As a result, Williams believed that the nation-state was an organ of cultural and political modernity.

Throughout the period from 1550 to 1850, there were relatively few opponents to the formation of a nation-state as such. Recent historians have examined the ways in which the modern British nation-state was constructed in such a way as to invite loyalty and attachment through the promise of social and cultural cohesion. Eric Hobsbawm for example has shown that all of Britain's supposedly national traditions were invented during the nineteenth century specifically to generate this feeling of loyalty.[6] Linda Colley's study *Britons* similarly explores how the nation-state was forged on the basis of a contract between political machinery and general population. According to this contract, the people of the nation would give their consent to the process of state-building in exchange for certain intangible features of nationhood: a feeling of belonging, the pageantry of monarchy, religious festivals, holiday entertainments and so on.[7]

Unlike Hobsbawm, and later Colley, Raymond Williams did not devote much attention to the precise history of the political machinery of Britain's nation-state. This is not because he was not interested in that history, but because he was interested in how other histories interweaved with it to create the modern British nation. Williams, for example, was aware that the ideological aspect of nation building coincided with the creation of new means of communication and transport. These appeared to offer people unbounded possibilities for social and physical mobility, while also meeting the need for relationship on a broader scale than had previously been possible. Such a situation was naturally conducive to the reification of the nation-state as the primary form of social and political organization. Since Williams was interested in how cultural forms relate to political and historical processes, he tended to concentrate more on these cultural and technological histories than on the history of the political state apparatus as such. He concentrated on the ways in which political apparatus, cultural forms and technological developments interacted in the generation of the modern nation-state.

The concept of nationhood possessed the minds of the majority of British people. This was so to the extent that the residual eighteenth-century concept of society, as totally separate from state apparatus, collapsed and disappeared. How was it possible for this to happen? How could the very people who had most to lose by the political organization of a centralized state evince such enthusiasm for it?

Williams believed that one answer to this might relate to the new conditions of urbanization that developed with the industrial revolution. He notes that

> by 1881 a majority of the British people were living in towns of 20,000 or more inhabitants. London had passed the million mark early in the nineteenth century; by mid-century its population was over two and a half million and by 1900 over six million. The new industrial cities were developing at often even more explosive rates.[8]

The conditions of living in these new, crowded conurbations, coupled with the hitherto unfamiliar experience of encountering dozens of strangers on a daily basis, created a need for new cultural forms, to enable people to understand the new ways in which they related to one another. This in turn impacted on the kinds of cultural experiences in which the new urban population engaged, as Williams notes:

> Within these unprecedented conditions, old oral forms, such as the sermon, were extended and developed; and relatively new oral forms – the outdoor and indoor political meeting, now often of vast size, and the popular lecture series – became central elements of urban culture. (*WCS*, p. 124)

If the archetypal nineteenth-century experience was one of a crowd, then this was reflected in the cultural forms of the time. The popular lecture and sermon, and above all the political rally, were kinds of cultural experience that incorporated a far greater number of people than had previously been the case. It was also the period during which modern large-scale spectator sports began to take off: 'Again, from mid-century, organised sport, especially football and horse-racing, developed within the new urban culture' (*WCS*, p. 125).

Such activities contributed to a situation where many more people than previously could attend or participate in the same cultural activity. These developments alone, however, do not explain how new cultural forms could enable a diverse body of people to conceive of themselves as part of a wider nation-state. Indeed, the drift away from earlier versions of the nation, identified by social relationships at a purely local level, was dependent on the replacement of this experience of assembly. The new large-scale concept of the nation-state rested on opportunities for people to participate in common cultural experience *without* the need for such mass meetings.

Raymond Williams suggested that one of the ways in which this began to occur was through the social extension of drama. Drama had residual associations with organized religion and worship, and consequently was rooted in earlier, pre-modern conceptions of society, where it had been religion – coupled with the social structure of a rural aristocracy – that had provided the main elements of social cohesion. At the same time, the technical improvements that transformed drama during the industrial revolution also affected its social reach. The new transport networks and comparable advances in commercial activity meant that the touring theatre company and the provincial playhouse became far more prominent elements of British culture. Thus, drama provided a bridge between older medieval concepts of community and the experience of modernization. As Raymond Williams puts it,

> It was in the sixteenth century that drama changed, as a social process, from an occasional to a regular provision. The performance of plays at set times of year, usually as part of a religious festival, came to be replaced by a repertory of productions in new kinds of theatre. In England, for example, the first commercial theatres were built in the last quarter of the sixteenth century, significantly at the approaches to the City of London, to catch a passing as well as a resident trade. Their physical structure followed precedents in performances in the courtyards of inns. Thus the transition from the occasional drama to regular drama was directly associated with a more mobile, trading society. (*WCS*, pp. 185–6)

This new drama enabled greater numbers of people over ever increasing distances to engage in the same cultural experiences and to com-municate those experiences with each other in new ways. Yet since the social provision of drama was still primarily dependent on the conscious assembly of people in one place at a time, it was not able to unify the nation synchronically.

Two developments became crucial to this process of unification: the new technologies of rail transport and the emerging cultural form of the modern daily newspaper. The railways, for example, were significant not simply because of their capacity to disseminate commercial freight and merchandise, but also because of the related cultural developments. As Williams points out, the new railway stations became places for meeting and for exchanging news and ideas. They also became mini-markets, and this perhaps was the crucial breakthrough, for it was in the new railway stations that the new cultural forms of the newspaper and the novel were primarily sold. The trains themselves carried these new cultural products around the country, creating a potential for simultaneous communion in cultural experience which far surpassed anything that had preceded it:

> it was in the bookstalls at the new stations, notably those of W. H. Smith, that the public could be reached in a new way. The cheap Parlour Library, and then the Railway Library, poured through this new outlet: the yellow-backs, with glossy covers, illustrated in colour, and carrying advertising on their backs.[9]

Of course, it was not only the transport of books and newspapers, but also the very opportunity for rapid long-distance travel that created a new sense of social relationship. Williams writes:

> there is almost certainly . . . a crucial differential between urban and rural people, and – within the urban – between London and other cities. Distribution methods, which would flatten these differentials, were not radically changed until the mid-century establishment of the railway network. (*WCS*, p. 123)

The emergence of a national rail network combined the modern technologies of transport with the post-enlightenment need to imagine human relationships on a secular basis. It not only transported people and goods, but also ideas. Williams's point is that the nationwide railway system did not simply emerge as a result of the new nineteenth-century sense of the British nation; it also played an active part in generating that sense.

He made a similar point about modern newspapers. The newspaper emerged from the eighteenth century as a local organ, capable of holding together a local community on a relatively small scale by enabling its readers to share communicative experiences. But then technical improvements in print and distribution combined with a commercial spirit began to consolidate local initiatives into nation-wide ventures. The new mass newspapers met the urgent contemporary need to explore the radically new kinds of urban experience that the industrial revolution had generated. Williams notes that

> steam printing of *The Times* began in 1814, and speed of production was steadily raised by mechanical improvements. The eventual combination of rapid steam production with the new, fast distribution system made available by the developing railway network, produced the conditions for major expansion. (*WCS*, p. 127)

The expansions that began to occur were twofold. First, the areas covered by a 'local' newspaper became greater and greater, as a result of new methods of transport and distribution. Subsequently, the local newspapers of the eighteenth century began to be bought up by fewer and fewer commercial blocks, so that even while the diversity of actual local newspapers remained the overall number of newspaper proprietors decreased:

> In the second half of the nineteenth century the ownership and control of newspapers moved, in the majority of cases, from small and often local family businesses to a more concentrated corporate stage, in which whole strings of newspapers and magazines were owned by a few powerful individuals or groups. (*WCS*, p. 181)

The result of this increasing centralization, coupled with increased combine ownership, would eventually be registered in the form of the national daily newspaper, or simply the 'nationals'. In this way, modern cultural forms and modern technologies each contributed directly to the growth of the new concept of the modern nation. The cultural materialist interpretation tells us that not only political institutions and technological innovations but also cultural forms have an important impact on the production and constitution of a society.

Raymond Williams was interested in showing how the histories of these different formative social features related to each other. He showed that cultural and technological developments are themselves in the last instance political developments, capable of playing a material part in the creation of a social order. Because it arose on the back of new forms of political institution, and because it was partly enabled by new technological and cultural forms, the nation-state was fundamentally an institution of cultural and political modernity. It therefore follows that to enter a historical period when these developments have either been concluded or have lost much of their importance is to enter a period when the national imagination too is up for renegotiation.

BENEDICT ANDERSON AND THE IMAGINED COMMUNITY

If these ideas of Williams seem rather abstract and theoretical, then they are perhaps better understood through recourse to the work of one of Williams's younger contemporaries. Benedict Anderson's study *Imagined Communities* (1982) explored in much more detail the ways in which the history of writing in general – and of print media in particular – overlapped with and informed the history of the nation-state. According to Anderson's argument, it was the technologies of printing and distribution that enabled the nation-state to imagine itself into existence as such.

Anderson argues that a nation is an imagined community, in the sense that it is a large-scale socially cohesive entity of which its members may feel themselves to be a part even though they may not, indeed probably will not, meet, encounter or learn of the existence of the majority of other members. He defines the nation as an imagined community in the following way:

> It is *imagined* because the members of even the smallest nation will never know most of their fellow-members, meet them, or even hear of them, yet in the minds of each lives the image of their communion . . . it is imagined as a *community*, because, regardless of the actual inequality and exploitation that may prevail in each, the nation is always conceived as a deep, horizontal comradeship.[10]

Anderson characterizes the nation as invoking a feeling of comradeship in the absence of any direct experience of one's comrades. The nation is an imagined community because its members assume the existence of each other without direct knowledge of such existence. Central to this conception of a nation is a materialist analysis of the means of representation that enable such large-scale imagining. The earlier systems of religion, and of intracontinental ruling dynasties, had prepared the way for the modern nation. But Anderson suggests that, even more than these, one factor was crucial in its imagining-into-being, namely print capitalism. As Anderson puts it:

> economic change, 'discoveries' (social and scientific), and the development of increasingly rapid communications, drove a harsh wedge between cosmology and history. No surprise then that the search was on ... for a new way of linking fraternity, power and time meaningfully together. Nothing perhaps more precipitated this search, nor made it more fruitful, than print-capitalism, which made it possible for rapidly growing numbers of people to think about themselves, and to relate themselves to others, in profoundly new ways.[11]

The nation-state could not have been imagined without the mobilization within the mind of a sufficient number of people of a concept of *nation*. This is where the fuller relations in which writing is also involved have additionally to be considered. To reach so many people, print products depended on such material processes as transportation, distribution and communication. In the full sense then, the history of the nation-state is analogous to the history of writing only insofar as the history of writing is itself understood as intersecting with other histories: those of the development of roads, railways and shipping, to name but the most obvious. Without these, there could be no widespread distribution of writing and hence no imagined community. The nation became imagined into being as a sufficient body of writing reached a sufficient number of people to enable such a cognitive association to occur. To understand this process materially we need to understand both the active properties of the writing at the level of content and the fuller material relations in which it is involved.

Like Raymond Williams, Anderson suggests that the two forms by means of which print capitalism would contribute most directly to the national imagination were the modern novel and the modern newspaper. The former, for example, addresses itself to a precise community of readers: a general 'we'. The members of this group can presume each other to exist without ever having met or heard of each other.

Indeed, this is the central premise of the nineteenth-century novel of personal confession. The convention of addressing the 'dear reader' became a dominant one in the nineteenth-century novel. The narrator speaks as an 'I' who assumes fellowship and membership of a general 'we' – a national collective of people unfamiliar to each other, yet sharing certain cultural knowledge and rituals.

As an example of how the 'I'/'We' novel enables its readers to form themselves into an imagined community, Anderson gives more detailed analysis of José Joaquín Fernandez de Lizardi's novel, *El Periquillo Sarniento* (*The Itching Parrot*, 1816). The novel was written shortly before Mexican independence from Spain. Indeed, Anderson describes it as 'evidently the first Latin American work in this genre'.[12] Although it was written prior to Mexican independence, the Mexican nation is already present, in embryonic form, within the structure of the novel:

> we see the 'national imagination' at work in the movement of a solitary hero through a sociological landscape of a fixity that fuses the world inside the novel with the world outside. This picaresque *tour d'horison* – hospitals, prisons, remote villages, monasteries, Indians, Negroes – is nonetheless not a *tour du monde*. The horizon is clearly bounded: it is that of colonial Mexico. Nothing assures us of this sociological solidity more than the succession of plurals. For they conjure up a social space full of *comparable* prisons, none in itself of any unique importance, but all representative (in their simultaneous, separate existence) of the oppressiveness of *this* colony.[13]

In this way, the novel operates as the locus for the unfolding of a precise relationship between writer and readers. The general typification of prisons, hospitals and so on militates against an insistence on the differential identities of each reader, and instead focuses on the realization of shared experience. In this way, the novel imagines the Mexican community into existence. The technologies of print, transport and distribution would serve only to augment this bond, by bringing the novel to every corner of the territory that would subsequently become identified as that of the Mexican nation.

Another novel Anderson considers is *Black Semarang*, published serially by the Indonesian Mas Marco Kartodikromo in 1924. There, the relationship between writer and a textually implied body of readers is cemented by the repeated use of 'our' and 'us', with the effect that again, the Indonesian national community was imagined into being before it became a geopolitical reality. It is not only the appeal to solidarity, or the invocation of common places, persons and experiences, that create this sense of communion.

Raymond Williams drew implicitly on Anderson's notion of the imagined reader when he reviewed an essay on the Welsh poet R. S. Thomas by Tony Bianchi. Bianchi showed that, as a result of the enthusiastic attempts made by his readers to claim Thomas as the nationalist spokesman of a Welsh poetic tradition, Thomas has been 'reconstructed in the image of his audience'. This bond between writer and imagined readers creates in turn a special kind of imagined community.[14] In his review of Bianchi's analysis, Raymond Williams suggested that this creation of an imagined community gave rise to the first seeds of political change in 'history, society and . . . nationalist politics' (*WSW*, pp. 35–6).

Williams and Anderson each suggest that fiction can be used to cultivate a symbolic bond between members of a theoretical readership, and that this bond can be elevated onto a national scale. If this is true of the novel, it is even more true of the modern daily newspaper. As Anderson says, 'in this perspective, the newspaper is merely an *extreme form* of the book'.[15] For not only does the paper mobilize familiar political, linguistic and cultural landscapes for common consumption, it is also read *simultaneously* by the majority of its readers on a daily basis. Consumption of the morning or evening daily national newspaper thus becomes elevated to the status of a kind of common ritual, capable of unifying the populace in unspoken – but communicative – congress across the land, just as the earlier rituals of religion had contributed to the prior imagined community of the church:

We know that particular morning and evening editions will overwhelmingly be consumed between this hour and that, only on this day, not that . . . The significance of this mass ceremony . . . is paradoxical. It is performed in silent privacy, in the lair of the skull. Yet each communicant is well aware that the ceremony he performs is being replicated simultaneously by thousands (or millions) of others of whose existence he is confident, yet of whose identity he has not the slightest notion. Furthermore, this ceremony is incessantly repeated at daily or half-daily intervals throughout the calendar. What more vivid figure for the secular, historically clocked, imagined community can be envisioned?[16]

The modern novel and the modern newspaper, then, were two of the main tools by which print capitalism contributed to the production of a national imagination. It is a matter of great significance that both of these examples are popular cultural forms, reproduced and disseminated in great numbers. Anderson does not discuss the minority literature of the intellectual elite, or even the reading habits of the bourgeoisie. Moreover, the examples of popular novels he discusses are all drawn from the colonial world, rather than from the metropolitan nations of Europe, and he shows how these novels play a direct and formative part in the anti-colonial imagination.

Anderson draws attention to the tendency of emerging nations to figure themselves as new. This was the case, for example, in post-revolutionary France and America. There was even an attempt in France to restart the calendar at Year One in the aftermath of the revolution, in order to enshrine this sense of novelty in the post-revolutionary nation's sense of itself. However, modernity would not allow this. Already, by 1789, Anderson points out, not only newspapers but also mass-produced watches, calendars, clocks, diaries and written records of all kinds existed. These militated against the cancellation of anterior time since the technologies of reproduction meant that the established measures of time were ineradicable. The plan to restart French history with Year One (for revolution) failed, because the French people already knew that the year was 1789.[17]

This gives rise to what Anderson calls the temporal paradox of nationhood. Emerging nations naturally figured themselves as new until they discovered that they were unable to do so. As a result, they sought instead to figure themselves as historical entities, on the basis of established history and antiquity. History itself became a new academic discipline in Berlin and Paris in the 1820s, and in America a little later. In the new national historiographies, 1776 in America and 1789 in France ceased to be seen as new beginnings. Rather, these modern moments of national self-recognition represented the re-discovery of ancient or mythic kinds of community which had already existed. Nationhood was thus legitimated by this invocation of the ancient past, rather than on the basis of novelty.

Anderson gives a detailed example of this process in the work of August Renan. In a famous paper entitled 'What is a Nation?' Renan had averred that the formation of a nation requires that certain things – conflicts, wars, disputes – be forgotten. Anderson quotes Renan's suggestion that the emergence of a unified French nation during the early modern period relied on a general forgetting of the Saint Barthélemy massacres of 1572, or the Midi massacres of the thirteenth century. If the nation is conceived as consisting in deep, horizontal comradeship, then memory of these things seems to detract from the emotional appeal of national unity. Yet in reminding the French people to forget such things, Renan assumed that everyone within the national community remembered what they were.[18]

To solve this apparent paradox, Anderson suggests, a precise kind of writing emerged in the new historiography of the nineteenth century. This took the form of a retrospective rewriting, wherein, for example, the thirteenth-century massacres cease to be figured as violent conflict between Avignon and the Catalans, and the sixteenth-century conflicts cease to be figured as bitter fights between Catholics and Protestants. These conflicts instead are retrospectively rewritten as fratricidal conflicts *between Frenchmen*. Out of this arises a common (national) history. Anderson refers to the kind of historiography he finds in Renan – and throughout the nineteenth century – as the 'reassuring use of fratricide.'[19] It removes the specific differentials from a violent history and creates instead this harmonious whole.

Anderson detects similar examples in American history (including the Civil War), and the Norman conquest of Britain. In the novels of Fenimore Cooper, for instance, or Melville, or even Mark Twain, conflicts between early settlers and native Americans, or again between established settlers and Negro slaves, are not figured as violent interracial conflicts. They are instead figured as aspects of the shared experience of early Americans, each trying to survive in a hostile environment.

Raymond Williams picks up on the Norman example when he draws attention to the irony whereby modern British history is often taught as though it began 'somewhere around 1066, when a Norman-Frenchman replaced a Norse-Saxon monarch' (T2000, p. 193). Again, in such histories, William the Conqueror ceases to be figured as a violent alien invader and is presented instead as the original English – and later British – monarch. This erases a sense of difference or disunity from history and legitimates an historic sense of British nationhood through invocation of an early imaged unity. As Anderson puts it, the actual record of war and violence on which the nation is founded must be forgotten as such, and then remembered differently, as part of 'our own' history.[20] This myth of unity can itself be perpetuated only in narrative, and this underlines the extent to which the modern nation-state is articulated not only by its political institutions, but also by its cultural forms: newspapers, novels, school textbook histories.

Benedict Anderson's notion of the *imagined community* helps us to understand what Raymond Williams means by cultural materialism. Each writer emphasizes the materially active part played by cultural forms such as writing in the generation of a social order. Implicit in this is the idea that to generate a new narrative of identity is to contribute to the formation of a new or alternative version of the nation.

TOM NAIRN AND THE CAPITALIST STATE

To a certain degree, a new perspective on national self-definition in Ireland, Scotland and Wales was provided by Michael Hechter's *Internal Colonialism: The Celtic Fringe in British National Development, 1536–1960* in 1975. Hechter ceased to see these peripheral nations as part of a putatively united British state, and instead developed a historical frame-work where these separate nations could be understood as colonies of ruling-class England. As such, they had importantly different histories, or importantly different perspectives on the common history.

In *The Break-Up of Britain*, Tom Nairn provides more detailed analysis of those different perspectives on the common history. Nairn argues that a key date in the history of the British state is the revolution of 1688. This ended the system of rule by absolute monarchy and gave rise to a period of bourgeois consolidation of the machinery of economic and political control. In other words, the 1688 revolution enabled the state apparatus of monarchy to continue, while also inviting the population to forget the worst excesses of the monarchy's past. Two distinct elements, potentially violent revolution followed by bureau-cratic consolidation, produced the British nation-state as an organ of political modernity while also retaining a common history on which a sense of national community could be founded.

Nairn argues that arising out of these developments in the 1680s, the British state was the first national state formation to come into existence anywhere in the world. Because of this, he suggests, the historic trajectory of state formation in Britain cannot be considered typical of the formation of nation-states in general: '[t]he multi-national state-form that has ruled there from 1688 to the present time could not be *typical* of general modern development simply because it initiated so much of it.'[21]

In other words, to Nairn, the British state is the prototypical institution of cultural and political modernity, a blueprint to be copied by other constitutions and other formations in other states. Arising out of the transition from feudalism to modernity, the British state could not be fully modern itself. It is, Nairn goes on to argue, a unique blend of the feudal with the two key factors of modernization: the bourgeois capitalist class and the nascent forces of industrialization. This blend makes it unlike the other European nations, which sought to copy the blueprint provided by the British state without precisely being able to replicate it, lacking the historical combination of archaism and modernity:

> Because it was first, the English – later British – experience remained distinct. Because they came second, into a world where the English Revolution had already succeeded and expanded, later bourgeois societies could not repeat this early development. Their study and imitation engendered something quite different: the truly modern doctrine of the abstract or 'impersonal' state which, because of its abstract nature, could be imitated in subsequent history.[22]

This sets up an interesting question about the temporal placing of modernity. To Nairn, the British state was the first-born child of modernization. Because of this fact, it was unable to slough off its traces of the pre-modern world in which it remained rooted. The paradox then presented is not that the process of modernization was completed in Britain before it arrived in other nations. It is not that Britain's period of modernization has already been concluded. The problem is, on the contrary, that Britain's constitution remains not modern enough. This paradoxical definition of the temporal location of modernity would provoke Raymond Williams, in one of his last ever public lectures, to ask 'When was modernism?'[23]

Tom Nairn uses the term 'priority' to describe this situation whereby Britain became the first nation to arrive into the modern world, and as a result was unable to develop along the same lines as other nations which sought to imitate it. He says of the British constitution:

Although a developmental oddity belonging to the era of transition from absolutism to capitalist modernity, its anomalous character was first crystallised and then protected by priority. As the road-making state into modern times, it inevitably retained much from the medieval territory it left behind: a cluster of deep-laid archaisms still central to English society and the British state. Yet the developmental position encouraged the secular retention of these traits, and a constant return to them as the special mystique of the British Constitution and way of life. Once the road-system had been built up, for other peoples as well as the English, the latter were never compelled to reform themselves along the lines which the English Revolution had made possible. They had acquired such great advantages from leading the way – above all in the shape of empire – that for over two centuries it was easier to consolidate or re-exploit this primary role than to break with it.[24]

The concept of priority has two meanings here. First, it refers to that process whereby the British state became the first modern state in the world. Related to this, it refers to the conscious policies adopted by that state: a logic of economic priority. This is where the history of the British state intersects with the history of its empire, revealing a mutually constitutive relationship. As Nairn points out, the primary affluence created by the British empire meant that for more than two centuries there was little pressure to reform the state apparatus. This gave rise to the 'special mystique' of the unwritten British constitution. It justifies seemingly archaic elements of British political life such as the wearing of gowns and wigs in Parliament, national ceremonies such as the State opening of Parliament, and the anomalous longevity of an unreformed upper chamber. Raymond Williams would, following Walter Bagehot, refer to these as the 'theatrical elements of the constitution' (*RH*, p. 259).

This mystique of Britishness, coupled with the economic prosperity generated by imperial practices, forestalled and deflected some of the pressure to reform the British political state until long after the revolutions of the seventeenth century, which might otherwise have gained momentum. In other words, Nairn argues that those revolutions provided other peoples with a blueprint to copy, and actually enabled them to go even further in their political reforms than had been possible in the initial revolutions in Britain. Thus 1789 in France was a copy of 1688 in England, but able to go much further than England because, having got there first, England was still at the transitional stage away from absolutism and feudalism.

The British state apparatus that emerged from 1688 was nowhere near as radical as that of Paris in the 1790s. The settlement following the 'Glorious Revolution' was moderate, capable of treading the middle ground between a feudal aristocratic culture and the demand for much more general social reform. This blend enabled the capitalist bourgeoisie to prosper by dominating the apparatus of state. This was done through the alliance of the landowners with members of the industrial bourgeoisie, *against* the proletariat. Thus the bourgeois revolution of 1688 was not much of a revolution at all. Nairn, like Anderson, concludes that the abolition of the monarchy in 1649 had far greater potential for democratic revolution. The effects of *that* revolution, however, were vitiated by the restoration of the monarchy in 1660. Nairn argues that Britain has been in need of a second political revolution ever since:

> There was no second political revolution, so that the more radical tendencies of the bourgeoisie were diverted and absorbed into the dense machinery of civil hegemony. As this happened the new working class was also diverted and repressed: the defeat of early nineteenth-century radicalism forced it into a curious kind of social and political *apartheid*. This condition was almost the opposite of the active intervention from below which figured in so many modern revolutions; so, therefore, was the mythology, or underlying political consciousness, which it generated.[25]

This is different from the nationalisms discussed by Benedict Anderson, where nationalist revolution comes from 'below'. Anderson's idea of nationalism is that it implies that power comes from a popular base in the people who thereby seek to control themselves. In the context of nineteenth-century Britain, this was generally absent. We know from the work of Hobsbawm and Colley that the masses – where they were mobilized at all – were mobilized from above, rather than by themselves. Britain's nationalism accordingly had to be based on conservative myths of the organic society.

The 1640s had absorbed the radical end of the bourgeoisie into civil society, and the nineteenth century saw a weakening of the potential for working-class revolt, culminating in the defeat of Chartism in the 1840s. The working class itself was then absorbed into the political and economic order of Britain's civil society. This was achieved via a consciously generated emphasis on the public sphere, and on the traditions, customs and cultural practices that the public could hold in common. It is for this reason that Raymond Williams emphasizes the importance of modern communal or widely disseminated cultural forms such as the theatre, sport, newspapers and the new practice of long-distance travel in the development of the modern nation.

The priority attached to maintaining the cohesion of civil society continued into the twentieth century. Meanwhile, the need for the second revolution to which Nairn draws attention became latent rather than manifest. On the other hand, that need would never entirely disappear either. For more than half of the twentieth century, the affluence generated by empire coupled with the continued functioning of civil society would ensure a measure of social cohesion and forestall in advance further pressure for social, economic and democratic reform.

With the end of empire came two related developments. First, the public national rituals associated with empire – coronations, anniversaries, national holidays of all kinds – were no longer available to play their part in the generation of social cohesion. Secondly and more importantly, the removal of the imperial hinterlands which for so long had provided the economic affluence conducive to civil cohesion revealed tangible differences in material standards of living and in access to real political power between increasing numbers of British people.

The latent need for a second revolution which for so long had been bought off by a combination of civic cohesion and economic prosperity finally emerged into the open again in the 1970s, in the form of trade union militancy across the country, racial antagonisms and Scottish and Welsh opposition to the unitary British state. Thus, nationalism in Scotland and Wales was in part generated by the wider push towards socialist democracy, in opposition to the capitalist state.

Nairn concludes that there are thus two tenable views of the unitary state:

> If one does not recognise that it is moribund . . . then naturally Scottish and Welsh nationalism will appear as destructive forces – as a basically irrational turning back towards forgotten centuries, as involution at the expense of progress. Whether conservative or socialist, belief in a continuing unitary state of the British Isles entails viewing these movements as a threat.[26]

On the other hand, if we take the view that the state had never ful-
filled its offer to bring Britain into the modern world by providing for
the first time a proper measure of democracy and equality to all the
peoples of Britain, then these movements appear in another light. As
Nairn says:

> if one perceives the United Kingdom as an *ancien régime* with no
> particular title to survival or endless allegiance, then the breakaway
> movements may appear in a different light. The phrase 'We must preserve
> the unity of the United Kingdom' is currently intoned like a litany by
> most leaders of British public life. Its magic properties are obviously
> derived from the cults of Constitution and Sovereignty. Merely to refuse
> this sacrament allows the observer to begin, at least, to acknowledge some
> positive side in the cause of the smaller nations.[27]

The positive side that Nairn detects in the nationalisms of Scotland and
Wales is aligned to the activity of trade unions and labour militancy
that also erupted in the English industrial regions during the same
period. It is not a matter of abstract chauvinism, but of advancing the
cause of functioning democracy. The history of the British state tells us
that the moderate revolution of 1688 failed to end a kind of political
absolutism. Nations where this has been the case have taken the first
step towards modern social democracy, without being able to cross the
threshold into it. Such nations are left at the gateway to modernity,
and this is how Nairn understands the whole history of the British
state. It is a state whose modernity is both already concluded and yet
to arrive.

When the crisis of a global recession emerged in the 1960s, this
became manifest in the form of popular anti-imperial revolutions.
These took the form of nationalisms of various kinds around the
world, because nationalism was the only available historical precedent
for revolution. Thus there was suddenly an emergence of, for example,
revolutionary Cubans; republican Irishmen; and a host of nation-bound
revolutionary proletariats in Angola, Mozambique, Korea, Vietnam
and others.

Nairn understands the emergence of socialist nationalisms in
Scotland and Wales in this context. Crisis in capitalist society generates
– or exacerbates – the need for revolution. The only existing historical
model for revolution is the nationalist model. Thus revolutionary

nationalisms arise to face the crises thrown up by capitalist society. This accounts for the socialist character of nationalist movements in Scotland and Wales. In each case, an emerging nation imagines its people into a national formation, and narrative plays a central part in that imagination. We would thus expect new nationalist movements in Scotland and Wales to be accompanied by new kinds of narrative in those nations.

UNOFFICIAL NARRATIVE: WILLIAMS AND BHABHA

Raymond Williams, Tom Nairn and Benedict Anderson are all interested in how the concept of a nation-state as the fundamental unit of political relationship achieved hegemony. The nation-state was imagined into being as an organ of its ruling class, for the benefit of expanding power and control over the working classes at home and over colonized societies abroad. Literature plays a part in making this power relation possible. To produce a kind of writing that disputes this imperial construction of the nation is thus to play a material part in undermining the unitary make-up of the nation itself.

In a more recent study entitled *Nation and Narration*, Homi K. Bhabha has sought to complicate Benedict Anderson's notion of the *imagined community*, which he perceived as too deterministic. Indeed, in Anderson's account, the creation of the nation-state and hence of a social order can seem like something of a *fait accompli*. Bhabha also seeks to draw attention to the ethnic and gendered constituents of the modern nation-state, which are rather absent from the work of Nairn.

Bhabha draws on the field of language and semiotics. He uses the French feminist semiotic writer Julia Kristeva to show that all language is multi-accentual.[28] The language in which any given narrative is created is always amenable to multi-accentual interpretation: all words mean different things in different contexts. If any piece of narrative can be interpreted in a number of different ways, this must be true of the narratives on which modern nation-states are founded. This enables Bhabha to argue that the very narratives that drum up hegemonic attachment to the nation-state can also be used to rupture connections to that state and so negate the hegemony of the ruling political order.

An example Bhabha elsewhere gives of this process is the work of the British-Indian novelist Salman Rushdie. Bhabha suggests that in his novel *The Satanic Verses*, Rushdie portrays the life of the sub-cultural community of a group of working-class Indian immigrants and their second- and third-generation offspring in East London at around the time of the Brixton race riots of the 1980s. The characters are mostly from low-income backgrounds, so that they are losers of the get-rich-quick ethos that characterized Britain in the 1980s. In the novel, this is made explicit when some of the characters gather to burn effigies of their nemesis, Margaret Thatcher. The strength of the novel, Bhabha suggests, is that it shows how matters of class, race and national interest intersect in complicated and sometimes contradictory ways. Moreover, in writing the novel, Rushdie gives fictional realization to the kind of working-class Indian community that had previously made little impact on the novel tradition in Britain. This is not, Bhabha points out, because such communities had not previously existed, but because they lacked access to the means of representation. Bhabha suggests that by writing a novel about a community of people previously excluded from the literary record, and explicitly in opposition to the dominant political tones of the period, Rushdie enables us to imagine 'how newness enters the world'.[29]

In *Nation and Narration*, Bhabha explores the possibility of using writing to imagine new forms of national identity. He shows that this need not necessarily take the form of counter-nationalisms in Scotland and Wales; and that the British identity can also be renegotiated on grounds of race and gender. Bhabha explores these different kinds of cultural emergence by invoking Raymond Williams's vocabulary of *dominant*, *residual* and *emergent* cultural practices.

Williams had developed this critical vocabulary in *Marxism and Literature*, arising out of his interest in both Marxism and semiotics. What Williams calls the *dominant* cultural forms in any society are those cultural forms or products which are related to ruling-class hegemony. In modern societies dominant forms are typically tied in to large-scale institutions of broadcasting and cultural production, and perpetuate the images of society that these institutions implicitly ratify.[30] *Residual* cultural forms are not only archaic or out-dated elements of a culture. The term also refers to those elements of the dominant which have become less visibly active in the daily life of a society, while at the same time retaining a latent power of their own. Examples Williams gives of residual elements in British society are rural communities, the established church and the monarchy (*ML*, p. 122). It is only *emergent* practices that can operate as truly oppositional forms, able to contest social and political processes. The emergence in the nineteenth century of the radical popular press is an important example (*ML*, p. 124).

This sense of how emergent forms can be used to contest or dispute the make-up of a social order is a necessary corrective to the too exclusive emphasis that would otherwise be placed on the role of the ruling class. Bhabha and Williams show that the nation is never as straightforwardly unified as its official narratives would suggest. Alternative nationalisms in Scotland and Wales, the creation of ethnic subcultures, dissemination of class-consciousness and understanding of how gender plays a con-stitutive role in kinds of cultural and political experience are all ways in which the possibility for narrating a different kind of nation are now being explored.

These cultural and political emergences taken together comprise the process that Tom Nairn describes as 'the break-up of Britain'. Nairn's study of that title is an attempt to understand dominant, emergent and residual cultural practices in contemporary Britain. The unitary British state of which Nairn's account remains the most thoroughgoing critique has been *the* dominant cultural form in Britain for centuries. It may be in the process of becoming residual. If this is so, it is only because certain other formations which would seek to supersede it are in the process of emerging. Clearly, the historical processes at work involve a complex interplay between dominant, emergent and residual forms. While maintaining a sense of how Williams developed this critical vocabulary within the context of a range of left-wing political theorizing on the subject of nationhood, therefore, it is to those processes and formations that we must now turn.

1

Towards a Materialism of Culture

What is cultural materialism? The question is not a flippant one. Much recent theoretical work in English studies has proven remarkably unable to answer this question, and has at times served only to confuse what it seeks to clarify.

Cultural materialism has become identified with a kind of Lacanian approach to literary texts. Such an approach typically defines *materialism* as a process of language acquisition. It analyses the process of subjectivity formation as it is worked out in the dialectical relationship between the ego and the social environment. This relationship is registered in and through language, so that the Lacanian approach demonstrates how individual subjectivities are materially generated in the process of language acquisition. It then goes on to extrapolate the extent to which the manifestation of this process in literary texts is also a material affair. It is an approach that draws on Freud's theory of sublimated sexual desire, and transposes this into a general textual economy of desire.

Scott Wilson's 1995 study, *Cultural Materialism*, follows this trajectory. Wilson begins by using Freudian psychoanalysis as an instrument for understanding the process of self-fashioning. He then goes on to extrapolate the Freudian concept of desire, elevating it into a general principle for the interpretation of literary, especially Shakespearean texts. Broadly speaking, this extrapolation follows the subtler modes of thinking introduced into the field of psychoanalysis by Jacques Lacan, and moves away from the perhaps rigid deterministic approach of

Freud.[1] The same could be said of Alan Sinfield's *Faultlines: Cultural Materialism and the Politics of Dissident Reading* (1992) and John Brannigan's *New Historicism and Cultural Materialism* (1998).[2]

So far so good. Whence the confusion? *Cultural materialism* is a term coined by Raymond Williams in the introduction to his 1977 study, *Marxism and Literature*. It is, in Williams's own words, a 'Marxist theory' of culture (*ML*, p. 5). Williams did not write about Freud, or Lacan, very much at all. Indeed, over the course of thirty-four published books and countless journal articles, Williams's references to Freud are few and far between. Williams appears to have been suspicious of what he saw as the bourgeois, individualist and anti-historical tendencies that could be said to exist in Freud.[3] As a result, the emphasis of Williams's cultural materialism is all about the correspondingly socialist and historical tendencies to be found in Marxism.

This is the confusion: recent work on cultural materialism is heavily indebted to the work of Williams. Wilson, Sinfield and Brannigan all acknowledge Williams as the founder of the field – cultural materialism – in which they operate.[4] Yet their approach is often explicitly psycho-analytic or semiotic, drawing far more on the instruments of Freud and Lacan than on Marx. This theoretical approach is not clearly used in the work of Williams, despite the assertion of these theorists that his work was the cornerstone of their own. He appears not to have founded the field that they credit him with having founded. Cultural materialism as Williams understood it was a Marxist theory of culture. Cultural materialism in the guises mentioned here appears to be a psychoanalytic approach, drawing more on Freud and Lacan than on Marx. Which then is the 'real' cultural materialism?

Raymond Williams developed his materialist theory of culture over a long period of time and through recourse to several different areas of research. Although cultural materialism as Williams defined it is rightly identified as a Marxist theory, Williams's work also overlapped more with the field of semiotic theory than is often acknowledged – hence the recent confusion as to how to define cultural materialism. Cultural materialism evolved as an analytic theory that combined the work of Marx, Freud and Lacan, transforming each in the process, in order to arrive at a sophisticated theory of culture.

THE FIRST TURNING POINT

Raymond Williams's early intellectual formation is best understood through reference to the intellectual milieu in which he operated. Three names spring immediately to mind: I. A. Richards, F. R. Leavis and E. M. W. Tillyard. When Williams arrived in Cambridge as an undergraduate in 1939, not much more than a decade had elapsed since the publication of Richards's *Principles of Literary Criticism,* which had established 'practical criticism' as the dominant method of the Cambridge English tripos. Leavis had published his pamphlet *Mass Civilisation and Minority Culture* in 1930, urging the social and literary elite to defend its way of life against the encroachments of the degraded masses. Williams's own tutor, Tillyard, was somewhere around the height of his career, producing studies of Elizabethan and Victorian poetry, emphasizing the organic, harmonious and supposedly timeless nature of idyllic English society.[5]

The best word to describe the approach to literature which was dominant when Williams arrived in Cambridge is literary idealism. Practical criticism as Richards defined it was a way of viewing the literary text, as it were, in isolation. It had been developed partly out of the dictates of the English course. Typically, the object of practical criticism was a short poem, or, exceptionally, a short passage of prose. This had the advantage of being capable of being transmitted to students quickly in advance of a tutorial. During the exercise of practical criticism, the students were supposed to examine the text for its innate properties: What did the text mean? How did it generate this meaning? How successful was it as art?

The question that practical criticism did not address was *how* students were to arrive at these judgements. Indeed, it seemed to require them intuitively to know what constitutes great art, and how. This value was taken to reside in the works themselves somehow, rather than in the students' estimation of them. This was more or less by definition true, since, in order for the students to have been presented with a poem or passage of prose in the first place, the piece had a priori been selected as a specimen of great literature worthy of appreciation.

This selection would of course have been made by the tutors and committees of the English faculty, and it is here that Richards's practical criticism intersects with the work of his colleague, F. R. Leavis. Leavis at this time was already beginning to develop the ideas that would culminate in the publication of his classic study, *The Great Tradition*, in 1948. In this work, Leavis sketched out what he took to be the finest representative works from the continuous organic tradition of the English novel. *The Great Tradition* depended essentially on a circular argument. Anything that Leavis discussed in it, from Austen to Conrad, was by definition great literature. Anything that was understood as great literature was by the same token discussed. As Leavis himself put it, 'by *great tradition* I mean the tradition to which what is great in English fiction belongs'.[6] Raymond Williams recalls in *Politics and Letters* in 1979 that the Leavis approach to literary history remained the 'going position' in Cambridge for decades (*PL*, p. 245).

Practical criticism and *The Great Tradition* rely heavily on a notion of literary idealism. These approaches assume that the literary text is best considered in isolation from any separate kind of knowledge or understanding. Each approach assumes that the literary text innately contains its own meanings and values, and that these cannot vary from reader to reader. In other words, it disavows the possibility that readers might call those same meanings and values into question. This is especially true of *The Great Tradition*, which is constructed to define all of the best qualities of Englishness as they are manifest in five centuries of classic literature, in a continuing harmonious culture. Any values which did not adhere to those defined by the great tradition were considered not worthy of consideration. This meant in practice that literary texts which expressed alternative values were rejected altogether. It meant also that students and readers who wanted to bring alternative values to bear on their interpretations of the 'great' works were generally discouraged, if not actively prevented, from doing so.

Literary idealism is a curious thing. It assumes that it is possible to approach a literary text with no more knowledge of the world than that which is generated by the text itself. At best, this requires readers to 'pretend' not to know the things that they do know about history, about politics, and about the world, in order to prevent these 'debased' and 'materialist' factors from impinging on their assessment of the work of art. At worst, it actively disavows the knowledge of the world brought into the process of reading, as if the people bringing that knowledge into their reading somehow did not count, or were not worth knowing about. The great tradition is composed primarily from a precise sector within English society. It assumes that to be anything other than ruling class, male and Anglican is automatically not to count.

When Raymond Williams, who was neither ruling class nor Anglican, nor English, began to bring his positively working-class and (at least putatively) nonconformist experience to bear on the ways in which he read literary texts, he was mildly rebuked by his tutor, E. M. W. Tillyard, for not playing the great tradition game. Before sketching out the process by which Williams developed his historical and materialist approach to the understanding of written texts in contradistinction to the dominant perspective of literary idealism, however, it is worth exploring the ways in which that perspective informed his own early critical work.

Williams's study at Cambridge was interrupted when he went to serve as a tank captain in Normandy during the Second World War. Upon discharge, he completed his degree and then went to work as an adult education tutor in the extramural delegation of Oxford University. During this period, he began work on what was in effect his first book of literary criticism, *Drama from Ibsen to Eliot* (although by the time he had managed to get it published in 1952, he had already published *Reading and Criticism* in 1950).[7]

Williams's selection of T. S. Eliot as the terminus for his own take on the great tradition is not an arbitrary one. For if Richards, Leavis and Tillyard can be seen as the key theorists of literary idealism, then Eliot was its main practitioner. Despite the many frustrations Williams encountered as an undergraduate grappling with the great tradition, this choice of culmination therefore implicitly reveals the extent to which that idealistic approach had taken hold within Williams's own mind.

In the introduction to *Drama from Ibsen to Eliot* Williams sets out an early critical and methodological position. His approach is a textual one, concentrating on isolated individual works of drama:

> It is literary criticism also, which, in its major part is based on demonstrated judgements from texts, rather than on historical survey or generalised impressions: of the kind, that is to say, which is known in England as practical criticism. Practical criticism began, in the work of Eliot, Richards, Leavis, Empson, and Murry, mainly in relation to poetry. It has since been developed, notably by both F. R. and Q. D. Leavis, in relation to the novel.

In the drama, apart from the work of Eliot on Elizabethan dramatists and of other critics of Shakespeare, the usefulness of practical criticism remains to be tested. This book, in addition to its main objects, is intended, therefore, as a working experiment in the application of practical critical methods to modern dramatic literature.[8]

Williams's approach at this early stage is a literary-critical, or idealist, one. He sets out to test the applicability of practical criticism to studies of drama. The thesis Williams propounds in *Drama from Ibsen to Eliot* is that drama is best understood in terms of its capacity to communicate an experience to an audience. Williams suggests that the overall design of a dramatist is best realized when he or she retains direct control of the play. That is, high art requires strict policing:

> It seems to me that the most valuable drama is achieved when the technique of performance reserves to the dramatist primary control. It does not greatly matter whether this control is direct or indirect. In an age when it is accepted that the centre of drama is language, such control is reasonably assured. For when the centre of the drama is language, the *form* of the play will be essentially literary: the dramatist will adopt certain conventions of language through which to work. And if in such a case, the technique of performance – methods of speaking, movement and design – is of such a kind that it will communicate completely the conventions of the dramatist, the full power of the drama is available to be deployed. (*DIE*, p. 29)

The vague reference to 'the age' is counter-intuitive. For in the 1950s it was by no means clear that the centre of drama was language. Williams's whole argument about naturalist drama was that it represented a turn away from the powerful controlling language of the playwright that we find in Shakespearean and Jacobean drama, towards an elaboration of costume, set, prop and action. These he terms 'substitute effects' (*DIE*, p. 75) for they deflect attention away from the controlling power of language. Only the best of contemporary drama, to Williams, retains this controlling power. This shows Williams caught in an impasse between high minority art and degraded mass culture. There is a real fervour with which he advocates the dramatist's tight control over language, and the implied need for a strict policing of high art.

Williams believed that communication is best achieved as a process when the dramatist finds the forms and conventions which are most appropriate to the experience he is seeking to convey. These conventions must be recognisable to the audience as such, rather than appearing as mere reproduction of lifelike behaviour. An example Williams gives of such dramatic convention is the chorus of mythical Greek Eumenides in T. S. Eliot's play, *The Family Reunion* (*DIE*, p. 245). Use of convention generates dramatic tension between the familiar and the innovative, and so enables drama to function as a profound source of communication. This interplay between novelty and the familiar was the basis of Eliot's own dramatic practice. As Eliot wrote:

> One error, in fact, of eccentricity in poetry is to seek for new human emotions to express, and in this search for novelty in the wrong place it discovers the perverse. The business of the poet is not to find new emotions, but to use the ordinary ones and, in working them up into poetry, to express feelings which are not in actual emotions at all.[9]

Eliot argues that the job of the poet or verse dramatist is to work everyday emotions up into a new kind of experience. This sounds very much like Williams's idea of the intensification of what is already familiar.

Williams's positive valuation of Eliot and his recapitulation of I. A. Richards's practical criticism points to an early difficulty which is both theoretical and methodological. The argument of *Drama from Ibsen to Eliot* is that communication can only really be achieved by the utilization of a form appropriate to the experience being communicated and to the receivers of the communication. Not only is it theoretically compromised and hamstrung by a strenuous emphasis on the defence of a minority culture, but this theoretical blindness impacts on the construction of the argument itself. Williams's attempt at finding means for expanding access to cultural forms recapitulates and extends the idea of a minority culture in danger of being swamped:

> The pressure of a mechanical environment has dictated mechanical ways of thought, feeling and conjunction, which artists, and a few of like temper, reject only by conscious resistance and great labour. That is why all serious literature, in our own period, tends to become minority literature . . . It will never become majority drama if it is to wait on the spread of universal beliefs. But its communication may be extended, and its writing made possible, if developments in society (the sum of individual developments)

make possible the re-creation of certain modes of living and of language against which such complexes as industrialism have militated. (*DIE*, pp. 27–8)

The nostalgia evinced in this passage for the putatively harmonious days of a pre-industrial society underlines the extent to which Williams's early work was shot through with the traces of Leavis and Eliot.[10] It is harder to imagine any writer in the English language who more fully idealizes feudal and medieval society than those two, and Williams, at the beginning at least, seems taken in.[11]

The abstractions Williams employs here fall short of a seriously engaged sociological critique. Williams announced in the introduction that his method would be essentially a literary-critical one, so that by the parameters of investigation which he has set himself, he is unable to relate the literary forms to the social, economic and political formations with which they are involved.

What could have become a dynamic and radical exploration of the impact of a minority culture on a wider social scale thus becomes foreshortened. Instead of a textualizing strategy à la Leavis and a developed sociological inquiry into the processes of communication through critical literacy we end up with a book compromised on both fronts. The compromise is manifested in the vague formulations 'such complexes as industrialism'; 'mechanical ways of thought'; and 'certain modes of living and of language'. What are these complexes and how do they relate to each other? These were the questions which Williams would attempt to answer throughout his subsequent work.

The key turning point for Williams came with publication in 1958 of his career-making *Culture and Society*. This is quite unlike his early work, which remained in thrall to the defence of a minority culture against the invasion of a degraded mass. In *Culture and Society*, Williams's whole argument is that the extension of participatory culture is not only a matter of taking preformed cultural forms to the masses. Williams insists that there are in reality no masses – only 'ways of seeing others as masses'.[12] The defence of a minority culture against the incursions of an unappreciative mass is no longer his theme.

Williams began *Culture and Society* by drawing attention to five words which had come into English usage at around the end of the eighteenth century: *industry*, *democracy*, *class*, *art* and *culture*. To

Williams, the emergence and historic variation in meaning of these words was evidence of a wider shift in social relations. *Industry* had ceased to be understood as a general term for work, or even a personal quality of conscientiousness. It had come to refer solely to the mechanized production of material goods in factories, with implications of danger, dirt and poor living conditions. *Class* was then a term used in a rather rigid and deterministic way to refer to the people involved in this work – usually with negative connotations, as in the nineteenth-century phrase, *lower class*, and in contradistinction to the assumed refinement of a social elite, the *upper class*.

At the same time, *art* had ceased to mean *skill*, and had instead come to refer to things such as painting, literature and music – although the extreme vagueness of definition was one of the stimuli to Williams's dissatisfaction with these terms. The same is true of *culture*, which had ceased to be used to refer to the cultivation and growth of crops, and was now being used instead as a synonym for *civilization*. Yet the metaphoric appeal of the earlier meanings, *growth* and *cultivation*, still retained a powerful general appeal, so that *culture* had implications of natural growth, beauty, harmony and peace. *Culture* was in short the opposite of *industry*. It was radically dissociated from the lives of people who worked in industry – that is, from the lives of the majority of people in Britain. *Democracy* on this reckoning was tantamount to a dirty word. By offering to include people in social, political and cultural formations, it appeared to threaten the very structure of those formations.

The work Williams undertakes in *Culture and Society* is twofold. He initially sets out to probe the process by which it became possible to understand *culture* as somehow separate from majority human activities. At the same time, he attempts to overcome this separation. Thus there are two methodologies at work in the text. A kind of literary archaeology, whereby Williams probed the emergence of the terms under discussion, is accompanied by a strenuous reinterpretation of that whole tradition, in order to overcome it. Thus the opening chapter, 'Contrasts', shows that the separation between culture and life was initially active in the work of Edmund Burke and William Cobbett. Yet these two writers are contrasted with a pair of more politically progressive figures, Robert Southey and Robert Owen, in order to show that the two different perspectives on culture run right through.

The two positions can be described as *idealism* and *materialism*. Idealism was the dominant position when Williams was writing in the 1950s. It has strong implications of social exclusion and political reaction. Politically, Williams explores its development in the work of Burke, J. S. Mill, Thomas Carlyle and Matthew Arnold. Culturally, the important moment is that of Romanticism, for Williams suggests that it was the Romantic artist who first developed a self-conscious separation from daily social life.

Reference to the two distinct categories of *politics* and *culture* is somewhat misleading, since the point of *Culture and Society* was to reveal that these areas of life are far more interrelated than the practice of literary idealism would suggest. When Williams looked back on the goals of the work, in the interviews published in *Politics and Letters* in 1979, he stated explicitly that the aim of *Culture and Society* was to 'reconnect' the concepts of art, literature and culture with the daily lives of the people of the country (*PL*, p. 110). The chapters of *Culture and Society* devoted to Pugin, Lawrence and T. S. Eliot all show that this separation remained the dominant ideological practice at the time of writing. Thus Williams points out in *Politics and Letters* that the work of *Culture and Society* was 'oppositional' (*PL*, p. 97) in this ideological sense.

As we have seen, the main theorists of literary idealism were I. A. Richards and F. R. Leavis. Thus in opposing that dominant institutional practice, Williams was also seeking to modify the work of those two men. Accordingly, the section of *Culture and Society* about Eliot is followed by a strong critique of Richards, which is tantamount to the conclusion of the book:

> There is an element of passivity in his [Richards's] idea of the relationship between reader and work which might in the end be disabling . . . [H]e has not offered enough really convincing examples of the intense realisation of a rich or complex organisation, which in general terms he has often described. He often notes the complexity, but the discussion that follows is usually a return on itself, a return to the category 'complexity', rather than an indication of that ultimate refinement and adjustment which is his most positive general value. One has the sense of a manipulation of objects which are separate from the reader, which are *out there* in the environment. (*CS*, pp. 244–5, emphasis in original)

Williams here exposes the circular argument on which practical criticism and *The Great Tradition* depend. Great literature is defined by its complexity; complex texts are taken to be examples of great literature. This recapitulates the separation between writing and society which Williams wrote *Culture and Society* specifically to overcome. To achieve this, Williams tried to break down preconceived notions of the *literary* and sought instead to open up English studies to broader forms of writing, and hence to value a greater range of human experience. He sought to decentre literature as a discipline, and open it up to a broader range of objects of study:

> Leavis might reasonably reply, to what I have written, that to see literature as a specialism among others is not to see literature at all. I would agree with this. But the emphasis I am trying to make is that, in the work of continuity and change, and just because of the elements of disintegration, we cannot make literary experience the sole, or even the central test. We cannot even, I would argue, put the important stress on the 'minority', for the idea of the conscious minority is itself no more than a defensive symptom against the general dangers. (*CS*, p. 254)

The concept of *literature* is in effect demolished by the conclusion of *Culture and Society*, and with it the implicit defence of an elite minority culture is opened up to political and sociological critique. In *Culture and Society* Williams pinpoints the historical process by which *art* became separated from *society* and constituted as its own fully autonomous field. A materialist approach to art would seek to overcome this separation. This is what happened during the subsequent decades of Williams's career.

MARXISM – AND LITERATURE

The Great Tradition is founded upon a circular argument. Anything that Leavis writes about is by definition great literature. Anything which he considered great literature is included in his study. Raymond Williams's frustration with this was that there was no externally verifiable definition of 'literature'. Indeed, the term seemed to exclude more kinds of writing than it included. Not only were any kinds of non-imaginative works (journalism, diaries, letters) out of the equation, but the majority of imaginative works also were excluded from the canon. To reject literary idealism was thus to reject 'literature' as a categorical essence, and open up cultural analysis to more varied forms of writing.

In a curiously paradoxical move, the new approach to writing which Williams propounded both under- and over-valued the role played by literature in society. As a categorical essence, the concept of *literature* was rejected. This rejection led Williams to explore the ways in which literature – now defined as *writing* – is materially active in society, and helps cause social and political changes to occur. Thus, literature is somewhat devalued as a concept, at the same time that actual literary works are shown to have more material power than had previously seemed possible.

This material turn depends strongly on Williams's engagement with Marxist theory – and what he perceived as Marx's inability to develop a sophisticated theory of culture. As he put it, 'an increasing number of Marxists now believe that cultural theory has become even more important, in modern social and cultural conditions, than it was in Marx's own day' (*WCS*, p. 196).

According to Marx, human societies consist of a controlling economic base and a controlled superstructure – the domain of culture.[13] The crucial activity not assigned by Marx to the category of superstructure is that of commodity production and exchange. It is the basic premise of classical Marxism that whoever controls the means of production in any given society controls ultimately also much broader conditions of social and cultural life. This influence can be extended to cover the entire scope of human activities and hence Marx assigns to the economy a causal position in relation to those activities which are regarded as superstructural or secondary and dependent.

It is easy to see how the secondary and dependent view of cultural products can be aligned with the literary idealism outlined above. In each case the literary text is assumed to be zoned off from material contact with the outside world. This congruence exists despite the wildly different political perspectives of Marx and, later, Leavis and Richards.

Williams acknowledges the causal power of the economy. But he suggests that the economy is only causally effective because its power is manifested through a range of other social and material practices. In *The Long Revolution*, published in 1961 as a companion volume to *Culture and Society*, he identifies four systems crucial to the development of social and cultural life. These are the system of decision; the system of maintenance; the system of learning and communication; and the system of generation and nurture (*LR*, p. 133). Roughly speaking, by these systems Williams means politics, the economy, education and care for others.[14] In Marx's work, most of the emphasis is placed upon the first two. Williams refers to this as a 'conditioned reflex to various forms of class society' in which 'the true nature of society – a human organization for common needs – was in fact filtered through the interests in power and property which were natural to ruling groups' (*LR*, p. 131). To acquiesce to this filtered view of society is to remain entrapped by the power of the economic base. For if we were able to reveal the extent to which this power can only operate by suppressing the systems of communication and generation, we would be able to rethink social determinism.

When looking back on this point in *Politics and Letters*, Williams tried to clarify what he meant by this. He considers the example of the industrial revolution – and refuses to see it solely as a transformation in economic relations:

> For the industrial revolution was among other things a revolution in the production of literacy and it is at this point that the argument turns full circle. The steam press was as much a part of the industrial revolution as the steam jenny or the steam locomotive. What it was producing was literacy; and with it a new kind of newspaper and novel. The traditional formulations that I was attacking would have seen the press as only a reflection at a much later stage of the economic order, which had produced the political order which had then produced the cultural order which had produced the press. Whereas the revolution itself, as a transformation of the mode of production, already included many changes which the ordinary definitions . . . said were not economic. The task was not to see how the industrial revolution affected other sectors, but to see that it was an industrial revolution in the production of culture as much as an industrial revolution in clothing . . . or in the production of light, of power, of building materials. (*PL*, p. 144)

Williams examines the notion that an economic order produces a political order which in turn produces a cultural order. The advantage of this differentiation of societal activities into different levels is that – *contra* literary idealism – it emphasizes that there is a relationship between political/historical processes and literature. Williams does not stop there, however. This three-stage reflection theory posits a view of the written text which is entirely passive, as if it is entirely dependent on other processes worked out in advance. To Williams, the writing of a literary text is already a process in itself, rather than a mere reflection of other processes. Rather than positing a model where all the important developments in a society are elsewhere, and are merely reflected second-hand by written texts, Williams developed a position whence he could argue that the writing of a text itself is an active process in society.

The name Williams would later give to that position is cultural materialism. It tells us that the forces active at the economic base have no power in the abstract. They are effective only because they operate in and through systems of communication and nurture as well as through the systems of decision and maintenance.[15] In the words of the French Marxist Louis Althusser, these systems then retain a *relative autonomy*.[16] There is thus no two-tiered structure of economic decision and super-structual reaction. There is rather an integration of all social activities, mutually constituting and informing.

Literature must then be seen as an inextricable element of much broader social processes. It contributes to the making and contesting of a social whole. At the same time, it is partially produced by other elements in that whole. Without the industrial revolution, we might say, no Dickens. But in a sense without Dickens, the kind of society that was produced by industrialization would also be qualitatively different.

Accordingly, what Williams refers to as the 'long revolution' is simultaneously a revolution in literary form *and* in social democracy. The changed conditions of industrial society simultaneously produced changed conditions of reading and writing. Adult literary was greatly expanded. This literacy expanded greatly beyond the strictly functional level, and encompassed a literacy of critical thinking. Throughout the long revolution, from the early nineteenth century, new kinds of writing played a precise part in this kind of critical consciousness and hence participated in a broader revolution – towards democratic change. Important examples Williams gives of this kind of writing are Godwin's *Caleb Williams*; Dickens's *Dombey and Son* and Gaskell's *North and South*.[17] The important point to emphasize then is that these texts are not considered in isolation. Williams reads them in the context of that broader revolution towards democratic forms, in which the writing is both reflection on social change and active stimulant towards further change.

Writing, and cultural forms in general, are thus revealed to be materially active within a society, rather than simply passive reflections on it. Stuart Hall suggests that the two texts in which Williams most fully probes this material relation between writing and social processes are *The Country and the City* (1973) and *Marxism and Literature* (1977).[18] In each of these texts, Williams draws parallels between the construction of specific social orders and the practice of specific kinds of writing. *Marxism and Literature* is an attempt to theorize the relationship between writing and the capitalist social order:

> The social and political order which maintains a capitalist market, like the social and political struggles which created it, is necessarily a material production. From castles and palaces and churches to prisons and workhouses and schools; from weapons of war to a controlled press: any ruling class, in variable ways though always materially, produces a social and political order. These are never superstructural activities. They are the necessarily material production within which an apparently self-subsistent mode of production can alone be carried on. The complexity of this process is especially remarkable in advanced capitalist societies, where it is wholly beside the point to isolate 'production' and 'industry' from the comparably material production of 'defence', 'law and order', 'welfare', 'entertainment' and 'public opinion.' (*ML*, p. 93)

Williams refuses to isolate the press, the police, industry or the economy. This is tantamount to a disavowal of the Marxist concepts of *base* and *superstructure*. To see cultural production as somehow secondary and immaterial would be to approach it from the idealist perspective from which Williams had struggled to depart. This would seriously limit Marxist analysis of cultural forms for it would prevent detailed analysis of the part played by cultural forms in the formation of a social order.

In *Marxism and Literature* Williams defines the social order as one of organized international capitalism. In his earlier study, *The Country and the City* (1973), he had equated the incubation of a capitalist order during the early modern period with the building of national states. These different versions of the social order are then mapped onto each other. The nation-state itself is revealed to be an important element of the capitalist order. This transposition from nation to capitalist order is analysed in *Marxism and Literature* through a rigorous critique of the concept of a *national tradition* in literature.

Williams was aware that the concept of *literature* had emerged during the seventeenth century. Initially, it had an emphasis on learning and observation, giving way to a valorization of works of creativity or imagination during the nineteenth century (*ML*, p. 48). The accompanying concept of *national tradition* emerged to embody and express the best of all cultural and literary production from a nation's history, in effect telling the nation all the best things about itself. By definition, works which did not or could not be made to conform to this model of the nation and its history had to be excluded from the national tradition, along with whatever experiences and values they expressed.

Argument over what is and is not 'literature' on this reckoning becomes much more than an academic debate over the ontological status of seventeenth-century documents. It becomes the terrain on which the whole question of what ideas and experiences are to be accepted and valued in the contemporary world is also fought out. If the notion of the literary retains any significance, it is by drawing attention to the different stories a society tells itself about who its members are and how they are constituted. Williams shows that this literary debate is ongoing and contested rather than finished and stable. To appreciate Williams's critique of the concept of national tradition fully, we must turn to the work on drama that he produced in the 1960s.

DRAMA, NATION, VOICE

As the *New Left Review* editors suggested to Williams in *Politics and Letters*, one of the earliest areas in which he had visibly departed from the organicist approach of Leavis and the practical-critical approach of Richards was that of drama (*PL*, p. 190). Williams had paid a great deal of attention to drama, from his earliest work in *Drama from Ibsen to Eliot*. Leavis by contrast was notably silent on that whole area.

This is a very curious phenomenon. One of the ways in which Leavis had asserted the continuity of his great tradition of English letters was through the manifest continuity of a linguistic inheritance. In *Politics and Letters*, Williams characterizes this Leavisite notion of linguistic heritage as the 'notion of language as a continuous legacy through the ages that carries the finest insights of community' (*PL*, pp. 176–7). One might expect that the spoken voice of drama could provide the kinds of evidence for the continuity of a harmonious linguistic community that Leavis asserted. His overlooking of drama thus seems to be a very striking one. This is the case unless we overhaul the notion of a continuous linguistic heritage, and reject with it the idealist reading of literary traditions and hence of national essence. It may well be that Leavis maintained a deep silence on the matter of drama precisely because, rather than evincing evidence of his cherished linguistic organic community, it actually evinced the opposite: a tradition of discontinuity and rupture.

This at least is what Williams finds in dramatic history. If, as Williams averred, *Drama from Ibsen to Eliot* was an experiment in the applicability of practical criticism to drama, it was an experiment which failed. Or, rather, it succeeded – in demonstrating the *inapplicability* of that approach. This chimed in with Williams's deepening realization that, for all its seductions, practical criticism was inappropriate as a means of understanding how writing works.

The significant thing about *Drama from Ibsen to Eliot* is that although its *methodology* is a practical-critical one, its *object* is greatly extended. It is the first text in which Williams analyses at length a body of writing other than the English canon. The drama in which he professes an interest is very much the drama of emerging peripheral nations: Scandinavia and Ireland. As he told the *Politics and Letters* interviewers, 'it is a historical fact that from the 1890s . . . the significant drama was always a minority breakaway from the majority commercial theatres' (*PL*, p. 194). In turning his attention to this minority theatre, he was already implicitly raising the kinds of question that practical criticism had not allowed him: why is the mainstream theatre of England and France so weak? Why is the emergent drama of these other nations so rich? What are the historical conditions relating to these developments? This questioning became more explicitly the case in his subsequent book, *Drama from Ibsen to Brecht* (1968).

Williams's enthusiasm for the marginalized drama of Scandinavia, Ireland and Wales is best expressed in one word: *polyphony*. He is interested in the kinds of drama that mobilize a variety of voices and that maintain this variety up to and beyond the conclusion of the dramatic action, so that the plays in question can be said to resist a narrative logic of closure. This is the case in various ways in the patterned voices of the drama of Sean O'Casey, Yeats, Ibsen, Strindberg and, in another context, Dylan Thomas.

Although Williams was professor of drama at Cambridge from 1974 to 1984, his writing on English drama is comparatively slight. No doubt this was because he believed the achievement of English dramatists since the renaissance to be comparably slight. In a late essay on 'English naturalism', Williams explored the reasons for this. He suggested that the drama of nineteenth-century England and France was relatively weak because historical conditions did not allow for innovative, oppositional or polyphonic vocal work. This is implicitly related to the conditions of stability arising out of the strongly imperial nature of Britain and France at the time: oppositional voices were not encouraged.[19]

Williams's interest in the emergent drama of Scandinavia, Ireland and Wales follows a precise trajectory. He is not interested in the mono-logical nature of English theatre in the nineteenth century because he thinks that the theatrical space had been occupied by anti-democratic tendencies and did not enable a multiplicity of voices on the stage. If monarchy produces monologue, we might say, then the emerging nations of democracy are better suited to dialogue.

This patterning of polyphonic voices was most fully realized in the expressionist plays of August Strindberg. Throughout *Drama from Ibsen to Brecht*, Williams discusses the writing for pure disembodied voice that Strindberg mobilized. This multiplicity of voices worked against a narrative logic of closure: in a real sense, it was hard to say how exactly these plays ended. *The Road to Damascus*, for example, 'yielded to a simultaneity of past and future' which enabled the play not only to reflect upon a precise historical experience, but also to posit a variety of multiple different potential futures.[20] *Dreamplay* employs the method of a dream as 'a means of serious analysis of the experience of identity' in which the only 'unifying mechanism' is the 'consciousness of the dreamer', and where the convention of utilizing several different voices militates against the resolution of singular identities at the play's conclusion (*DIB*, p. 95). *Ghost Sonata* achieves this multiplicity of voices in a 'persistent pattern', so that again no single voice is allowed to dominate (*DIB*, p. 99).

This kind of drama simply could not have been produced in imperial societies, where emerging and dissident voices would not become audible until later – as, for example, in Ireland. The process of industrialization in Ireland would create radically new relationships. Mass migration from rural to urban areas created conditions in which people for the first time became accustomed to encountering strangers on a regular basis. How they might relate to each other, in the conditions of relative crowding that characterized urban life, was then a major question.

When Williams praises the Irish drama of Synge and O'Casey, it is precisely because the plays of these dramatists did not only reflect passively the disorientating changes which had occurred. They also actively helped to develop new forms of relationship, and new forms of community, in which the people of Ireland could feel at home. Thus in both these writers, there is a 'sense of a specific social transition from rural to urban speech' (*PL*, p. 195). This was the history of Ireland at the time. The drama was then part of that history.

In *Drama from Ibsen to Brecht*, Williams praises the drama of W. B. Yeats in similar terms. Yeats too was able to 'draw on the source of vitality in Irish country speech' (*DIB*, p. 122). This new linguistic resource again existed in dialectical relation to the society from which it was drawn. By mobilizing the patterns of speech that he found in the contemporary world, Yeats was able to develop an understanding of the changes that were beginning to come over Ireland. Williams suggests that Yeats's most successful play was *The Death of Cuchulain*. He describes the achievement of Yeats in the following way:

> What he had done, in his theatre, and what he had encouraged others to do, was indeed just this: to think, to imagine, a dramatic figure, until it 'stood where they had stood'. And then it was not only Cuchulain (in the legends that remained, for the most part, an exploitation of local colour) but a contemporary Irish world. (*DIB*, p. 128)

The plays of Synge, O'Casey and Yeats are all understood as material elements within a general Irish history. The strength of the plays in question is that they provide a positive resource for the understanding of changed social relations, through the mobilization on the stage of a multiplicity of different voices. This both reflected the changed material circumstances of life in Ireland and contributed to further change – to the development of democratic forms of relationship and represen-tation.

Williams's interest in the voice, and its relation to historical processes, opens a rich vein of congruence between his dramatic criticism and the concurrent work of semiotics, which had itself arisen partly out of Freudian psychoanalysis. In semiotics, the whole object of investigation is language. Williams reveals in *Politics and Letters* that he was fully aware of the congruence between his work and that of semiotics, and of a precise historical reason for it. He points out to his interviewers that the historical conditions which had enabled the emergence of the expressionist theatre were the very conditions which had also given rise to Freudian psychoanalysis. The historical process of modernity had created conditions of unfamiliarity, mobility, exile and change at such a frighteningly rapid pace that the result was a discursive practice given over to exploring and understanding those changes. This is what Williams finds happening in the emergent Scandinavian drama and in the same manner – though in a different form – in the psychoanalytic theory of Freud. As a result, Williams likens Freud to a modernist writer:

> Freud's writings should be read, not so much as a body of science, as what are called in another category novels – and as such they are extraordinarily interesting, although of course they have an extraordinarily different status. One reads them as one would read the closely connected contemporary writing of Strindberg or Proust, granting no necessary prior validity because they were based on clinical experience, simply because between the clinical experience and the text there is the process of composition. After all, what is the validity of Strindberg or Proust? Their work articulates another kind of experience, an observation of experience, which preceded and continued into the process of observation. (*PL*, p. 332)

The reading of Freud as novelist is based on the idea that Freud produces a kind of writing unlike anything that had gone before, arising out of the precise historical experience of modernization. Williams wishes to strip Freud of the privileged aura of scientific authority, while at the same time drawing attention to the utility of considering Freud's work specifically as a body of writing which can then be understood historically like any other. What is interesting is that we then find – despite differences of form – an important area of congruence between the expressionist drama and Freudian theory, at the level of content, and specifically in the matter of the multiplicity of voice. This can be elucidated by considering Williams's interest in semiotics alongside the work of his younger contemporary, the French psychoanalyst Julia Kristeva.

CULTURAL MATERIALISM AND HISTORICAL SEMIOTICS

Kristeva is a psychoanalyst in the Lacanian mould: she is interested in how subjectivity is formed as a linguistic process and in how the self is always a linguistic construct. She interrogates the Freudian narrative of subjectivity formation as a journey from *nature* to *culture* founded on the civilizing repression of instinctive desire. She understands subjectivity formation, rather, as a process of *language acquisition*.

This is both individual and social, in the sense that language always precedes the individual. For the individual to acquire subjectivity by acquiring language, he or she must therefore enter into the social world which is always already formed. At the same time, to acquire language in this way – and to use it – is also a matter of individual expression, so that the speech act is always structured both socially and personally. Subjectivity is generated only through the speech act, with the implication that self-identification in language also turns out to be a process that occurs dialectically, through the interaction of the socially structured self with a linguistic field.

To acquire language is to enter into what Kristeva calls the *symbolic order*. Like any order, this order has its own rules and logic. The symbolic order of language tends towards a logic of closure. It enables purposive-rational communication founded on logic and rules, rather than emotion or expression.[21] It is this rational purposive communication which enables the social order to be constructed – and Kristeva finds evidence of this in a whole range of institutions from banks and building societies to parliaments and armies, schools and post offices. These are the physical manifestations of the symbolic order, and they are achieved via the action of the symbolic order in and through language.

At the same time, language is not so rigidly structured as to be not amenable to individual modification. On the contrary, language always precedes the subject, but the way in which the subject uses language is always a subjective process, bearing the hallmarks of individuality. Then again, the process of acquiring an identity is itself always a social and dialectical one, so that there is no such thing as simple individual identity. There is always, rather, a social process of identity formation.

Instead of a linear narrative of identity formation, Kristeva thus proposes an ongoing *process* of identity that can never be completed. Every speech act – every attempt at subjectivity – bears the stamp of the symbolic order because language is the bearer of that order. Yet each linguistic event also has the capacity to modify or elude the structure of that order, the structure of language itself. Kristeva thus proposes a second term, the *semiotic*, to refer to the capacity of language to elude the symbolic order even while entering it. The *semiotic* is the stamp of individual subjectivity operating within the symbolic order. It is never simply sloughed off. The symbolic order does not simply jettison the semiotic. The two elements of linguistic expression exist in ongoing dialectical relation with each other, with the result that the symbolic order – and the social order which is based on it – can always be negated by semiotic inversion.

The important point to emerge out of Kristeva's sense of the interplay between *semiotic* and *symbolic* is that language is always polyphonic. It is never a simple instrument of purposive-rational communication and does not simply tend towards a narrative logic of closure. There are no endings in language. There is only an ongoing process.

Raymond Williams shows himself to be aware of this social-subjective dialectic at work in language when he writes:

> The thing that is technically called *multiaccentuality* in a word, the fact that there really is more than one proper meaning, all the associations and root qualities and so on – this then becomes crucial, and one begins to see that use of words as almost material. (*WSW*, p. 83)

Williams's interest in language deepened as he read broadly in all kinds of social and cultural theory during the 1970s. Conventionally, this is understood as Williams's engagement with European Marxist theory, and in particular his reading of Goldmann, Althusser, Lukács and Gramsci, culminating in his own study, *Marxism and Literature*, in 1977.[22] This account of Williams is not untrue, but it is arguably incomplete. The longest section of *Marxism and Literature* is the section on language, and this reveals Williams's cultural materialism to have more in common with the practice of semiotics than has previously been acknowledged.

We know from *Politics and Letters* that Williams was reading the work of social-linguists Rossi-Landi, Chomsky and Benveniste at this time.[23] We know also that he was aware that their linguistic enterprise had been strongly informed by the psychoanalytic work of Jacques Lacan. *Marxism and Literature*, when approached in this light, is not so much the terminus of a long period of engagement with Marxist theory. It is, rather, the beginning of a process of combining that theory with semiotic work as it had developed after Lacan. Thus when Williams describes language as 'almost material', he is expanding his own understanding of *materialism* to include this semiotic element.

The early stages of Williams's career saw him caught between two poles: idealism and materialism. These modes can be understood alongside Kristeva's sense of the *symbolic* and the *semiotic* respectively. The *semiotic* refers to the capacity of language to elude formalization and hence to resist the rendering passive of communication acts within the symbolic order. Kristeva, like Williams, is interested in the poetics of emergence. In her study *Revolution in Poetic Language*, she asks:

> At what historical moment does social exchange tolerate or necessitate the manifestation of the signifying process in its 'poetic' or 'esoteric' form? Under what conditions does this 'esoterism,' in displacing the boundaries of socially established signifying practices, correspond to socio-economic change, and, ultimately, even to revolution?[24]

The historical point at which Kristeva suggests writers began to discover means of harnessing the semiotic in such a way as to produce art that was not orientated solely towards achieving rational communication was the middle of the nineteenth century. The implication of Kristeva's work is that all language and hence all writing has at least the potential to act in a polyphonic way, that refuses acquiescence in the symbolic order. The great modernists who developed new literary forms from the second half of the nineteenth century onwards are valued on this account because they take to an extreme what is implicit in such a concept of language: a polyphony of voice and a resistance to narrative closure. Kristeva values the modernist writers Dostoievsky, Joyce, Proust and Kafka highly for this reason. To be a polyphonic writer is to participate in Kristeva's revolution in poetic language. Indeed, it is tantamount to her definition of *modernist*.

That the period of these writers coincides exactly with Raymond Williams's long revolution is suggestive. What this account of Kristeva most usefully adds to an understanding of Williams is a sense of individual subjectivity and agency as it is constituted in and through language. This complements Williams's sense of social and collective forms of agency. Indeed, Kristeva reveals the two strands to be related in important ways. Having established the connection between rational

communication and the symbolic order in contradistinction to the semiotic state which constantly opposes it, she maps this opposition onto a
revolutionary history:

> The problem then was one of finding practices of expenditure capable of
> confronting the machine, colonial expansion, banks, science, Parliament
> – those positions of mastery that conceal their violence and pretend to be
> mere neutral legality. Recovering the subject's vehemence required a descent
> into the most archaic stage of his positing, one contemporaneous with
> the positing of social order . . . so that violence, surging up through the
> phonetic, syntactic and logical orders, could reach the symbolic order
> and the technocratic ideologies that had been built over this violence to
> ignore or repress it. To penetrate the era, poetry had to disturb the logic
> that dominated the social order and to do so through that logic itself, by
> assuming and unravelling its position, its syntheses, and hence the ideologies
> it controls.[25]

Banks, scientific institutions and parliaments are all manifestations of
the symbolic order. The symbolic order, in other words, becomes visible
in the external manifestations of the modern nation-state and its
different institutions, just as, to Raymond Williams, the nation-state is
synonymous with the development of a hierarchical capitalist structure.
In Kristeva's account, a revolution in poetic language would enable
an upsurge in linguistic violence directed against the rules of logic and
syntax on which the symbolic order is founded. It is a large claim for
the radical power of modernist poetry, but as we have seen, a fully
material account of literature operates in a paradoxical way, precisely
by both under- and over-valuing the power of literature.

When Kristeva writes of the epistemic violence directed by the great
modernist poets against the grammatical laws of the age in order to
penetrate their logic, there is an undeniable rhetorical element, which
we do not find in Williams. The substantive argument, though, is much
the same. Williams valorizes the writing for a polyphony of voice that
he found in Synge and Yeats, Ibsen and Strindberg and, in another
period, Dylan Thomas. His evaluation of this work is based precisely
on the potential of language to disrupt the symbolic order. He values
the poetic emergence of those writers in contradistinction to the
parliamentary, nationalist, imperial and authoritarian tendencies that
are found in the societies of England and France at the time, and
which also characterized the drama produced in those societies. To

Williams, as with Kristeva, this socially and politically transgressive element is tantamount to a definition of modernist writer. In each case, the polyphonic voice of modernist writing explicitly opposes and undercuts the imperialism of narrative monologue.

In Williams's account, the psychoanalytic work of Freud and the dramatic work of Strindberg have a common origin. The modernist writers emerged as a result of the historic experience of modernization and turbulent change – as did the comparably modernist writings of Freud. In the face of disorientating change, each writer had pursued the quest for a deeper understanding of identity formation right back into the human mind itself. If Freud can be understood as a kind of modernist writer like Proust or Strindberg then, by the same token, Strindberg can be understood as a kind of psychoanalytic dramatist. By showing that he is interested in the common historical origin of these radically diverse discourses, and by expanding his own understanding of the concept of materialism to incorporate the linguistic element, Williams developed cultural materialism as a theory of culture which combines elements of both Marxism and psychoanalysis, to their mutual transformation.

Semiotics provides cultural materialism with a useful framework for understanding certain historical processes. It is not understood as a science as such, in the sense that it is not accorded any greater sense of authority than other kinds of writing. This is precisely how Williams understood the earlier field of psychoanalysis. He saw Freud as a suggestive resource rather than a scientific authority. It is significant that, in *Politics and Letters*, Williams makes a similar point about Lacan: 'In the same way the work of Lacan should not be taken as a confirmatory authority, the provision of a framework within which other compositions are read, but rather itself as a composition which we all believe to be important' (*PL*, p. 332).

Williams maintains a sense of the importance of understanding psychoanalysis through the modifications to it propounded by Lacan, while at the same time de-privileging Lacan by undermining his authoritative position. In this way, Williams submits the category of psychoanalysis to a historical critique:

> I have great respect for Lacan, but the totally uncritical way in which certain of his concepts of phases in language development have been lifted into a theoretical pediment of literary semiotics is absurd, in a world in

which there is current scientific work of a non-philological kind with which all such concepts have to be brought into interplay. There has been such justified suspicion on the left of the dominance of behaviourism in the experimental social sciences that there has been an over-accommodation to the claims of psycho-analysis and its various derived schools, which have seemed much nearer and more radical, often precisely because of their literary qualities. What is needed is not a blending of concepts of literature with concepts from Lacan, but an introduction of literary practice to the quite different practice of experimental observation. That would be the materialist recovery. (*PL*, p. 341)

Williams had earlier considered precise pieces of writing separately from the categorical essence, literature. He understands Freud and Lacan in the same way. He considers the writing of these psychoanalysts separately from the category of psychoanalysis. Thus he is interested in Freud and Lacan as modernist writers, without treating them as scientific authorities in the abstract.[26]

This point emerges from two important late Williams essays. 'Problems of materialism' was a review of the work of Italian analyst Sebastiano Timpanaro, published in *New Left Review* in 1978, and again in the selection entitled *Problems in Materialism and Culture* (1980). 'Crisis in English studies' originated as a Cambridge lecture on cultural theory in 1981, and was subsequently published in the volume *Writing in Society* (1984).

'Problems of materialism' is Williams's recapitulation of the themes that had previously been latent in his work. Initially, this takes the form of a rejection of the categorical imperative: 'in the very course of opposing systematic universal explanations of many of the common-ground processes, provisional and secular procedures and findings tend to be grouped into what appear but never can be systematic, universal and categorical explanations of the same general kind' (*PMC*, p. 103). Williams's early literary work had frustrated him because it left no room to ask the question: How do people form their judgements of texts? This is also what he finds in the blind acceptance of behavioural theory, based on a crude version of psychoanalysis. The parallel between how ideas are formed in literature and in science is explicit:

What has ordinarily happened, even inside 'psychology', with its variation into what are often non-communicating schools, but even more in the general culture, with its eclectic reliance on 'scientifically founded concepts' derived from evidence and procedures never rigorously examined, is the diffusion of a set of systems which even when they are materialist in character – and many of the most widely diffused are evidently and even proudly not – take on the appearance of general humane explanations. Thus one can be asked, in the same mode as for an opinion of a film or a novel, whether one 'accepts the findings' of Freud or of Skinner or of Lacan, without any significant realisation that all such 'findings' depend on criteria of evidence, and on the (contested) theoretical presuppositions of both the evidence and the criteria. (These considerations would be relevant, of course, also to the 'opinion' of the film or the novel.) (*PMC*, p. 117)

Although Williams conflates the work of very different figures Freud, Lacan and Skinner in 'Problems of materialism', his general point is clear. He does not use psychology or psychoanalysis as definitive statements of timeless truths. There is no question to him of simply taking up the findings of psychoanalysis and mobilizing them uncritically. To Williams, it is inappropriate to talk of psychoanalysis in terms of its explicit findings, for the implication of taking such an approach would be entrapment within a strict genetic, biological and behavioural determinism. Rather than approach the matter in terms of stable findings, then, Williams approaches psychoanalysis as a specific kind of writing. As such, he is able to use it to interrogate some of his own concepts and postulates, without registering an unquestioning devotion to the discipline. Throughout 'Problems of materialism', Williams attempts to restore a sense of the material and ideological processes active behind supposedly neutral science, just as he had earlier done in literature. To do so is to extend the horizons of his understanding of cultural materialism, for the question implicitly raised by Williams throughout the essay is: Is psychoanalysis a kind of materialism?

The answer depends on what we understand by psychoanalysis. If psychoanalysis is mobilized uncritically through ratifying appeal to its apparently authoritative status, then Williams wants nothing to do with it. For to accept its 'findings' uncritically is to forestall the very questions of how ideas are formed which are the goal of cultural materialism. This uncritical acceptance would be a kind of psychic idealism, and as such, not properly materialist.

If on the other hand psychoanalytic work is taken as a suggestive set of ideas, rather than as the last word on identity formation, then it

interests Williams. This is because psychoanalysis so understood opens
up a series of questions as to how ideas and images are formed, and
this can properly be called materialist. Williams, as we have seen,
understood the psychoanalytic project as a kind of literary project, in
the sense that it was given over to trying to understand the conditions
of modernity out of which it had arisen. As a result, it is not timeless
or ahistorical; it has a material and knowable history and a particular
material framework within which its 'findings' have to be considered.

No doubt it is because of this ambiguous definition that Williams
preferred not to use the term *psychoanalysis* in his own work. Williams
concludes 'Problems of materialism' with an implicit call to broaden
the understanding of materialism so that it can incorporate analysis of
mental and cognitive processes, without being trapped in the idealist
mystifications of psychoanalysis. He concludes: 'analysis of these varying classes of concepts is fundamentally necessary, as a new form of
historical and cultural linguistics' (*PMC*, p. 118). Having rejected psychoanalysis as a categorical discipline, he suggests that it would be valuable
to hold on to some of the insights of that work, and understand them
alongside the insights of more conventional literary study. Implicitly,
then, Williams is in need of a new term, for a new kind of work, that
will enable him to take on the concepts of Freud and Lacan without
needing to offer blind obeisance to them.

In this sense, the essay 'Crisis in English studies' begins where
'Problems of materialism' concludes. Having originally intended to use
the material as a series of lectures on literary theory in Cambridge,
Williams was prompted by the MacCabe controversy to bring it
forward and deliver it as one condensed lecture.[27] Much of it is a recapitulation of the foregoing themes: the suspicion of psychoanalysis's
authoritative claim, tempered by the potential for certain concepts
from that work to offer suggestive ways of understanding subjectivity
historically. Again, this brings Williams to a point where he needs a
new term to refer to those elements of psychoanalytic work from which
he takes real value, in contradistinction to those which he mistrusts.

This time, however, the term is to hand. It is, in short, *semiotics*. This
is the term for the practice whereby literary study, psychoanalytic
theory and a whole range of work across all the human sciences can
be brought into useful dialogue with each other without overvaluing
disciplinary boundaries or the status of one or two leading figures in
each discipline. It is a way of rendering psychoanalysis literary, and of

rendering literature amenable to material psychological interrogation. Williams says:

> It was here, perhaps to our mutual surprise, that my work found new points of contact with certain work in more recent *semiotics*. There were still radical differences, especially in their reliance on structural linguistics and psychoanalysis, in particular forms; but I remember saying that a fully historical *semiotics* would be very much the same thing as cultural materialism . . . (*WS*, p. 210, emphasis added)

The embrace of semiotics arises out of Williams's methodological uncertainty as to how exactly to understand the status of psychoanalysis. Whereas psychoanalysis left Williams with the uneasy question – Is it material or not? – the interest in semiotics is unambiguously materialist. Unlike the tendency in psychoanalysis to posit final answers which cannot be questioned, semiotics represented to Williams a way of asking perpetual questions. A semiotic approach to literature, for example, would enable radical rereadings, where the known and reproduced historical conclusions offered by the text can be short-circuited by the tendency of semiotic analysis to question exactly what it is that is constructed in language:

> Thus the value of literature is precisely that it is one of the areas where the grip of ideology is or can be loosened, because although it cannot escape ideological construction, the point about its literariness is that it is a continual questioning of it internally. So you get readings which are very similar to certain recent *semiotic* readings, where you construct a text and subtext, where you can say, 'this is what is reproduced from the ideology'; but also, 'this is what is incongruously happening in the text which undermines or questions or in certain cases entirely subverts it.' This method has been used in very detailed and interesting analysis. (*WS*, p. 208, emphasis added)

It is this sense of subversion that had enabled Julia Kristeva's semiotic critique of Lacan's concept of the symbolic order. The same sense, understood as a resistance to narrative closure and hence to ideological containment, reveals cultural materialism to contain an important semiotic element. Semiotics, as we have seen in the work of Kristeva, explores the radical potential of language to subvert its own authority. This had also been an interest of Raymond Williams's from the earliest stage of his career, when he developed *Keywords*[28] precisely as a means of showing the historic variability and multi-accentuality of language. Thus the work of a semiotician such as Kristeva renders more explicit what had been present in the work of Williams in latent form.

NATION AND NEGATION

At the conclusion of the essay 'Crisis in English studies', Williams defines cultural materialism as 'analysis of all forms of signification, including quite centrally writing, within the actual means and conditions of their production' (*WS*, p. 210). For primarily institutional reasons, the object of Williams's analysis tended to be literature rather than other social forms of signification such as painting, music, art, architecture and so on. Within that context, Williams decentred the concept of *literature*, opening it up to the broadest conceivable definition. This process of inclusion is achieved by converting a preconceived notion of *literature* into the more broadly encompassing *writing*. It is the practice of cultural materialism to understand the material and historical processes at work in the activity of producing a passage of writing.

The shift is from a concept of literature which merely reflects the society in which it was produced, as it were passively, to a concept according to which literature itself is part of the material process by which society is generated. In terms expressed by Hungarian Marxist Georg Lukács, it is a shift from a version of literature which merely *describes*, to an idea of communication which actively *narrates*.[29] The crucial distinction is all about seeing literature as an active process, itself contributing to the creation of a social order which cannot be seen as complete without its literature. Once we have grasped a sense of continuing process as opposed to a mechanical model of social determinism, the estimation of the place of literature in society will be radically revised.

By operating in consciousness, literature – along with all other forms of signification – contributes to the active production of a specific social order. Thus Benedict Anderson was able to argue that the history of nation-states is analogous to the history of writing in general, and of print capitalism in particular. The nation-state is imagined into being by the writing which imagines its existence. This is as true of literature as of other kinds of writing and other kinds of signification. To understand the material history of writing is to understand the precise formations and relations in which it is produced. The claim that the history of nation-states is inextricable from the history of writing is true only in this full sense: not only the writing, but the material relations involved in the writing, enabled the nation-state to be imagined into existence.

This understanding of how writing operates in consciousness in an active way radically revises the Marxist dichotomy of *base* and *superstructure*. Raymond Williams undertook this revision, partly arising out of his frustration at Marx's perceived failure to produce a theory of cultural forms. Williams argued that cultural forms are themselves material and hence part of the *base* of society. If the activity of the social order is understood as the perpetuation of the nation-state then, as we have seen, this is crucially enabled by the operation of writing and other forms of signification in consciousness. Cultural materialism is the name given to analysis of those forms.

Because this approach seeks to analyse the material nature of mental processes, it can be argued that cultural materialism is partly analogous to semiotic analysis – which also investigates the tangibility of mental processes. Julia Kristeva's semiotic analysis implicitly reveals that the symbolic order is continually negated at the very moment of its assertion. Moreover, Raymond Williams's analysis of the Marxist concepts of base and superstructure explicitly overhauled any rigid distinction between these different levels of society, and showed instead how each fed into the other.

In other words, semiotic analysis shows us how the symbolic order and the economic base can both be subverted or negated. Given that the nation-state is identified in Williams's work with both the economic base, on one hand, and the symbolic order on the other, what does this tell us about the unitary state? Implicitly, the nation-state itself is also always in a process of being negated by the very means which assert its existence. That is, the ideological bonds which hold the state together have always to be actively generated. At the same time, the act of generating such bonds also throws up the possibility for generating a quite alternative set of ideas and hence for formulating quite different kinds of social and political relationship. The nation is always coming into being at the same time that it is permanently capable of being negated and broken into fragments.

2

The Welsh Identity of
Raymond Williams

Raymond Williams's project to articulate a critical cultural materialism could not be complete until he had taken on board a sense of the materiality of language itself. This vital element brought his work into creative dialogue with what he had previously thought of as bourgeois materialism – the work of semiotics, and an interest in the voice.

As with the emergent drama of Scandinavia and Ireland, it was in terms of a polyphony of voices that Williams couched his positive evaluation of the Welsh playwright, Dylan Thomas. Williams praises Thomas's *Under Milk Wood* for 'weaving a pattern of voices, rather than an ordinary conversational sequence' which can 'include not only things said, but things left unsaid, the interpenetration of things seen and imagined' (*DIB*, 1968, p. 217). That is, the play has an important capacity to serve in a subjunctive mood, allowing us to relate what we *know* about Welsh society to how we imagine it *could* be. Williams reminds us that *Under Milk Wood* 'grew out of a broadcast talk . . . which described the dreams and waking of a small Welsh seaside town' (*DIB*, p. 212). His analysis thus posits a distinct relationship between the emergent multiplicity of voices inside the play, and a non-fictional, indeed, a historical, emergence of Welsh consciousness outside the theatre.

The multiplicity of voice relates strongly to the onset of democracy, and the 'dreams and waking' to which Williams refers here could refer to twentieth-century Welsh history in general quite as much as to the individual play. The play's capacity to examine an implicit relationship between things which have been seen and things which as yet can only be imagined has for Williams an important general significance. It hints at the material role played by writing in historical and material processes.

The relationship between writing and history in the Welsh context can be explored in more detail using Williams as a guide. Like his comments on Dylan Thomas, it was very much in terms of the polyphonic voice that Williams stated his praise for the realist writing produced in south Wales during the 1930s. Moreover, when Williams came to write his own novels, he did so consciously in that tradition of socialist critical realism. This raises a question over how exactly Williams's work relates to that earlier body of Welsh industrial writing.

THE WELSH INDUSTRIAL NOVEL

Raymond Williams discusses the phenomenon of Welsh industrial writing in two major essays. 'The Welsh industrial novel' was prepared as the inaugural Gwyn Jones lecture at Cardiff in 1978. 'Working-class, proletarian, socialist: problems in some Welsh novels' was originally published in an anthology of articles about British working-class fiction in 1982.[1] Both pieces were recently reprinted in *Who Speaks for Wales?*

'The Welsh industrial novel' opens in characteristic Williams fashion, with an examination of different definitions of the genre. This is more or less the substance of the whole article, with questions of definition giving way to a relatively brief discussion of several different novelists: Gwyn Jones, Lewis Jones, Jack Jones, Alexander Cordell and Gwyn Thomas. 'Working-class, proletarian, socialist' is a more theoretical take on the historical emergence of the writing in question.

Williams's important definition of industrial writing is as follows. It is a kind of writing set in and around the kinds of place where industrial work takes place: mines, factories and mills. Its main characters are typically involved in this kind of work. In a fuller version of the industrial novel, the characters are also shown to inhabit typical lifestyles accompanying their working life, so that their leisure, their means of interaction and their ways of relating to one another are also seen to be characteristic of the industrial world to which they belong:

> What basically informs the industrial novel, as distinct from other kinds
> of fiction? Both the realist and the naturalist novel, more generally, had been
> predicated on the distinctive assumption . . . that the lives of individuals,
> however intensely and personally realised, are not just influenced but in
> certain crucial ways formed by general social relations. Thus industrial
> work, and its characteristic places and communities, are not just a new
> background: a new 'setting' for a story. In the true industrial novel they
> are seen as formative.[2]

This last point is important, for it has an important bearing on the
fullest available definition of the industrial novel. What matters most
is not the industrial work per se. Rather, the important ingredient is
the impact of this on the lives of the people. Thus, the mine, or the
factory, or the mill is not mere background setting for the unfolding of
a separate action. These are important inasmuch as their operations
and the relations they produce are shown to have a strong impact on
the kind of society in which the action takes place. As a result of this
formative element, the place of work takes on some of the properties
of a character within the novel: it relates to the people and to their
lives, and demonstrates that those lives are always involved in a process
of change.

> Social relations are not assumed, are not static, are not conventions
> within which the tale of a marriage or an inheritance or an adventure can
> go its own way. The working society – actual work, actual relations, an
> actual and visibly altered place – is in the industrial novel central. ('Welsh
> industrial novel', p. 103)

The brief references Williams makes here to marriage, inheritance
and adventure are important, because they show him associating the
Welsh industrial novel with a similar body of work that had been
produced in England during the early industrial revolution. Williams
had shown right back in *The Long Revolution* that unlikely marriages,
inheritances and overseas emigration are the desperate stratagems by
which Victorian novelists sought to foreclose the troubling questions
of social relationship which their novels had raised (*LR*, pp. 82–3).
This was the case in *Mary Barton, Shirley, Hard Times* and *Vanity Fair*.
     Williams underlines the shared genealogy of this classic English
writing with the Welsh industrial novel, when he writes:

the first phase of the industrial novel is a particular crystallisation within English culture, from the mid-1840s to the mid-1850s, when a group of middle-class novelists, for the most part not themselves living in the industrial areas, began to explore this turbulent human world. ('Welsh industrial novel', pp. 96–7)

The implicit kinship between forms of fiction produced in England in the 1840s and south Wales in the 1930s is this: that in each case, rapid industrialization had thrown up a changed set of social relationships, which the novelists in question used their writing actively to explore.

If there is this shared historical genealogy, then there is also an important historical difference between the Welsh writing of the 1930s and the better-known English examples of the 1840s. As Williams points out, Gaskell, the Brontës, Dickens and Thackeray were prominent members of the *middle class*. They did not belong to industrial communities and were certainly not involved in industrial work themselves.

The Welsh writers of the 1930s, by contrast, belonged to the communities of which they wrote. Lewis Jones and the poet Idris Davies had also actively laboured in the kind of work their writings narrate. This is not simply an interesting biographical detail, but an important theoretical element in establishing the definition of the Welsh industrial novel. Thus the Welsh industrial novels, 'unlike the English nineteenth- century examples . . . are, in majority, written from inside the industrial communities; they are working-class novels in the new and distinctive twentieth-century sense' ('Welsh industrial novel', p. 100). It is this written-from-within the working class element that gives the industrial writing produced in depression-era south Wales its distinctive character. Williams states the difference more succinctly in 'Working-class, proletarian, socialist: problems in some Welsh novels', when he writes: 'the writers and intellectuals of twentieth-century Wales are much more often working class in origin than their twentieth-century English counterparts'.[3]

The writers of Welsh industrial fiction were more directly involved not simply with the work but also with the broader lives, relationships and historical currents of which their novels treat. This opens up a further important bearing in the genealogy of the form, and this is again best demonstrated in contradistinction to the industrial writing of the English 1840s. Since Dickens and Gaskell were not intimately involved in the matters which they address, there is a tendency to abstraction in their work. This can be seen in the portrayal of Dickens's Coketown or the allegories of Thackeray's *Vanity Fair*. The history of the industrial revolution as an ongoing process is not realized in specific form within these novels. History is the vague and sublime process that is tangibly happening – somewhere else.

The Welsh industrial novel is not like this. Its writers – like its protagonists – are only too involved in the historical matters of which they write. As a result, there is not this sense of a separation from history. History enters the novels in a specific and verifiable – as opposed to an abstract and absent – way. The novels were written during a period of economic depression, which the writers sought to understand and, by understanding, ease. Neither the historical times nor the geographical locations are abstracted out of the novels in question. Gwyn Thomas's *All Things Betray Thee* demonstrably takes place in the Merthyr of the 1830s. Gwyn Jones's *Times Like These* again can be precisely placed, in the Rhondda Valley, in the 1920s. Moreover, since many of these novels were written during the depression of the 1920s and 1930s, it is this historic event that the novels continually invoke. Williams concludes:

> So then, if we have learned to look in this way, it is no surprise to find at the centre of so many of the Welsh industrial novels of this period one decisive experience: the general strike of 1926 in its specifically Welsh form; that is to say, the general strike followed by the long months of the miners' lockout, by the long years of depression, and very deeply, by the pervasive sense of defeat. ('Welsh industrial novel,' p. 104)

The precise historic and geographical placing of these novels in the Welsh valleys in 1926 gives them a historical specificity that is lacking in say *Hard Times* or *Mary Barton*. Examples Williams gives of this kind of fiction are Gwyn Jones, *Times Like These* (1936); Lewis Jones, *Cwmardy* (1937) and *We Live* (1939); and Jack Jones, *Black Parade* (1935). When Williams set his own novel, *Border Country*, around the general strike, he placed himself squarely in the tradition of Welsh industrial writing.

The general strike of 1926 is a precise crystallization of what, in the context of English writing, had been a much more general historical process in the 1840s: industrialization and the accretion of a specific capitalist order. The English novelists whom Williams had earlier examined appeared to sympathize with this suffering. Yet within the structure of their own society, they were unable or unwilling to imagine any really viable alternatives to it. Thus, as Williams noted, the conventions on which their novels depend are absurd inheritance, unlikely marriage and overseas adventure in the colonies. These stratagems provide narrative closure within the novels that would otherwise lack such closure. They do so often in favour of the existing class structure and of the ruling and owning classes. Solving the problems of inequality in the society was far more difficult.

The recurring conventions in the Welsh industrial novel are quite different. Their conventions are used in order to find ways of identifying a specific future for the society in which the novels were written. This, as we have seen, was particularly difficult in the work of the 1840s.

The Welsh industrial novels typically begin at or shortly after the moment of industrialization of the Welsh valleys. The rapid industrialization that occurs is dangerous and unchecked, in a world governed by little social legislation, so that the first recurring convention of the Welsh industrial novel is the mining disaster (Lewis Jones, *Cwmardy*; Jack Jones, *Bidden to the Feast*; Rhys Davies, *Jubilee Blues*; Menna Gallie, *The Small Mine*). In each case, any attempt at establishing the legal responsibility of the colliery owners for the disaster that has occurred is rapidly quashed by a nominal trial, as in Lewis Jones's *Cwmardy*.

The convention of the industrial disaster, in other words, is a way of exploring the gradual development of class-consciousness in the south Wales valleys. The paternalism of the ruling class is gradually eroded as the workers learn by experience that the colliery owners do not necessarily know what is best for the men. The myth that by benefiting their masters the workers will benefit themselves is rolled back by a deepening awareness that there is no common interest.

If the convention of the mining disaster introduces this element of consciousness in the Welsh industrial novel, then other conventions take it to an extreme form. Almost invariably in these novels, there is the portrayal of a strike action held in protest against low wages and high rents (Lewis Jones, *Cwmardy*; Jack Jones, *Black Parade, Bidden to the Feast*; Gwyn Thomas, *All Things Betray Thee*; Rhys Davies, *A Time to Laugh, Jubilee Blues*). At the same time, many of the novels are set at a historical period of war overseas – either the Boer War, or the First World War. Another feature of Welsh industrial writing is the absent relative who has gone to fight in the war. This was historically likely, in an area of depression and low employment, and of *de facto* economic conscription.

Along with the *strike action* and the *conscripted relative*, a concurrent element of much of the Welsh industrial writing is the portrayal of labour militancy and open class conflict. This is portrayed within the novels via the response to the strike actions by the ruling class. Time and again, the strike is broken through the mobilization of *military force*. This happens in Lewis Jones, *Cwmardy*; Jack Jones, *Black Parade*; Rhys Davies, *A Time to Laugh* and *Jubilee Blues*; and Gwyn Thomas, *All Things Betray Thee*.

The effect of these simultaneous actions is again consciousness-raising. On the one hand, the workers are supposed to believe that their masters know best. On the other hand, this belief is shattered by the turbulent experiences of the characters. The absent relatives are conscripted into the army through economic imperative. That same army is sent in to crush the strike in which that relative's family members are involved. The society is turned against itself. This forces the characters to ask much deeper questions about their place in society, and about their loyalty and solidarity.

This questioning of loyalty is intensified by another frequent convention of the Welsh industrial novel – the coronation. In *Cwmardy*, *Black Parade*, *A Time to Laugh* and *Jubilee Blues*, the coronation of a new English monarch is portrayed with profound social and historical ambivalence. The workers are invited to feel loyalty to this alien order, its empire and its monuments, at the same time that their experiences could hardly be said to cultivate such loyalty. In each case, the crowd who gather on coronation day enthusiastically celebrate the occasion. It is only one or two figures on the side who strike a note of discord.

The conventions that can be identified within the Welsh industrial novel are the mining disaster; the strike; the overseas war; the turning of the army against strikers; and the coronation. These are precise equivalents to the conventions of marriage, inheritance, and escape into the colonies that Raymond Williams believed characterized the English industrial writing of the 1840s. There is however one striking contrast. Those conventions tended towards a narrative closure where all social relations – and the social order itself – are rendered static and unvarying. The conventions of the Welsh industrial novel, written as it is from a working-class and socialist perspective – refuse to cohere in this way. The novels do not read like novels. At least, they do not 'end' with the kind of 'closure' that we find in *Mary Barton*. The Welsh novels in question then seem more open-ended, ambiguous and in that sense more 'literary' than the better-known examples of the 1840s. Yet a century and a half of canonization has come to exactly that opposite conclusion: that the fiction of the 1840s is to be valued as great literature, whereas the work of 1930s Wales is barely worth reading. What is the reason for this?

Raymond Williams attempts to answer this question throughout the slightly later essay, 'Working-class, proletarian, socialist: problems in some Welsh novels.' Williams provides two reasons why Welsh writers had rarely been able to produce works of sufficient merit to attract the 'literary' tag. One of them is the unfamiliarity inside Wales of the prose narrative form. After all, writing in English in Wales had really only begun to take off in the twentieth century. Although there were fifteen centuries of Welsh-language writing prior to this, the Welsh tradition was primarily a poetic one. As Williams says, it was 'a many-sided tradition which did not, however, include realist prose narrative. By the twentieth century that may have been old to the English; it was new to us' ('Working-class, proletarian, socialist', p. 150). The shift in Welsh history which saw Welsh become the minority language had occurred so rapidly that the impact of the Welsh literary tradition was to leave the new English speakers hamstrung, because the new language brought with it new literary forms – especially the novel – which had not existed in the old language and hence were unfamiliar to the general culture of Wales.[4]

More important, of course, was a preconceived idea of the *literary*. This takes Williams into an examination of the categories 'literature' and 'national tradition'. In contrast to the primarily ruling-class tradition of English literature, Williams knows that there was a long-established tradition in Wales of writing produced from within the working class. This writing existed mainly in various forms of auto-biography: diaries, letters and journals. That it happened not to include novels is an irrelevance to Williams. This underlines the extent to which the unfamiliarity of the novel form in Wales was related both to the class make-up of the population *and* to the linguistic inheritance which rendered that form unfamiliar. It is this distinctive historical inheritance that renders the Welsh industrial form distinct within the evolution of working-class writing more generally. But that writing had always been there:

all through the nineteenth century, there were working-class writers. Only they were rarely writing novels. Verse of several kinds, and some vigorous work-songs. In prose, pamphlets, memoirs, autobiographies. That is either writing in the direct service of the cause, or writing as a direct record of it. ('Working-class, proletarian, socialist', p. 151)

Of course there is no simple reason why members of the working class were not able to write novels. This undoubtedly takes us into a whole nexus of issues including worker education, political formations and local communities. We can, however, discuss general trends, and it is clear that the general trend from the Victorian period onwards was for adult workers to seek to educate themselves to the greatest possible extent and to write about their own experiences. The question as to whether this writing can be considered novelistic is then irrelevant. What matters is that it was written at all. Thus the Welsh industrial novels are virtually autobiographical: Lewis Jones, Jack Jones and the others wrote directly of their own daily lives, while B. L. Coombes's *These Poor Hands* (1939) is explicitly an autobiography. An equivalent example of an English industrial autobiography written from within the working class of the 1840s would be Alexander Somerville's *Autobiography of a Working Man* (1848) – which Williams discusses with enthusiasm in *The Country and the City*.[5]

The Welsh industrial novel flowered in depression-era south Wales in the 1930s. It was a period of poverty, poor standards of public health, social unrest and low rates of education. These are not favourable conditions for producing great literature. Literary or not, the Welsh industrial writing of the 1930s was valuable both because it recorded a precise experience and because it enabled those involved in it to develop their own consciousness. The flowering of the Welsh industrial novel – such as it was – is then perhaps best understood using Raymond Williams's concept of a 'formation':

a working class, at its most general, and in any socialist perspective, is really a *formation* within a much wider system: not only the much wider national and international economy; but also the relations between classes, including that other alien class, those other alien or indeterminate or irrelevant classes. ('Working-class, proletarian, socialist', p. 153, emphasis added)

Formation is the term Williams uses for a body of work, or group of people involved in a body of work, who have no formal, official or institutional affiliation with each other, yet who nevertheless evince structurally homologous tendencies within the general scope of their work. There is no necessary reason for the writers, artists or intellectuals within a formation to have collaborated on joint projects, or even to have met each other at all, in order to evince such a congruity. The whole idea of a 'formation' is that it was developed in contradistinction to just such officially sanctioned or institutional partnerships.

As an analytic concept, the advantage of using the idea of a formation is that it allows us to consider similar work being produced within a specific society at a specific moment, even if, strictly speaking, there is no extant relation between the components of which that work is comprised. It has a further advantage of empowering unofficial or non-institutional kinds of work. Williams writes:

> This is why, in any analysis, we have also to include *formations*. These are most recognisable as conscious movements and tendencies (literary, artistic, philosophical or scientific) which can usually be readily discerned after their formative productions. Often, when we look further, we find that these are articulations of much wider effective formations which can by no means be identified with formal institutions, or their formal meanings and values, and which can sometimes even be positively contrasted with them. (*ML*, p. 119)

This definition depends on a circular argument: A formation is defined as an informal and extra-institutional articulation of a 'much wider effective formation'. What Williams seems to mean is that the informal formation can be taken as an association which has not been formally made by its members. Rather, a group of writers becomes identified as a 'formation' by an exterior commentator, outside the formation itself, on the basis of the perceived overlap of interests or concerns among the members. Williams then takes 'formation' to be a measure of wider tendencies and experiences operating in the broader society of which the formation is a part. Examples he gives elsewhere of this kind of formation are the political brotherhood that met around William Godwin in the late eighteenth century, and the 'Bloomsbury' group of intellectuals, including Virginia Woolf, E. M. Forster and J. M. Keynes, in the 1920s.[6]

The Welsh industrial novel is just such a formation. It incorporates writers as diverse as Lewis Jones, Jack Jones, Gwyn Jones, Gwyn Thomas and Menna Gallie. These are writers of no common institutional origin and who were not necessarily personally acquainted. Their work is certainly not collaborative in the institutional sense. These novelists comprise a 'formation' in the sense that their work can be taken as a general articulation of even more general historical tendencies. When the general broadening of the educational franchise, combined with a favourable family and school environment, gave Williams the chance to go to Cambridge and become a professional man of letters in 1939, he took it. His novels (1960–90) are direct successors to that tradition of industrial writing.

BORDER COUNTRY AND UNFINISHED NARRATIVE

The realist texts Williams discusses in 'The Welsh industrial novel' and 'Working-class, proletarian, socialist' have the capacity to help readers develop a critical consciousness. This is also the case in Raymond Williams's autobiographical first novel, *Border Country* (1960).

The novel opens with Matthew Price, a university lecturer in London, being summoned back to his family home in Glynmawr to attend to the illness of his elderly father, Harry. As he travels home, a series of flashbacks narrate Matthew's childhood life in that Welsh borders village: living through the general strike and the depression of the 1930s, up to the triumphant climax of part one, which describes the winning by Matthew of a place at Cambridge University and his departure to it.

Those sections of the novel that are set in the present make it clear that Matthew has lost some of the closeness with which he had earlier related to the people of Glynmawr. This is underlined by the fact that they continue to refer to him by his childhood name, Will, whereas after going to Cambridge, he had adopted the more adult name, Matthew. The scenes where he comes across his former sweetheart, Eira, are frigid and bitter. Most revealing of all is how the returning Matthew relates to his father's old friend, the petty businessman Morgan Rosser.

Border Country does not simply narrate a homecoming. It profoundly dramatizes the difficulties involved *both* in leaving a familiar home *and* in returning, and of continuing to return. Matthew Price in his adult life must live on both sides of the border, in metropolitan London and local Glynmawr, without ever belonging in either. He exists in a perpetual border zone, shuttling between different places, different relationships and different ways of life.

An important example of this occurs at the climax of the novel. The returning Matthew attempts to rationalize to Morgan Rosser his rejection of his father's way of life. The father, Harry, has continued to work on the railways in Glynmawr. Matthew has gone away to receive an education, and chosen to pursue a quite different career. Matthew explains that it is not that he has rejected his father, but that he has chosen a different kind of work:

> a father is more than a person, he's in fact a society, the thing you grow up into. For us, perhaps, that is the way to put it. We've been moved and grown into a different society. We keep the relationship, but don't take over the work. We have, you might say, a personal father but no social father. What they offer us, where we go, we reject.[7]

As Matthew's rejection of his father's way of life suggests, there is continual interplay between different experiences. This is manifested in the writing as a relationship between industry and education, standing in for the relationship between father and son. Matthew insists that he has not rejected his father as a person; merely as a destination. He does not want to perform the same kind of work as his father. The nature of their relationship is both embracing and antagonistic, and the antagonism can never finally be resolved. Thus the climactic scene between Matthew and Morgan Rosser concludes without a sense of closure:

> 'It's late. I'd better be going.'
> 'With nothing finished?'
> 'We shan't finish this, Will. It's a life time.' (*BC*, p. 277)

Morgan tells Will that this dialogue cannot be resolved because it is in the nature of dialogue to be open ended and ongoing. The novel itself similarly refuses to draw firm conclusions. The continual shuttling back and fore, across the borderland and between different ways of life, is epitomized by the disjointed manner in which *Border Country* concludes. It appears as though Harry has recovered from illness, and Matthew catches the train back to London, to his own wife and children. However, he only gets as far as Newport, before a message catches up with him: Harry has suffered a relapse, and in fact is soon dead.

At the funeral, Matthew meets the vicar Pugh for the first time in years. It was Pugh who had originally advised the young Will/Matthew to go away to Cambridge. Rather as though he has waited years to ask the question, Pugh asks Matthew if the universities really are the great institutions he had wanted them to be. Matthew's reply is vague:

> 'I don't know. Yes, in many ways. But at times it makes sense, this dialogue of the centuries. As an outpost of that it's important: keeping that conversation alive. And then clarifying, sometimes, where we live ourselves.' (*BC*, p. 321).

Rather than answering the question about Cambridge, Matthew suggests an abstract metaphor. The metaphor he uses is one of dialogue: the encounter between different places, different peoples and even different histories. This is appropriate, for it has in effect been Matthew's life. He understands the university as it relates to these other peoples and places which appear distant from it.

Border Country concludes without the sense of an ending. There is considerable irony in this, for there can be few more final events in life than that which concludes the novel: a funeral. Yet, even here, we detect a resistance to narrative closure. On the eve of Harry's funeral, all of his relatives stay at the Price house. Feeling cut off from the other mourners, Matthew discusses his emotional response to his father's death with his cousin, Glynis:

> 'If I say what I feel I find many of my feelings are common.'
> 'I guessed that. It's what they said about Uncle. Your Dad.'
> 'Did they say that?'
> 'Yes, he always was a bit of a stranger.' (*BC*, p. 323)

The novel implicitly concludes with a pair of questions: Who was Harry? Who is Will? Their subjectivity cannot be understood aside from a social process of identity formation which can never end. This process of social-individuation is the one whereby Matthew discovers that his most personal and seemingly unshared feelings are also very commonly felt. The fact that Harry Price is described as 'a bit of a stranger' has the effect of positing the heart of the novel as something ultimately unknowable, as a mystery. This form allowed Raymond Williams to explore the ongoing and open-ended nature of subjectivity formation.

For throughout Williams's fiction, it is when the mystery appears to be solved that all the real questions of identity and subjectivity begin. As Williams's novels became more ambitious, he would return to this structure again and again.

THE 'SIMPLE' MYSTERY: *MANOD*

In *Border Country*, Raymond Williams poses the relationship between father and son as a mystery which can never really be solved. His subsequent novels elaborate on this basic mystery structure, where conclusions fail to offer closure. *The Fight for Manod* (1979) and *Loyalties* (1985) are more explicitly investigation or thriller novels. *The Fight for Manod* can be understood as a thriller in the sense that it combines political machination and intrigue with a process of investigation: in this case, of industrial espionage. *Loyalties* poses the relationship between two of its main characters as a central mystery, which is investigated by both protagonist and reader – again, with a sense of political intrigue. Raymond Williams appears to have found the investigation plot a useful device by which he could put various questions to a contemporary social order. *The Fight for Manod* is the novel where Williams really begins to use that plot to explore questions of commitment and belonging.

At the start of *The Fight for Manod*, Matthew Price and Peter Owen arrive in the depressed Afren Valley near Gwenton, Wales, as consultants to the Whitehall government on a proposed project to develop a new city there: Manod. In his role of consultant, Price will live there for a year to see if the project is viable. He discovers that the local builder, Dance, has already started to try and manoeuvre his company into a position from which he will be able to profit from the Manod project by winning certain important contracts.

The local people are suspicious. Modlen Jenkins asks Matthew about the Manod project. Since she has heard only a very general whisper about what is being planned, she is unable to ask the right questions: she does not know what to ask. All she can do is ask in very generalized terms if the planned development – whatever it is – will have any real impact on Pont Afren:

'Will it be round here then?'
'Well, along the Afren, that's the general idea. That is, if it ever gets built.'
'Only I hope it's round here. Like we need it at Manod, bring a bit of life.'
She shifted her bag on her knees. He glanced across at her as the pitch straightened.
'You want it to come then?'
'We want more people anyhow. And some work for us here.'[8]

Modlen both wants and does not want the project to come to fruition. Certainly she is suspicious of outside influence on the life of the valley. Yet she also does not want to feel that the valley is being overlooked. She does not know what to make of it all, does not know how to ask the appropriate questions to allay her anxieties, and so falls back on a kind of defensive hostility.

This is the general reaction encountered by Matthew and Peter. District planning officer Bryn Walters finds it hard to believe that Price is neither for nor against the project, but only consulting. Bryn discusses the work of Matthew's superior, Robert Lane, in a way that clearly shows that he is suspicious of both Lane and Matthew. Matthew tries to establish Lane's credentials as an urban planner through recourse to Lane's list of academic publications. Walters responds:

'Yes, I read the big one soon after it came out. I've been meaning to read it again. The title fascinated me: *Social Method*. Of course in work like my own . . .'
'Yes?'
'I see social method in the raw. It cuts down the time for books.'
He again stared intently.
'The rawer the practice,' Matthew said, 'the more need for theory.'
'Of course, of course. A very gifted man.' (*FM*, p. 31)

Bryn is wary of the likelihood of the Afren valley's being manipulated from outside. He sees Price as an alien intellectual, the kind who disavows in advance earnest questioning or exploration of political commitments. There is a great irony in the suspicion which Price and Owen provoke. Within the parameters of the investigative thriller genre that Williams is using, their work should point through Matthew and Peter to the shadowy goings on at Whitehall which inform the Manod project and hence the novel. Yet this is exactly what does not happen, because of the locally fixed suspicion of Matthew and Peter, which in effect posits them as the dangerous outsiders to be distrusted, rather than the real manipulators in government.

The already existing tendency to see Peter and Matthew as alien intellectuals is exploited by the builder, Dance, in order to throw the community behind his development project. When Matthew refuses what amounts to a bribe from Dance, Dance refuses to see his offer in those terms. He construes it instead as the expression of a warm and well-motivated feeling of goodwill, which would be understood by the members of the tightly bonded community of Pont Afren, but which the alien interlopers Price and Owen cannot appreciate:

> 'It's not our way, you know that,' he said hoarsely.
> 'Not whose way?'
> 'Not our way, you know what I mean. Not how we live down here and get on with each other, because this is our place, this is all we have.'
> 'I could comment on that but I won't.'
> 'You see. No comment. You've learned up all that. So that you can't talk to us, not as if you're one of us. You've come back as an official, one of the government's people. One of this caste that controls us, but that lives off our living.' (*FM*, p. 170)

It is an ironic turning of the tables. Dance as one of the people makes Price seem the villain. This poses Price's presence in the valley as a mystery. Dance states this explicitly: 'a mystery from the beginning, your coming to Manod' (*FM*, p. 169). He is only echoing Bryn's suspicion of Matthew's political commitment. Yet to us as readers he is not a mystery. We are familiar with both Price and Owen from *Border Country* and Williams's second novel, *Second Generation*, and do not feel that there is anything untoward in their presence.

Thus the mystery of the novel is not for us as readers the same mystery as that experienced by the characters contained within it. Williams uses the mystery plot to refract different commitments across the text. *The Fight for Manod* enacts a process of investigation and detection, where the conclusion of the investigation leads not to known answers but to endless questions. Unlike the classic detective novel, here, where detection concludes, uncertainty begins.

The mystery of Matthew and Peter gives way to the deeper mystery of Dance and his business activities. Price and Owen investigate every aspect of the Manod project. They discover that it has been encouraged by

Dance. He has set up 'Afren Agricultural Holdings' (*FM*, p. 123), part of the larger Anglo Belgian Community Developments, or ABCD (*FM*, p. 157), to buy up land so that he is well-placed to take advantage of the development – once government investment gets it off the ground. Peter Owen realizes that this could be done only if information about the development was leaked from the relevant government department to the company. He calls this 'an organised rip-off for an oil company subsidiary and a merchant bank' (*FM*, p. 192), because it is in effect an attempt to finance a private venture out of the public purse. In the final climactic meeting of consultants, Owen storms out and resigns because he refuses to accept an official cover-up.

More explicitly than *Border Country*, this is a thriller. Dance's mysterious dealings are more dramatic than the mystery of Matthew Price's relationship with his father. The investigation carried out by Price and Owen takes them into the world of secret insider deals, tantamount to industrial espionage. The cover-ups and cloud of secrecy go all the way to the highest echelons of government.

Yet the mystery is comparatively easily solved. A few telephone calls, a few meetings and one trip each to London and Antwerp are all it takes Price and Owen to point the finger at the mysterious figure of Dance. Dance seems oleaginous and despicable from the beginning: Susan Price instinctively refuses to 'trust' him (*FM*, p. 123), while Matthew tells her that he thinks him a 'dreadful man' (*FM*, p. 166). Dance is a 'know-all' (*FM*, p. 40) and seems 'shady' (*FM*, p. 143). At Megan and Ivor's wedding he stands 'alone' in a corner while the other guests – dance (*FM*, p. 164). From the beginning, he seems like a conventional novel villain to us and, sure enough, he turns out to be one. There are no complications in the investigation and none of the plot twists we might expect of a political thriller.

What, then, is the point of envisaging the plot as a process of detection? Arguably, the point is that it opens up questions. The ease with which the ABCD company is exposed forces us to ask not 'what is this sinister industrial crook doing?' Rather, as soon as we know this, we ask 'what can it mean for us?' This is more or less the conclusion – if conclusion is the word – to which Matthew and Peter come: that they know exactly what has been happening, but it is exactly then that 'the problems start' (*FM*, p. 135). The process of investigation does not end with answers, but with questions. All they can do is 'use the inquiry to develop an alternative strategy' (*FM*, p. 137). This strategy, it seems, will be one of asking troubling questions about the suspicious deal that is going through, or using the answers provided by the inquiry to open up those questions. This is the very strategy that had not been available to Modlen Jenkins, who did not know what questions to ask.

Analysis does not posit stable answers that are presented unproblematically. Knowing what Dance is up to does not enable Owen and Price to combat his ruthless measures, and does not enable them to beat him. Investigation, and the novel, therefore break off not with answers, but implicitly with a question: if knowing how multinational capital works is not enough to defeat its power, what will? It is when the positing of stable answers and meanings breaks down that the interminable process of asking questions begins.

A 'FULL BLANKNESS': *LOYALTIES*

In Williams's novel *Loyalties* (1985), what appears to be the end of the investigation again turns out to be the opening up of questions rather than the positing of answers. The novel follows two families over the course of several generations. Each episode is associated with a precise historical moment. The first section, 1936–37, ties together the political culture of south Wales with the onset of the Spanish civil war, thus placing the quest for socialism in a wider context. The third section, 1955–56, demonstrates the involvement of political activists in London with what is happening during the Suez crisis overseas. The final section is set during the miners' strike in 1985. Williams uses these events both to open up questions about loyalty and commitment and to affirm his own loyalty to that earlier generation of Welsh socialist writers who had written similar work.

Loyalties opens in Danycapel, south Wales, in 1936. Emma Braose, her brother Norman, and their associates Georgi and Mark Ryder have come to the Welsh valleys for a socialist conference, having met at Cambridge and in Vienna – where Emma's parents were in the diplomatic service. Among the local delegates at the conference are Bert Lewis and the brother and sister Jim and Nesta Pritchard.

Norman has an affair with Nesta, who becomes pregnant. Emma and the Communist Party pressure Norman to give up this inexperienced working-class girl. Emma thus comes to the Pritchard family and arranges for the child to be born in Westridge nursing home. Abandoned by Norman, Nesta subsequently marries Bert Lewis, who has suffered horrific facial injuries in a tank battle in Normandy. When Nesta visits him in Salisbury American Hospital, she brings with her his adopted son, Gwyn (Nesta's child by Norman), and also Dic, a second son who has been born to Bert and Nesta.

In the establishment figure of Norman Braose and the scarred working-class man Bert Lewis, Gwyn clearly has two different kinds of father. This relates the structure of *Loyalties* to that earlier structure of *Border Country*, where Matthew Price discussed two fathers, a personal father and a social father. In *Loyalties*, Williams does not clearly delineate each role. It is tempting to equate Bert with the personal father and Braose with the social father. Yet the actions of Norman Braose impact on Gwyn in a direct way throughout his life. Likewise, the absence of Bert, to fight in the war during Gwyn's infancy, gives him a social and historical perspective on the family's development, which is not the exclusive domain of the upper-class figure Braose. In this way, Braose and Bert can both be said to occupy each role: personal and social father. The antagonism between the two strongly recalls that of *Border Country*. In *Loyalties*, this becomes transposed into an examination of how individual ambition relates to social and political commitment, and opens up the question: Where does Gwyn's loyalty lie?

In the 1968 section, Gwyn and his half-brother Dic go on an anti-Vietnam protest, where Dic is arrested and Gwyn must pay a fine for his release. This is arranged by the mysterious American Monkey Pitter, a some-time colleague of Norman's. In fact, the relationship between Monkey and Norman is the mystery of the novel. It also represents a complication of the doubled filial relationship. Arguably, Monkey himself is another kind of father figure to Gwyn. He is certainly of the same generation as Norman, having known him at Cambridge. He also takes a direct (though intermittent) involvement in the bringing-up of Gwyn. Through this means, the father figure is again seen to be ultimately unknowable, forcing Gwyn to ask all manner of questions about who he is, without arriving at definite conclusions.

Having paid for Dic's release, Monkey takes him to Emma's house, where Nesta and Gwyn can pick him up. This is where Gwyn meets Monkey Pitter for the first time. Yet it is also strangely not like the first time, for these two have been co-present in each other's lives for decades. Monkey tells Gwyn:

'When I said that I have known you all your life I was not joking. Your life,
I mean, has been there all the time as a central, an essential, fact. But what
I have further to say is what you do not yet know: that you have been
deprived of your history.'
'I don't agree. My mother was very honest about it.'
'About herself, of course, and as far as she knew. But let me put it in this
way. You have been deprived not only of your natural father but of what he
was doing and has done.'
'I don't understand.'
'That's just what I'm saying. But I would like you to believe that it has been
heroic in its way.'[9]

There are direct parallels between history, society and the father figure.
History and society are kinds of father. Yet they cannot be simply opposed
symbolically to the personal-natural father who eludes symbolization.
For, as Monkey tells Gwyn, it is in losing his natural father that he also
loses access to his own history as social father. Thus the personal father
is already one kind of social father. The symbolic father and the personal
father are thus different functions, co-present in each of these different
figures of the father: Norman Braose, Bert Lewis, Monkey Pitter.

Gwyn Lewis cannot understand what Monkey Pitter tells him because
final understanding is not possible. Gwyn wants to know who his father
is, and hence gain access to his own history and identity, which would in
turn enable him to work out where his loyalties lie. Yet the structure of the
novel frustrates this hope, and again provides not answers, but questions.

The unsettling nature of these (non)revelations sends Gwyn to his
mother, Nesta, and a further search for answers. When he asks her about
his father, her response is to show him two paintings she has kept secret
for years: a portrait of Norman from the time of their affair back in
the 1930s and a picture of Bert horrifically scarred during the war.

These provide some of the answers Gwyn needs about his own identity,
but he still does not understand them. He says the portrait of Bert is
beautiful – because of the love Nesta put into painting it. But she rebukes
him: it is not beautiful. Bert was a cripple, made unbeautiful by the world
of war:

'I said that the painting is intensely beautiful, it is –'
Nesta screamed suddenly. He stared at her, bewildered. She pushed him
hard away. He staggered slightly as he went back. Nesta screamed again.

'Mam,' he said, 'Mam, what is it?'

She was staring at him, angrily. He was bewildered because he had never seen her in even ordinary anger. She had always been so contained and quiet and pleasant, always younger than her age, self-possessed and slightly withdrawn.

'*It is not beautiful!*' she screamed, in a terrible high voice.

'Mam, please, I didn't mean that,' Gwyn struggled to say.

'Do you understand nothing?' she screamed. 'Do you know nothing? Have you learned nothing?' (*L*, pp. 347–8)

The paintings are supposed to provide answers. 'Who is your father? Look, and see.' But, when Gwyn looks, he sees not one father, but two. An answer is again deferred. The canvas of a painting is a suggestive metaphor here. It is a blank space which appears to be filled up by the act of painting, so that when the portrait is complete the image is finalized, and fixed for posterity.

These paintings, however, are radically incomplete, existing in an ongoing dialogue with each other and opening a space out of which meaning can pour. The canvas expresses, as it were, a *full blankness*. It expresses not too little meaning for Gwyn to understand, but too much. If there was only one painting, he could arrive at an answer. It is because of the dialogue between the paintings that he cannot do this. The form that appears to offer conclusions fails to do so. It can only open up further questions.

Raymond Williams found this structure appropriate to a turbulent period – the Cold War – in which it was continually necessary to define one's own political commitments by measuring them against an externally changing political history. Monkey had referred to Gwyn's father Norman as heroic because of Norman's work for the Communist Party, and the attempt to contribute to class transformation in society. At the conclusion of *Loyalties* it is strongly suggested that Norman – and even Monkey Pitter – have travestied the socialist ideals of their youth by agreeing to work for a capitalist government. Where Gwyn's loyalty lies then remains an open question. Williams's own socialist commitment to putting deep questions to the capitalist order is replicated by the form of his novels, which undertake similar work. *Border Country*, *The Fight for Manod* and *Loyalties* all generate a series of questions and problems which cannot be conjured away.

CULTURAL MATERIALISM: THE WELSH EXAMPLE

Williams's novels, like the emergent drama of Scandinavia, Ireland and Wales, resist absolute closure. This brings his work into constellation with the earlier generation of Welsh industrial writers, who had similar political commitments. It could be argued that Williams's television play, *Public Inquiry*, makes the conjunction between emergent drama and critical-realist fiction even more overt. In that play, Williams dramatizes the aftermath of a railway accident. By using the convention of the industrial disaster in his play, Williams explicitly aligns himself both with the emergent drama which he valued so highly and with the conventions of Welsh industrial writing identified above.[10] Yet it is not clear at which point in his career Williams read the Welsh industrial novels, so that the alignment is not one of straightforward influence or homage. What then is the precise relationship between Williams and those earlier writers?

In January 2006, the Welsh Assembly Government launched the Library of Wales book series. This initiative can be seen as a process of cultural reclamation: twentieth-century Welsh writing in English quickly becomes unfashionable and out of print. The ostensible goal of the Library of Wales is to make some of the writing produced in Wales over the last century available again. The first five titles included Raymond Williams's novel *Border Country*, and a much earlier pair of working-class novels from south Wales, Lewis Jones's *Cwmardy* and *We Live*.

The Library of Wales was launched by the Assembly specifically as a nation-building initiative. The emphasis on sustaining and developing a sense of nationhood through writing had been a commonplace of Welsh-language culture for centuries. Similarly, the assumption that writing has socio-political power of and for itself, rather than simply reflecting anterior power relationships, had been a prevalent element of Welsh-language culture for many generations. In his *The Taliesin Tradition*, Emyr Humphreys recorded the contribution made by Welsh-language poets and epic writers to an elaboration of Welsh cultural nationhood since the tenth century. Raymond Williams's enthusiastic reviews of *The Taliesin Tradition* and Tony Curtis's *Wales: The Imagined Nation* were recently republished in *Who Speaks for Wales?* Nevertheless, the extent to which Humphreys's exploration of a national, politically endowed poetic tradition coincides with Williams's thinking on the subject is a complicated question. Certainly, we know that Williams was suspicious of the concept of a national tradition *per se*.[11]

The emphasis of the Library of Wales is very strongly on reinforcing a sense of Welshness in the majority anglophone communities of the (formerly) industrialized Welsh valleys. As such, it could be described as a corrective to, or at least an effort at redressing, Humphreys's almost exclusive emphasis on the contribution of Welsh-language writing to national developments. Raymond Williams appears to have believed that some such corrective was necessary. He concluded his review of *Wales: The Imagined Nation* by suggesting that it is 'not only the Welsh who have to discover and affirm an identity by overcoming a selective tradition.' (*WSW*, p. 36). The selection of industrial fiction and valleys writers for the opening titles in the Library of Wales series could be seen as a step towards overcoming the selective tradition which Williams describes. The writers chosen belong to the twentieth century rather than the distant past; they come from urban as opposed to rural areas; and belong to the working class rather than the bourgeoisie.[12]

Arguably, this emphasis on valleys writers and industrial fiction indicates a particular ideological construction of Welshness that could be said to have swung too far away from the Welsh-language tradition to which it serves as a corrective. The exclusive attention to urban, working-class and mostly male writers appears to endorse a sense of Welshness that is not necessarily generally applicable. At the same time, the opening titles published in the Library of Wales give us a chance to rediscover or re-evaluate the tradition of Welsh industrial fiction that flowered in the 1930s – a tradition to which Raymond Williams as novelist consciously belonged. This rediscovery has only been possible because since 1997 Wales has had some self-rule and hence the capacity to develop such projects.

It is also in a real sense true that Wales only has self-rule partly because the writers of Wales spent time and effort exploring their identity and culture. This contributed to an increase in the cultural confidence of a notoriously unconfident Wales. In this sense, Williams's emphasis on the material contribution made by writing to historical processes tunes in with the earlier assumption of the Welsh-language tradition, that writing has a certain political power of its own. The Library of Wales emphasis on industrial fiction may seem like a corrective to prior notions of Welshness as manifested in an exclusively Welsh-language tradition. A sense of the socio-political power of writing is retained from that tradition by the Library, which is published under the auspices of the National Assembly (now the Welsh Government).

Williams's emphasis on the material role played by writing in society implies that Welsh writing – in either language – does not simply follow on from political and historical developments. It also contributes to them. In Wales, the drift can be seen by comparing the two referenda, of 1979 and 1997. In 1979 the Welsh electorate overwhelmingly rejected the principle of self-rule. The narrow margin by which Wales then embraced devolution eighteen years later represented a 'huge shift'.[13] The different factors contributing to this swing are of course multifarious and complex. It seems that an increased confidence in Wales's sense of national identity was an important contributory factor. This growing sense of cultural nationhood had been augmented by the contribution made by Welsh artists, actors, musicians and writers to the general culture.

Clearly the real claim for the power of literature is a modest one: the results of the two referenda are not only caused by the reading of novels, and in fact owe a greater debt to more direct political campaigning. Yet the demarcation between the overtly political and the cultural spheres is not so clearly drawn, if we get rid of the idea of literature as an idealist realm and explore its material properties. This is particularly clear in the case of Williams, who was for a time member of the Welsh political party, Plaid Cymru.[14] He was a political activist within Wales on the one hand, a Welsh novelist on the other, while all the time refusing to draw such a strict line between the two spheres. Williams declares these twin elements of his work for Welsh consciousness when he says:

> The central point about Scottish and Welsh nationalism is perhaps this: that in Scotland and Wales we are beginning to find ways of expressing two kinds of impulse that are in fact very widely experienced throughout British society. First, we are trying to declare an identity, to discover in fact what we really have in common, in a world which is full of false identities . . . And second, but related to this, we are trying to discover political processes by which people really can govern themselves – that is, to determine the use of their own energies and resources – as distinct from being governed by an increasingly centralised, increasingly remote and also increasingly penetrating system: the system that those who run it, for their own interests, have decided to call 'Unity'. (*WSW*, p. 188)

Williams wants to reveal what socialists 'really have in common' in a world which is 'full of false identities'. If this is applied to Wales, the implication would be that some versions of Welshness are 'more Welsh' than others. This in turn would be to overlook the constructed and mediated nature of *all* national identities. By contrasting official narratives of British identity ('false identities') with 'what we really have in common', Williams seems to affirm a notion of authenticity which might not survive rigorous theoretical critique. The implication of his words here seems to be that if we could strip away the official narratives of the modern state, we would arrive at a version of the nation that somehow exists prior to the means by which it is constructed.

This notion of authenticity overlooks the constructed nature of all identities and might be disabling. This is particularly relevant to Williams, to whom the process of representation creates the possibility to construct alternative forms. The process of discovering an identity is in part the work of fiction and cultural production. The demand for politically separatist institutions then belongs to the more strictly political sphere. Yet Williams does not draw such a tight demarcation between the two. Instead, he makes an argument about the relationship between culture and politics that is openly dialectical and mutually determining.

Separatist political institutions create the conditions under which it becomes possible for Scotland and Wales to support their own cultural production: their own writers, dramatists and artists. At the same time, it is also partly because those cultural figures have the courage and confidence to explore their own identity with differential regard to the British whole that the nations in question develop the self-confidence required to demand political institutions of representation. Rather than being side-tracked by a notion of authenticity, this emphasis on how writing has the capacity to generate alternative formations implies that all identities are constructed and mediated. This is particularly important to Williams, who was concerned to generate such alternative forms. When he is writing about the interrelation between writing and social change, therefore, he is on much surer ground than when making vague references to 'true' and 'false' versions of national identity. The materialist emphasis on the kinds of formation that can be constructed by writing overcomes the total separation of politics from culture. In a way, therefore, Raymond Williams *was* campaigning for Welsh devolution while sitting at his desk writing novels. These participated in the general rise in Welsh consciousness during the period 1979–97.

In retrospect, it is possible to argue that even the overwhelming 'no' of 1979 was not the huge defeat that it is usually described as. Compared to the situation in the 1930s, to have organised a vote at all represented a significant step forward for Wales. The cultural confidence necessary to ask for things like political institutions of representation increases in part because of the work of cultural production in allowing an exploration of Welsh identity. The formation of the Welsh industrial novel was an early contribution to this exploration.

Using Raymond Williams's concept of the interplay between *dominant*, *residual* and *emergent* cultural forms, the Welsh industrial novel formation can be described as the *pre-emergent* stage in the development of Welsh critical thought. The *pre-emergent* is a category Williams used to refer to those areas of oppositional cultural or political work which initially appear in such minor and dormant form as to be virtually invisible within the dominant culture. It was developed in *Marxism and Literature*:

> What matters, finally, in understanding emergent culture, as distinct from both the dominant and the residual, is that it is never only a matter of immediate practice; indeed, depends crucially on finding new forms or adaptations of form. Again and again what we have to observe is in effect a *pre-emergence*, active and pressing but not yet fully articulated, rather than the evident emergence which could be more confidently named. (*ML*, 126–7)

The *pre-emergent* is valuable because it is the stage at which the first tiny movements for change begin to become active inside a society. As a result, it may well be that the pre-emergent forms by which a society is gradually changed can be identified only as such retrospectively. We might say that the desire in certain small quarters of British society to abolish the monarchy could be defined as pre-emergent.[15] Yet we will only really be able to say this retrospectively in the future, from the standpoint of a moment at which abolition has been achieved.

This retrospective mapping is certainly the case with the Welsh industrial novels, and the general militancy that was felt in the Welsh valleys during the 1930s. The point could be made with regard to those Welsh industrial novels such as *Cwmardy*, where a new monarch is crowned and where most of the crowd fervently celebrate, with just one or two figures questioning the need for Welsh people to honour an alien monarchy. The emergence of the Welsh industrial novel formation from the 1930s onwards demonstrates that oppositional forces to the unitary British state in general, and to the alien capitalist order in particular, were already beginning to develop. This is why they can be considered a pre-emergent formation.

The political commitment to socialism and unionism in which those novels played a part opened up a broader commitment to extending the nature of British democracy. This would become manifest in 1997 with the achievement of provisional self-rule in Wales. The period between referendum defeat in 1979 and eventual success in 1997 is then the 'emergent' period. It was during this period that Welsh self-confidence grew at a sufficient pace for real change to become manifest in 1997.

Yet, in the 1930s, it could not have been clear that devolution as such was the natural endpoint of this kind of activism. Thus it is only retro-spectively that the industrial novel formation can be identified as pre-emergent. It is because of this near invisibility that Raymond Williams felt that pre-emergent forms were the most important oppositional forms in a society. This is because they are so latent as to be precarious in the extreme.

A well-known Williams article, 'The tenses of imagination,' can help us map the terrain of Welsh consciousness in this way. It was published in the collection *Writing in Society* in 1984, having originally been delivered as a series of papers at the University College in Aberystwyth in 1978 – the year before the referendum.

'The tenses of imagination' is frequently invoked, primarily because it offers a series of generally applicable insights into a materialist theory of culture. What is less often noted, however, is the precise cultural history in which the paper was an intervention. The general applicability of the theory has tended to occlude the moment of production. In other words, the precise past, present and future that Williams was trying to imagine when he delivered 'The tenses of imagination' in Aberystwyth in 1978 were *Welsh* pasts, presents and futures. It is not only the case that the paper can be used to understand the political activity that was occurring contemporaneously with it. That political and historical moment itself provides the key context in which we have to understand the development of the paper. The Welsh identity of Raymond Williams is then a crucial element to our understanding of cultural materialism. Not only does that analytic theory enable us to understand Welsh history; Welsh history itself helps us to understand the genesis of the theory. This underlines the dialectical way in which forms of writing relate to social processes.

Williams opened 'The tenses of imagination' by considering various different definitions of the concept of *imaginative* works. He notes that the term is usually used to refer to acts of creativity or original composition, with the strong implication that the works in question have been imagined up without regard to any external social or historical reality.

Doubting that it is really possible for any kind of imaginative process to function in this way, he goes on to consider a related second definition of *imagination*, that of empathy. This kind of imaginative process in effect asks us to put ourselves in a certain situation. It says 'imagine if . . .', and then extrapolates a certain situation with which first writer and then reader seek to cultivate an imaginative affinity. Williams rejects this definition of imagination, again because he suspects that it is simply not possible for imagination to function without regard to a prior set of images in the mind. These images can of course only have been produced socially through interaction with the human landscape. Williams rejects definitions of imagination which present the mind as having no existing relationship with that landscape.

In moving away from idealist versions of imagination, Williams introduces two important new definitions of imaginative work. First, he attempts to examine the relationship between the imagination and the 'real'.[16] Secondly, he suggests that imagination is not simply a matter of dreaming up new kinds of image, as if from nowhere. On the contrary, the imagination is then a process of demonstrating connections between what can be thought and what already exists.

Accordingly, the imagination becomes important as it bears on helping us realize the kind of *future* that might be achieved. No socialist change could occur without a prior concept of the possibility of change, and an accompanying sense of what new kind of society might be built by change. Imagination plays a tangible part in helping desirable futures become a reality. The imagination is thus 'real' in this active sense of enabling potential futures to be brought forward. It is also 'real' in the important sense that the desired futures must always be shown in advance to be achievable. That is why imagining the future is not in Williams's account a matter of psychic idealism. Rather, it is a matter of demonstrating how a desired future might be rooted in a contemporary present, and is hence a possible destination arising out of it. Imagination is then not a break with contemporary reality, but a continuation of it.

'The tenses of imagination' was based on material delivered in Wales in 1978. At this point, Williams had one very particular desirable future in mind. That is, the possible future of a Welsh society in which some kind of democratic home rule would become a reality. Reading in this way enables us to reconstruct the precise occasion on which the paper was delivered.

When devolution was realized in the referendum of 1997, the large swing that had been required to overturn the defeat of 1979 was in part due to the raising of Welsh confidence that comes about through an exploration of Welsh culture and identity in writing, in film and in other cultural forms.[17] Williams himself had been involved in this work, so that although he did not survive to witness the moment of devolution, in some senses, his lifetime *was* that moment. Thus it is perhaps no coincidence that at roughly the moment of devolution, the Library of Wales has brought Williams's own novel, *Border Country*, back into print. Williams, that is to say, *is* still present during the process of devolution – in his writing, which was a contribution to it.

The relationship that exists between cultural production and social processes is a dialectical one. This can be gauged by examining the complex historical sequence in which these cultural emergences have occurred. On the face of it, it seems as though The Library of Wales (2006) was launched *after* political change had occurred (in 1997). This would suggest that cultural production is passively dependent on anterior political change, which it then reflects in a secondary manner.

On the other hand, not only had a relative step towards devolution already been taken much earlier on, with the holding of a referendum in 1979, but some of the literature itself had also been published at an earlier period, in the 1930s. The question as to which came first, the Library or the Assembly, is then a very much more complex one than it may first have appeared.

The Welsh case is a particularly clear example of a more general materialist theory of culture. On the one hand, it has become possible to revalue Welsh writing of the 1930s (and since) because the Assembly exists to finance such projects. On the other hand, the fact that the Assembly itself exists is in part due to activities like the writing. Cultural forms do not only reflect society. They play an active part in societal processes. There is no linear relationship between culture and historical change. These things are related to each other in a complex dialectical manner which opens beyond the simple constructs of cause and effect.

3

Universities – Hard and Soft

At the same time as being concerned with the tradition of Welsh industrial writing, Raymond Williams was also involved in a quite different tradition – of university writing. This is generally English and middle class. Such involvement is significant, because it shows Williams always crossing disciplinary, generic and national boundaries.

Concepts of education were of direct and central relevance to what Williams called the *long revolution* towards a participatory democracy. Education, the curriculum and access to the university system are highly prominent themes in his writing, and university campuses feature frequently in his fiction. Williams's theoretical interest was always in finding ways of transforming the dominant social order. Accordingly, he gives the classic campus novel formula a twist in the attempt to imagine a university different in kind from those he found in more conventional campus novels. Reading Williams's fiction as university fiction requires keeping a careful eye on the proposals he made for education in his non-fiction.

CAMBRIDGE ENGLISH

In Britain, universities arose as institutions capable of generating a sense of unified national culture during the late eighteenth and nineteenth centuries. As Bill Readings succinctly puts it in his study, *The University in Ruins*, the nineteenth-century university 'gives the people an idea of the nation-state to live up to, and the nation-state a people capable of living up to that idea'.[1] Universities contributed to the dissemination of national culture both via informal networks of personal relationship within the political class and via formal means of communication, most notably the print media. This enables us to glimpse again the importance of Benedict Anderson's argument, that the history of those media *is* the history of the nation-state.

Raymond Williams explored the relationship between universities, literary study, national culture and the imperial formation on one specific occasion. 'Cambridge English, past and present' was delivered as one of Williams's retirement lectures in 1983, and was subsequently included in the volume, *Writing in Society*.

'Cambridge English, past and present' begins with a preliminary survey of the history of English as a university subject. Notably, Cambridge was one of the last British universities to introduce a degree course in English. The stimulus towards introduction had been much greater and much more successful in 'newer' universities. Moreover, Williams draws attention to two important formations outside the university that were crucial in bringing about the establishment of the new discipline: the new adult workers' education movement and the contemporary movement for the education of women.

Williams points out that one of the major obstacles to the establishment of English as a Cambridge degree subject was that it was seen as 'the women's subject', lacking 'sufficient rigour' for a course at Cambridge.[2] Terry Eagleton has pointed out that when English finally broke through as a Cambridge subject, it did so on the basis of having demonstrated a rigorous, 'masculine', demanding syllabus.[3] Throughout the late nineteenth century, the dissemination of a certain sense of national identity had been accompanied by a corresponding sense of masculinity. This perception of strength and heroism had enabled the British Empire to allot to itself the role of guardian of societies the world over.

The establishment of English as a Cambridge subject was predicated on the overcoming of the perception of it as effeminate. This could be done partly by outlining a rigorous syllabus of examination. Such work could only go so far, however. A more general solution was to demonstrate the utility of mobilizing literary education to contribute to the formation of national culture and the national political order.

In 'Cambridge English, past and present,' this is what Raymond Williams suggests eventually happened:

> The interests that came to be defined as aesthetic and cultural, or earlier as spiritual and historical, turned readily to so much available and valuable work. It was indeed these interests which produced the new nineteenth-century sense of Literature, as a body of imaginative writing which represented these most general human qualities. Behind that again was the late eighteenth-century sense of *English* Literature, a *national* literature, as distinct from the earlier classical and European emphases. English studies in the schools, in the nineteenth century, included the history and geography as well as the literature and the language of this self-conscious and consciously taught *nation*. ('Cambridge English', p. 179)

If literary study was required to demonstrate its own worth, the capacity of literature to provide the conscious teaching of a national formation was the surest ground on which it could carry out such a demonstration. Williams showed that during the national and imperial period, literary study became accepted precisely because it enabled the nation to be imagined into being.

> The term *Nationalliteratur* began in Germany in the 1780s, and the histories of 'national literatures', with quite new perspectives and emphases from older and more general ideas of 'humane letters', were being written in German, French and English from the same period, in which there was a major change of both ideas of 'the nation' and of 'cultural nationality'. (*WS*, p. 195)

Through the institutions of education in general, and through literary study in particular, the nation could be consciously taught into existence.

Two important points emerge from this. First, Williams emphasizes that this kind of teaching of national identity through recourse to a literary tradition can only be a partial and selective process. The selection of literature for study thus had certain bearings on what kind of nation was being imagined. This in turn opens the whole practice up to a notion of *intention*. Who is doing the teaching and for whom? Williams thought literary teaching was brought about as an extension of ruling-class policy during the national and imperial period. The history of education in the nineteenth century thus has a very particular relation to the history of the nation and of the empire. As Tom Nairn puts it, 'the progress of schools and universities measures that of nationalism, just as schools and especially universities become its most conspicuous champions'.[4]

It is interesting to note in this context that English was taught in universities in Scotland before it was taught in England. There are complex historical reasons for this, but undoubtedly one of those reasons was that the distinctiveness of an already defined Scottish culture posed a significant threat to the putative unity of Britain's national culture during the national period. Teaching English literature within Scottish universities was one way of extending this unity. In 'Cambridge English, past and present', Williams highlights the propensity of early literary study to eliminate Celtic otherness from the canon of literature, and hence from definition within the national culture:

> What was being traced, of course, was a genuine ancestry of thought and form, with the linguistic connections assumed from the habits of the private schools. It is not so much this cultural *connection* that counts; it is the long gap, in the culture, history and languages of these islands, across which this persuasive formulation simply jumped. 'We should know the poets of our own land', but then not Taliesin or Dafydd ap Gwilym. 'Of our own people', but then not the author of *Beowulf*. ('Cambridge English', p. 181)

The selective tradition in literature was extended by structural congruence into a selective version of national identity itself. The ostensible justification for this was linguistic coherence: the tradition as selected comprised a body of works in the *English* language. The corollary of this was that the alternative traditions in Celtic writing, and hence in Celtic self-definition and nationhood, were written out of the record. The conflation of *literature* with *English* in effect bolstered the homogeneous sense of English nationhood that had been much more broadly propagated since the nineteenth century, when, as Eric Hobsbawm points out, England's national traditions were actively invented.[5]

If the slippage from *literature* to *English* was a means of effacing the threat presented by Celtic otherness to British national unity, it also brought up another challenge for the national formation. Not only was English taught as a degree subject in Scotland before it was taught in England, it is also true that it was taught in certain colonies before it was taught in either Scotland or England. In *Masks of Conquest: Literary Study and British Rule in India*, Gauri Viswanathan notes that, by entering a commitment to 'undertake the education of the native subjects' in India, Britain's imperial government accepted 'a responsibility which it did not officially bear even towards its own people'.[6] Benedict Anderson points out that Parliament mandated to the East India Company the 'allocation of 100,000 rupees a year for the promotion of native education' as early as 1813.[7]

In the early period of the empire, colleges in the colonies were used to serve a hegemonic purpose. Macaulay's notorious minute on Indian Education (1835) advocated the teaching of English literature as a means of producing a class of peoples 'Indian in blood and colour, but English in opinion, in taste, in morals and in intellect'.[8] The cultural mission of the colleges around the empire was thus specifically to augment the bonds of the empire in an ideological manner. As Gauri Viswanathan puts it, 'raising Indians to the intellectual level of their Western counterparts constituted a necessary prerequisite to . . . forestalling the danger of having unfortified minds falsely seduced by the "impurities" of the traditional literature of the East'.[9]

The historic emergence of English as a university subject interacts with the history of Britain as an imperial power in a dynamic of mutual transformation. The extent of its empire brought Britain to a global pre-eminence that was mirrored in the prevalence of the English language around the world. English had spread relatively rapidly in the nineteenth century partly because of the use of English education in the colonial colleges to serve a hegemonic purpose.

There was at least one unsought consequence of this. One result of mobilizing literary study in the colonies was that by the end of the nineteenth century there was a substantial body of works in English produced from within nations other than Britain. Were these then to be considered a part of the 'English' tradition? If so, this would contradict the historic role of the university: to create a sense of unity within national culture. Raymond Williams draws attention to the contradiction in his late essay 'Crisis in English studies':

> Not just Literature, but English Literature. This is itself historically a late construction, since for medieval writing, at least to the seventeenth century, it is obviously uncertain. Is 'English' then the language or the country? If it is the language, there are also fifteen centuries of native writing in other

languages: Latin, Welsh, Irish, Old English, Norman French. If it is not the language but the country, is that only 'England' or is it now also Ireland, Wales, Scotland, North America, Old and New 'Commonwealths'? ('Crisis in English studies', *WS*, p. 194)

As a result of literary education in the colonies, there arose a powerful and interesting literature demonstrably in English yet from societies and nations other than Britain. This was at odds with the ostensible purpose of teaching English as a university subject. At home, that teaching had been carried out to propagate a sense of nationhood. In the colonies, the aim was to augment the cultural bonds of empire. Yet the teaching of English in the colonies had resulted in the rise of another kind of literature, and hence the possible imagining-into-existence of other kinds of nation. In other words, the means that enabled the nation to be consciously taught through its literature also enabled other nations to be written into the record.

When the empire was faced with a faltering history, it needed to resort to more direct means of control and administration. In *Masks of Conquest*, Viswanathan explores the various measures that were brought into the Indian education system as a result. Entrance to the Indian Civil Service became predicated upon success in competitive public examination, in contradistinction to the ad hoc basis on which appointments had previously been made – primarily on the basis of personal acquaintance within the political class. Provision for the education of Indian subjects was organized along state lines from 1854, and proposals for a network of university colleges in Madras, Bombay and Calcutta were forwarded in 1857.[10] These measures represented a professionalization of Britain's entire approach to education and empire during the second half of the nineteenth century.

The business of colonial colleges was no longer primarily to perform the cultural and ideological work of the empire. Rather, colleges were now required to produce a number of highly trained functionaries to carry out its administrative, legal and communicative work. Viswanathan notes that 'with the extended use of English as the language of commerce was brought into existence a much larger class of Indians willing to co-operate with the British in the exploitation of India's resources'.[11] She suggests that education in India became progressively more utilitarian, with a large working class being educated solely in the 'mechanical arts and skills of agriculture' along with the skills required to meet specific regional needs such as 'land measurement and land registration'. Meanwhile, the new network of national university colleges fostered 'a small but influential intellectual' group, which was 'drawn largely from the indigenous learned class' and 'was targeted for eventual induction into government service'.[12]

Education, in other words, acquired a new utilitarian aspect at the same time as it sloughed off its cultural and ideological prerogatives: it was 'pursued as a means to an end'.[13] A new generation of educated Indians was garnered to provide the empire with the lawyers, civil servants, administrators and even doctors, on whom its continued survival would depend. Chinua Achebe has drawn attention to a similar need for the university colleges to produce a steady output of highly trained professionals in the latter stages of colonial rule in Africa.[14]

There is thus a shift from conceptions of the university within the colonial context. The initial emphasis on cultural and ideological work was replaced by a nascent ethic of professionalism where students were prepared to carry out specific tasks in the system. This transition from *cultural* university to *professional* training would only subsequently take place inside Britain itself. This underlines the extent to which the colonies played a leading constitutive role in the historical development of British culture.

The implication of this is that, since education was imbued with an imperial and ideological ethic which was subsequently to decline, educational institutions came to occupy a vacuum. The university arose in order to create and distil a sense of harmonious national identity that could then be disseminated in the colonies. In a period where the colonial imperative no longer obtains, the historic mission of the university must clearly be modified. Bill Readings has referred to the university as being in this sense a 'post-historic' institution, having lived on long after its historical *raison d'être* has become obsolescent.[15] In the light of this obsolescence, the structural function of the university system has changed, from performing general cultural and ideological work to fulfilling a professional ethos where specific individuals are trained to perform specific functions.

These changes were beginning to take place during the early years of Raymond Williams's career. As empire began to decline, conceptions of the university would undergo historic variation, shifting from the organ of hegemonic and ideological work, to the provider of a specific set of skills to shore up Britain's faltering global role. The transition from a university of historic nationhood to the university of corporate professionalism within a transnational economy can be seen by examining the ideas of a university that were prevalent in Williams's own time.

BANKING EDUCATION

The shift from university of cultural nationalism to college of technical or professional training began during the 1950s. This was partly connected with a relative economic decline brought on by the period of decolonization. It was also related to a general economic downturn following the war. Rather than generating a sense of cultural nationalism – as at an earlier period – the specific aim of universities and colleges was now to equip the country with a sector of trained professionals who would enable British businesses and other institutions to survive and expand in a market economy that was in the process of going global.

Raymond Williams was concerned with education as a carrier of asymmetry which prepares its students for participation in the competitive sphere. In a system that asserts the incontrovertible right of a competitive free market ethic, education can be used in conjunction with social and political structures which promote the primacy of the individual over all social concerns. This kind of education promotes certain students and keeps certain others back, thus exactly mirroring and underlining the competitive world into which it is assumed the students will enter once their education is complete.

The dominant view of education in Williams's day was one where students were instilled with the spirit of competitive individualism at every point, thus actively generating a social order founded on these assumptions. This approach to education is an entirely instrumental one, as if its students simply go to a certain place of instruction for a certain amount of time and emerge from that institution once the period of instruction has expired, fired up to face the world of competition.

Brazilian educationalist Paulo Freire calls this a 'banking' concept of education, depositing in students only so much knowledge or so many skills as are necessary to perform certain tasks. Freire defines banking education as follows:

Education thus becomes an act of depositing, in which the students are the depositories and the teacher is the depositor. Instead of communicating, the teacher issues communiqués and makes deposits which the students patiently receive, memorise, and repeat. This is the 'banking' concept of education, in which the scope of action allowed to the students extends only as far as receiving, filing, and storing the deposits.[16]

The banking model has deep roots in nineteenth-century utilitarian approaches to education, of which Charles Dickens provided fictive critique in the novel *Hard Times*. The utilitarian model sees education as a short-term transfer of specifically deposited units of information or skills, which will equip students to perform specific tasks within a society. Raymond Williams expounded a critique of nineteenth-century utilitarianism when he extrapolated the bourgeois individualist assumptions of T. H. Huxley's 1877 metaphor of education as a ladder. The ladder, Williams argued, was a perfect metaphor for bourgeois competitive capitalist society: 'the worker holds the ladder for the boss to climb'.[17]

Freire uses the term 'banking education' to draw attention to the relative shift from education as a *process* of cultural hegemony to education as an *instrument* of international capitalism. This occurs at two inter-related levels. There is the manifest *content* of an educational programme. This is inseparable from the cultural and institutional *carrier* in which that content is conveyed. Banking education instils in its students the skills necessary to fulfil a particular role within the capitalist order. At the same time, the competitive system of examination by which that education is assessed also instils simultaneous assent to the world of competition. 'Verbalistic lessons, reading requirements, the methods for evaluating "knowledge", the distance between the teacher and the taught, the criteria for promotion: everything in this ready-to-wear approach serves to obviate thinking', writes Paulo Freire.[18] The system of banking education occupies a specific place within the capitalist social order. It prepares its students to perform certain tasks within that order by equipping them with specific skills. At the same time, it nurtures them into a general acceptance of that order through the gradual exposure to a system of hierarchical relations where individual progress is measured by competition. The manifest content of banking education is thus mirrored in latent form by the institutional carrier of that education. The world of competition to which students are exposed in education is precisely the world they will encounter outside it. Banking education, in other words, promotes the virtues of free market competition. As a result it systematically fails – often despite the commitments and efforts of individual teachers – to communicate anything beyond these concerns. Williams says:

> The failure is due to an arrogant preoccupation with transmission, which rests on the assumption that the common answers have been found and need only be applied. But people will (damn them, do you say?) learn only by experience, and this, normally, is uneven and slow. A governing body, in its impatience, will often be able to enforce, by any of a number of kinds of pressure, an apparent conformity. (*CS*, p. 302)

The meaning of 'conformity' within the history of the education system is historically variable. During the imperial period, the institutions existed to carry out the dissemination of a strongly unified sense of national culture. This is the legislated unity that Williams thought was the specific goal of early literary study. Following the end of the colonial project, the new order that emerged was one of increasingly international capitalism. Conformity within this order is now understood in a more flexible way, as *assent* to the world of free market competition.

Williams's idea of conformity describes the phenomenon whereby the transfer of education on a top-down model instils in its recipients a kind of assent to the fundamental structuring of competitive society. Williams was opposed to this instrumental concept of a university, and sought ways to replace it with the kind of institution that might be used to promote thinking more sceptical of the capitalist order. As Fazal Rizvi says, it is not only that Williams wanted to use education to democratize society. Williams also showed that 'education itself has to be democratised'.[19]

Paulo Freire opposes the banking concept of education with a *problem-posing education*, where dialogical relations are indispensable. Problem-posing education disavows the idea that educational authorities can limit in advance what knowledge and skills are to be transferred to the students. It disavows, in Raymond Williams's words, the idea that the correct answers about how to structure education have been found and need only be applied.

This alternative kind of education can only function when the hierarchical separation of teachers and students is dissolved and each is willing and able to enter into dialogue with the other. The teacher ceases to be a figure of distant authority, and will become instead a promoter of critical social and cultural thinking. Freire says:

> Those truly committed to liberation must reject the banking concept in its entirety; adopting instead a concept of men and women as conscious beings, and consciousness as consciousness intent upon the world. They must abandon the educational goal of deposit-making and replace it with the posing of the problems of human beings in their relations with the world.[20]

Freire's problem-posing education points towards a dialogic approach. He advocates the ongoing asking of questions between teacher and student, as a means of dissolving the hierarchical relationship between the two. In his approach to education, Williams too comes down on the side of open-ended questions.

The most significant proposal Williams makes for education is to teach discussion. This models education on an idea of exploration and mutual interchange of ideas. This is in sharp contrast to banking education, which is a tool of the competitive capitalist order that relies on the all-knowing teacher handing whatever knowledge or skills are deemed appropriate on to the passive students. A discussion-orientated education will remain constantly open and flexible, able to modify its curriculum as the needs, interests and abilities of the students vary. The kind of education system Williams envisages runs something like this:

> [C]hanging the educational system from its dominant pattern of sorting people, from so early an age, into 'educated' people and others, or in other words, transmitters and receivers, to a view of the interlocking processes of determining meanings and values as involving contribution and reception by everyone. (*RH*, p. 36)

Williams's terms *transmitters* and *receivers* recall the deposit boxes of Freire's banking education. Freire's seminal book *Pedagogy of the Oppressed* has direct relevance to Williams's interest in the long revolution towards an educated participatory democracy. To both writers, the important theme is education as a site for resistance to cultural domination.

Williams showed in *Marxism and Literature* that the contest between dominant, residual and emergent cultural forms is never simply and decisively won, but involves the constant making and unmaking of ideas. This conflict is what Williams, following Gramsci, calls hegemony: the putting into circulation of ideas, and the gradual build-up of assent to them through their construction and recognition as norms. The kind of hegemonic work that universities can perform has undergone historic variation, from disseminating a unified sense of national culture in the nineteenth century, to generating overall assent to the capitalist structure of the world order in the twentieth century and beyond. Because of this variation, Williams modifies Gramsci's notion of hegemony, and points out that there are several *hegemonies*, in the plural:

> We have to emphasise that hegemony is not singular; indeed that its own internal structures are highly complex and have continually to be renewed, recreated and defended; and by the same token, that they can continually be challenged and in certain respects modified. That is why instead of simply speaking of 'the hegemony', 'a hegemony', I would propose a model which allows for this kind of variation and contradiction, its sets of alternatives and its processes of change. (*PMC*, p. 38)

The notion of different kinds of hegemony underlines the historic variation in how social orders are constructed. The early emphasis on social order as a self-contained nation-state evolved historically into a social order of transnational capitalism. Universities played specific and different parts in the material construction of the social order in each period.

The multiplicity of hegemonies enables us to realize that no dominant system can entirely resist different modes of opposition to it. In the imperial period, literary study in India could not ultimately prevent an alternative critical consciousness from developing, even though the ostensible goal of such study was to forestall oppositional thinking. Raymond Williams believed that, in the later period too, political hegemony is not able to exhaust all of the forms of opposition to it. If the university is understood as a tool of the competitive capitalist social order, then there remains the possibility of transforming this into the site for the promotion of critical thinking. The challenge then is to find a kind of university where this is possible.

HARD AND SOFT UNIVERSITIES

What form could such a university take? A clue is provided by Williams's novel *The Volunteers*. The Volunteers of the title are a covert group of revolutionary activists. They have realized that in an age of technologically enhanced surveillance of the social organism, mere surface raging or unsustainable lashing out at the individual offices of power will not enable revolution. Their strategy is to infiltrate the organs of state power – parties, committees, anywhere where decisions are taken – and work to achieve change from the inside.

Rosa, an insider of this covert group, explains to the investigative journalist Lewis Redfern how their infiltration works. Aside from what she calls the 'hard' parts – the strikes, the marches, the visible campaigning – she also says: '[t]here are soft parts. The universities, the schools, the operative parts of the media.'[21]

This distinction between the hard and the soft can be used to generate a distinction between different kinds of education. The Volunteers imagine all universities as 'soft' components of the social order – in contrast to the 'hard' elements of the military-industrial complex. French Marxist Louis Althusser makes a similar distinction between what he calls the 'Repressive State Apparatus' and the 'Ideological State Apparatus', where the former correspond to the 'hard' elements of a social order and the latter to the 'soft.'[22]

It was precisely to show that aspects of the ideological apparatus such as the media, publishing houses and universities carry out a material role in generating a social order that Raymond Williams developed his cultural materialism. This theory overcomes the distinction between 'material' and 'ideological' components of a social order, by showing that all the components are materially active.

The vocabulary employed by Rosa in *The Volunteers* can therefore be usefully modified. All universities constitute a material part of the make-up of a society and are therefore not to be seen as 'soft' or idealist elements of that order. On the other hand, universities have the capacity either to support the social and political order dogmatically, or to operate as a site for the promotion of critical cultural and political thought. The terms *hard* and *soft* can therefore be used to refer to these contrasting conceptions of a university.

A hard university practises a programme of banking education and contributes to the continual reproduction of the dominant ideology through mobilization of a competitive ethic and selective promotion. Its courses last for a fixed (and predetermined) period of time, after which the process of education is assumed to be complete. Its syllabus is also preselected and, barring the occasional choice of course, varies little according to the needs or ideas of the individual student.

This is not how Williams imagined a university. Williams's concept of the university can therefore be referred to as a 'soft' university. A soft university is not restricted to one location, like a hard university. On the contrary, if it is really to be democratized, then what happens in the university must have an active relation with all the rest of the society. Williams's valuation of the Open University, which he thought was the most important legacy of Britain's Labour government of the 1960s, makes it an example of a soft university.[23]

Tony Pinkney describes the planned city of Manod in Williams's novel, *The Fight for Manod*, as a 'soft' city. Pinkney makes this point in order to draw attention to the conflicts that Williams portrays in the novel over how the city will be built, and for whose benefit.[24] This point can also be drawn out of the discussion of different kinds of university. Rather than simply acquiescing in the construction of a capitalist order, the whole role of universities within society is still actively contested.

Unlike a 'hard' university, a 'soft' university would not determine in advance how long it will take students to reach an acceptable level of educational fullness. Instead, it would enable students to continue learning at the same time as they engage in important creative and critical work. Again, the Open University can be seen as an example of this. Moreover, whereas a 'hard' university selects the content of its programme in advance, giving its students little or no input into that selection, a 'soft' university equips students with the resources to decide for themselves what educational programme has most direct and immediate relevance to their own lives. An example of this in Williams's writing would be his praise for the Centre for Contemporary Cultural Studies at Birmingham University, which drew its materials from different aspects of contemporary British culture and continually updated its syllabus.[25]

Williams was aware that no form of cultural dominance can ever entirely exhaust the modes of opposition to it. This enabled him to make continual proposals about how to reform and revolutionize education. *The Long Revolution* (1961), *Communications* (1966), and *Resources of*

Hope (1988) all contain specific proposals for how to transform education. This in turn would enable education to elude the dictates of the capitalist order by teaching its students scepticism towards that order. Historically, the establishment of this kind of oppositional university was not realized in full, even in the Open University. The task was then a matter of trying to demonstrate, against certain political and economic pressures, the possibility of creating such a system. That possibility was best demonstrated by Williams in his fiction.

WILLIAMS VERSUS THE 'MOVEMENT'

Raymond Williams did not comment on the work of his contemporaries very much. He characterized the mainstream kind of writing produced during the 1950s and 1960s as the fiction of *personal pleading* (*LR*, p. 310). This was because the mainstream fiction of the time was often centred on the life of one individual, and tended towards a narrative logic of closure, to the detriment of wider social commitments. A good example of this kind of fiction is the work produced by the so-called Movement group of writers, including Philip Larkin, D. J. Enright, Kingsley Amis and John Wain. Although the Movement is normally thought of as a group of poets, these writers also attempted fiction and, in particular, university novels. It is significant that the Movement writers were among the few of his own contemporaries on whose work Raymond Williams commented in detail. His books *The Long Revolution*, *Orwell*, *Raymond Williams on Television* and *What I Came to Say* all contain passing swipes at the dominant fictional form of the 1950s and 1960s as it was practised by Movement writers (*LR*, pp. 310–11; *WCS*, p. 25).[26]

Williams gives the genre of university writing a radical new twist, using his fiction to imagine a new kind of university and hence a new set of social relations. Unlike the campus fiction of the Movement writers, much of the action in Williams's work takes place off campus, opening up connections to a much broader political world. When Williams departs from the Movement writers' fictional portrayal of the university, he also takes exception to the political and ideological associations that come with it. The difference is between the closed and elitist world of the *campus novel* and the open and dialogic mode of Williams's *university fiction*. Williams's detailed engagement with the work of the Movement writers, in other words, can be traced in such a way as to highlight how he proposed to use education to democratize society.

For example, in an article published in the *New Statesman* in 1961, to which he and Raymond Williams both contributed, Kingsley Amis described as 'leftist fallacies' the notion that 'the competitive element could, or should, be taken out of education'.[27] In the banking system of education, assessment and advancement are selective and competitive from a very early stage. To Amis this is necessarily so, since it is the essential way of preparing students to slough off the merely educational stage and enter the real (competitive) world. Education within the spirit of aggressive competitive individualism is thus to Amis 'an essential step towards doing something for ourselves'.[28]

In his response to Amis in the *New Statesman* article, Williams puts his own argument for breaking 'the deadlock between the abstract *individual* and *society*'.[29] He strongly resists the idea that the assimilation of all spheres of society to the competitive world of capitalism is either necessary or desirable. In his pursuit of a democratic future he suggests that there should 'be no assimilation, but transformation'.[30] That is, where Amis sees the individual working to obtain the maximum of self-determination within the panoply of society, Williams wants to rethink relations between human beings and society. The difference in conception of education between the two men stems from this. Amis believes in an education system with an element of selection through competition built in. Williams seeks ways to remove the hierarchical element from education. Amis's university is a place to which by definition few people have access and which denies any association with the outside world. Williams's university, by contrast, is commensurate with a degree of universality.

The difference is visible in the fictional portrayal of the university mobilized by each writer. Kingsley Amis's first novel, *Lucky Jim* (1954), is the kind of campus novel that portrays a 'hard' university. Junior lecturer Jim Dixon is plagued by a student, Michie, who wants to know what special subject Dixon is offering, so that he can decide whether to subscribe to it. Dixon wants to keep Michie out. The reason is that 'Michie knew a lot, or seemed to, which was bad' because Dixon himself 'wouldn't be able to go on seeming to know' the answers 'while Michie was there, questioning, discussing and arguing about them'.[31]

The central premise of a 'hard' university is this: the lecturer is there to *know*, and to impart this knowledge uninterrupted by the irritating questions of the students. This view of a university is not necessarily endorsed by Amis. On the contrary, *Lucky Jim* satirizes the hierarchical structure of academia: 'No firsts this year for us,' explains Dixon's colleague Beesley, 'four thirds, and forty-five per cent of the first-year people failed. That's the only way to deal with 'em.'[32] In this mocking of the groves of academe, Amis is unable to break beyond the bounds of comic writing. He is unable to make any serious suggestion as to how else a university should be organized. Despite lampooning what has been described as a 'hard' university, Amis has no corresponding sense of a 'soft' university, and his satire is rendered powerless as a result.

A 'hard' university envisages education as one step on a journey from home to education to work to world. In other words, this reckoning imagines education as a stage of life that, once finished, cannot be returned to. A 'soft' university, on the other hand, is all about the interpenetration of work and education. When Jim Dixon gives his public lecture at the end of *Lucky Jim*, he remarks that the audience 'seemed to contain everybody he knew or had ever known apart from his parents'.[33] By contrast, Matthew Price in Williams's *Border Country* returns to his family. He tells his father:

> I can't just be a delegate, sent out to do a particular job. I've moved into my own life and that's taken me away. I can't just come back, as if the change was water. I can't come here and pretend I'm Will Price, with nothing altered. (*BC*, p. 297)

Yet come back he does. This is the fundamental difference from a 'hard' campus novel. There, education simply equips individuals to do specific jobs, and takes them away from the earlier stages of their development. In *Border Country*, by contrast, education and work are both dialectical processes, they take place everywhere.

Border Country is an autobiographical novel. Williams used it as a kind of vehicle for the exploration of his own experiences. The relationship between the distant university and the local community is shown to throw up a series of challenges, because the necessity to exist in a series of different environments renders Matthew Price, like Williams himself, perpetually homeless. He is not quite at home in the new university world he has entered. Neither can he simplistically return to his prior way of life.

Williams expressed this dilemma elsewhere as the conflict of ideas between educated thought and customary feeling, or, again, between an attachment to place and a new experience of mobility. The first English novelist whom Williams suggests registered the experience of this conflict was Thomas Hardy. Williams's evaluation of Hardy's *Jude the Obscure* could be taken as a commentary on *Border Country* itself. Williams draws attention to the continuity of experience in the kinds of writing from *Jude* to *Border Country*:

> It is more than a matter of picking up terms and tones. It is what happens to us, really to us, as we try to mediate those contrasted worlds: as we stand with Jude, but a Jude who has been let in; or as we go back to our own places, our own families, and know what is meant, in idea and in feeling, by the return of the native. The Hardy country is of course Wessex: that is to say mainly Dorset and its neighbouring counties. But the real Hardy country, I feel more and more, is that border country so many of us have been living in: between custom and education, between work and ideas, between love of place and an experience of change. This is of special import-ance to a generation, who have gone to the university from ordinary families and have to discover, through a life, what that experience means.[34]

The anguished dilemmas experienced by Jude outside the towers of Christminster were repeated almost a century later in the anguish felt by Matthew Price in *Border Country*. Williams's moving description of Hardy's life and work has a particular resonance in the context of university education in Britain in the 1950s and 1960s.

There is a further element of kinship between *Jude the Obscure* and *Border Country*. Christminster in Hardy's novel is not simply a university. It is a disguised version of Oxford, cathedral city and university town. When the young Price in *Border Country* goes to the Reverend Pugh to discuss the idea of going away to an Oxbridge College, Pugh expresses fear that he is not the best person to advise. He is 'isolated' from the village, 'sad and indifferent' (*BC*, p. 213). He cannot relate to most of the villagers who are chapelgoers, rather than members of his Anglican church. His retreat from the daily life of the village into his own private study seems to parallel the studies and combination rooms of classic campus novels. Pugh draws an explicit comparison between his church and education: 'Formerly, you know, Matthew, I should have been educating you, and then sending you on, later, to the cathedral' (*BC*, p. 213). Yet if his church somehow corresponds to a university, it can only be to a 'hard' university. He tells Will that he is just a kind of 'outpost' with 'no roots' in Glynmawr (*BC*, p. 214), whereas the roots of a 'soft' university snake out and reach everywhere.

Pugh wonders if there is really any difference between the greatest cathedral or university and the chapels and schoolrooms of Glynmawr. 'Perhaps they are only the Glynmawr chapels better built. Only as institutions, sometimes, they seem more.' (*BC*, p. 216) There is a difference between the great cathedrals and universities and Glynmawr's chapels and schoolrooms. It is the difference between a 'hard' and 'soft' university, or between an education which connects and an education which divides. *Border Country* shows Williams beginning to question the inherited divisive dominant mode of education without imagining what he could replace it with. For that, he would have to try his hand again, in *Second Generation*.

OXBRIDGE, THEIR OXBRIDGE

Lucky Jim's college is situated on 'College Road'. In other words, it is entirely self-enclosed. Williams's barely disguised Oxford of *Second Generation* shows his protagonists living on 'Between Towns Road'. Interaction between university and world is always already inevitable.

Amis too wrote an Oxford novel, *The Alteration* (1976), comparison of which with *Second Generation* is instructive. *The Alteration* imagines an England in which the Protestant Reformation – and much subsequent social reform – never took place. The setting must appear simultaneously as both a backward unregenerate past and the contemporary world of 1976. Amis achieves this by marrying every conceivable relic of Merrie England (shires, and lords, and markets, and taverns, and ale) with such features of modern life as trains and cars. The effect is of a culture caught up in a parody of itself, slowly suffocating.

The plot runs thus: talented choirboy Hubert Anvil is discovered by his abbot, who wishes to castrate him so that he can sing as a boy soprano forever and so bring glory to the Abbey school. The pope gets word of all this from his envoys Viaventosa and Mirabilis, and wants to bring Hubert to sing in Rome. Hubert runs away, is kidnapped by lowlife vagabonds, and escapes to the New England embassy where the American ambassador Cornelius Van Den Haag smuggles him out of the country and enables him to avoid the 'alteration' that is to be inflicted upon him.

At the same time the 'alteration' that is imagined to come over England, the Protestant Reformation, is avoided by the papacy. But, by this very logic, which invites us to imagine how things might be different, we are compelled to accept that such a reformation has already benefited our own world. It is a gesture of ratification and evasion. The choirboys talk about a scientific novel they are reading, which imagines the 'ridiculous' scenario of a modern, post-reformation England, free of tyrannical rule.[35] This invites us as readers to celebrate the fact that we really do live in such freedom.

In the 1976 of Amis's novel, women are not free to speak in public.[36] Officers of the oligarchic state have unfettered power of interrogation derived from distant papal authority. The coercive apparatus of the tyrannical state employs torture and sexual exploitation to harness control over people.[37] At the same time, the state authorities stir up disease and war, as ways to reduce the size of the troublesome population.[38]

This is the world before the Protestant Reformation and before the extension of democracy, brought right into 1976. Amis's characters can only imagine the democratic post-reformation future which we as readers must presume ourselves to inhabit. The implication is that we are living at the end of history. That is, to us, the characters belong in a historical past which has now been forgotten, as if all problems and cruelties have now been solved and as if history itself has reached its destination. It is a historical deflection that forestalls in advance the possibility of questioning the social ordering of our own present. Anything that might need questioning has already been questioned.

Raymond Williams's emphasis on different kinds of hegemony shows us that a social and political order has always to be actively generated. It is never simply a given. Amis's novel seems to imply that since all the facets of medieval absolutism which he portrays had ended by the twentieth century, then the social order which arose in its place was natural and spontaneous, rather than actively generated. Yet the social order of free market capitalism is not a given. It is not the way the world looks when it is simply stripped of the trappings of a prior historical period. It is in itself an actively generated social order. It is perhaps no coincidence that *The Alteration* concludes with Cornelius

Van Den Haag's plan to ship Hubert over to New England. The end-point of progress away from the medieval absolutist state is that haven of free market competitive individualism – America.

Raymond Williams took issue explicitly with this. In the *New States-man* article, he warned – *contra* Amis – against seeing 'the United States as a kind of universal future' which can be seen as 'a process of modernisation' but in reality is a much more ideological gesture towards the capitalist order.[39] Williams's Oxford novel *Second Generation* posits a quite different culmination to the process of education.

Peter Owen is a research student on Welsh population movements in a thinly disguised Oxford, to which his parents Kate and Harold, and aunt and uncle Myra and Gwyn, had earlier moved to seek employment at the car factory. American academic Professor Kissler has heard about Peter's research and proposes to ship him over to California to carry out further work in population studies. Yet Peter ends up deciding to concentrate his efforts on the 'real' work of relating to his own com-munity, and writes to Kissler to decline.[40] America as universal future, and as metonym for competitive capitalist society, is explicitly rejected. University education is not envisaged as an instrument to enable participation in the capitalist sphere.

Second Generation is Williams's attempt at a 'soft' university novel. He wishes to disavow the notion of education as an autonomous sphere. This is done by portraying the work of the university directly alongside that of the factory where Peter's father and uncle work. Events in one locale shape and inform events in the other. When Peter's super-visor Robert Lane asserts an absolute distinction between the two spheres, Peter shouts it down: 'No Robert. This is not two cities but one.' (*SG*, p. 251) Against this, Lane launches a counter-offensive, pointing out that the two communities do not mix with each other at all. 'But,' Lane continues, 'I can rage against the feel of the university and yet still respect the work that it's doing.' Peter retorts: 'Because you've sold out to it, surely. You daren't make the connection . . . The questions you learn not to ask. The questions I was taught not to ask.' (*SG*, p. 251)

The concern throughout *Second Generation* is with the questions that a certain kind of education specifically teaches its students not to ask. *Lucky Jim* satirizes the university system without being able to imagine an alternative kind of education. Raymond Williams appears to have thought this was generally true of the university novels of the Movement writers. 'Haven't you determined / the answer with your question?' he rhetorically asks them in his poem written on the occasion of 'On First Looking into *New Lines*' (*WCS*, p. 257). *New Lines* was a Movement anthology, and the doggerel Williams wrote in response to it was an implicit swipe at the values expressed by that formation of writers. Williams was suspicious of the tactical disinterestedness that the poems seemed to express. As he told *Poetry Wales* in 1977, what he objected to was the Movement writers' vitiation of literature as a social process. Literature in this practice is hollowed out and deadened, replaced by 'quite attractive verse of its kind, light social verse – a sort of shrug, polite, carefully not going beyond the emotions of what was probable' and therefore also ruling out 'emotional intensity and the kind of writing that goes with it' (*WSW*, p. 88).

In contrast to this tactical disavowal of self-interest, it is necessary to recall Paulo Freire's concept of education as learning to question. This was also the way in which Raymond Williams envisaged a dialogical practice within the classroom. The point must be understood as a continuing conflict over the definition and role of the university, which is then also a conflict over the construction of the capitalist order.

Williams's fictional approach to the university shows him taking exception to a whole tradition in English writing. The Movement novelists by contrast are the custodians of that tradition. Indeed, Edward Lobb says of the Movement that it 'has an importance out of proportion to the quality of the work' precisely because it 'crystallised tendencies which were already at work' and 'set the tone' for British writing 'for several years'.[41] Although Lobb is talking about the dominant tone in British poetry, his comment could apply equally to the production of novels, for the number of Movement writers who attempt 'hard' university novels is striking. Other examples would be Philip Larkin's *Jill* (1946), John Wain's *Hurry on Down* (1953) and D. J. Enright's *Academic Year* (1955). These novels imagine the university as an instrument of the capitalist order and are inculcated with a kind of competitive ethic. This in turn had arisen out of the nascent shift in conceptions of the university, from disseminator of national culture to organization of rigid professionalism.

The transition from *cultural* to *professional* university had already started by the 1950s. As a result, a commitment to the competitive market underlies the Movement novels. J. P. Kenyon has noted the congruence between university fiction and novels about trade and commerce:

'if you substitute for "professor" the term "managing director", or for "College Council" or "Faculty Board" the term "Board of Directors", you realise that many university novels are in fact "business-like", in a literal sense'.[42]

John Wain's 1958 novel *The Contenders* is a good example of the business-university novel. It tells the story of three friends, Joe Shaw, Robert Lamb and Ned Roper, who have all recently left education and find themselves deliberating which professional field to enter. Robert and Ned are the contenders of the title. They have always been rivals – academically, emotionally, in sport and now professionally. Their constant one-upmanship culminates in Ned Roper's stealing Robert Lamb's wife, Myra. The novel's narrator, Joe, appears to eschew this competitive ethic. In the opening paragraph of the novel he tells us that '[t]his is the story of two men, Robert Lamb and Ned Roper. I know them both and I'm going to tell the story as I watched it happen.'[43]

In the figure of Joe the narrator, Wain appears to admonish the competitive ethic that has converted human relationships into the mere raw material of success. Joe, the reasonable narrator, sets out to tell things simply as they happened, as if he has no interest in the events being narrated. Yet Wain's narrator is simultaneously inside and outside the game. For Joe – uncompetitive Joe – is nevertheless assured of promotion in his own industry, journalism.

Joe is a reasonable narrator. Unreasonable is Robert, railing against the establishment to which he yearns to be admitted, and then drowning his grievance in alcohol and becoming obnoxious. Or, to put it another way round, unreasonableness also is Ned Roper asking Robert with studied inhuman politeness to run along from the house where he (Ned) has set up home with his (Robert's) ex-wife, and stop making a spectacle. Between these extremes of obnoxious or studied inhuman unreasonableness, the middle ground occupied by reasonable narrator Joe Shaw appears the firmest ground. Anything can be described as long as nothing is really communicated as a process. Nothing can be discussed in a serious engaged manner because that would lead on to the fanaticism of Robert or else the studious inhumanity of Ned.

The reasonable narrator Joe is a level-headed, friendly, approachable figure. Talk about serious matters of the day he will not, so that near the conclusion of *The Contenders*, even home rule for Scotland becomes a mere nicety, something to talk about in a queue for the telephone with a stranger:

When I got to the box there were a couple of chaps standing quite con-
tentedly outside it . . . One of them was a Scotsman, and he was able to add
variety and breadth to our little symposium by giving the characteristic
north British view. I began to question him keenly about the nationalist
movement, and the extent to which he, personally, considered Home Rule
desirable or feasible. Now and again we glanced at the woman inside the
box; she didn't seem to be talking much – if she was, we could only conclude
that she had learnt some technique of talking without moving her mouth;
from a ventriloquist, no doubt. This led our discussion naturally into the
realms of entertainment and the arts, our Caledonian friend contributing a
spirited defence of the traditional songs and dances of his native heath.[44]

The patronizing tone of this passage towards Scottish culture hardly
needs pointing out. The Scot, we are told, is 'spirited' and this implicitly
contrasts with the calm and decorous demeanour of the questioner.
We are not told what either party really thought about home rule. Such
conclusions do not matter in situations like these. It does not matter
what is discussed as long as they are discussed reasonably, without
seeking to generate any social effect. Throughout *The Contenders*, the
real business of communication is forestalled so that nothing is allowed
to fracture the competitive world this novel inhabits. Education exists
simply to provide the tools for success in the competitive world.

English as a university subject had been taught in Scottish universities before it was accepted in institutions in England. This enabled
the nineteenth-century university to carry out some of the cultural
and ideological work of nationalism – and ultimately, of empire. The
dissemination of an undifferentiated British culture through the teaching
of subjects such as English, history and geography in the Scottish
universities was one way in which the putative unity of the British
state could be augmented. This in effect is what Amis and Wain do to
Scotland and Wales. Wain's Scotland is swallowed up by the putative
entity, 'north Britain'. Similar representations of Wales can be found in
Wain's *A Winter in the Hills* (1970) and Amis's *The Old Devils* (1986).

A Winter in the Hills and *The Old Devils* are both university novels.
In *A Winter in the Hills*, London philologist Roger Furnivall heads to
north Wales to study Celtic languages, believing this will equip him to
gain admittance to the institute for Celtic study in Uppsala, Sweden,
where he dreams of being surrounded by attractive women. In north
Wales, Furnivall gets drawn into local gangster conflicts and a series

of romantic escapades, before returning to London and his academic career. In other words, *A Winter in the Hills* satirizes the work of the university professor, yet without making any serious exploration of its role in a democratic society.

Amis's late novel *The Old Devils* describes the lives of four retired couples in the south Wales area where, years earlier, they had attended university. Their relationships are complicated by the arrival of another former acquaintance, the poet and literary professor Alun Weaver, who has made a name for himself in England as *the* poet of Wales. Yet, where in Hardy's *Return of the Native* or Williams's *Border Country* we find a serious commitment to exploring the effect of living continually in different kinds of community, *The Old Devils* does not perform this work. In satirizing the nationalist pretence of the 'poet of Wales', it carries out similar work to *Lucky Jim*. That is, it holds the world of academia up to biting satire, but without being able to suggest alternative forms of relationship, so that in the end, the satire itself becomes blank and meaningless.

The derisive representations of university work that occur in Movement fiction may be traceable to the shifting national and imperial fortunes experienced by the British state during this period. In the face of the dissolution of empire and relative decline in Britain's fortunes, the last preserve of national culture was to cling to the spurious unity of a multi-national state formation, despite the pressure for self-government that was slowly beginning to rise in Scotland and Wales.

Thus in the work of Britain's established novelists of the late imperial period we can discern an appeal to the putative unity of the British state. This really belongs to an earlier historical period. It is in Raymond Williams's vocabulary a *residual* element in British society. This is true in the very specific sense that the appeal to unity through the castigation of Celtic difference continues to exert limited real power, even though the historical moment at which it arose has long passed.

Raymond Williams's portrayal of Welshness in *Border Country* and *Second Generation* is again associated both with cultural identity and with the work of the university. In his work, however, the role of the university is quite different. Instead of an appeal to national unity, there is a continual exploration of the relations between communities in England and Wales. There is moreover an absolute rejection, in the work of Peter Owen in *Second Generation*, of the use of education to provide success in the capitalist market. Raymond Williams, in other words, rethinks the university. He envisages it neither as an organ of national-imperial consciousness nor as an instrument of the transnational capitalist order. He understands the university as a place that promotes critical cultural and political thinking, from which the unequal structuring of capitalist society might be countered. The difference springs ultimately from a fundamentally different conception of the university: a university that divides, or a university that connects. The difference, that is, between 'hard' and 'soft' universities.

4

Postcolonial Britain

Modern British history reveals a gradual variation in the scope and nature of university education. Universities started out as institutions imbued with a national and imperial ethos during the colonial period. With an economic downturn brought on in part due to decolonization, the emphasis behind university education became more instrumental, providing training for the new professionals who would enable British businesses to compete in a global economy. In other words, the history of universities in Britain reveals a subtle overlap between national interest and capitalist economics.

To Raymond Williams, the nation-state was an institution of cultural modernity and imperialism. The text in which Williams explores these ideas most fully is *The Country and the City* (1973). Here he attempts an examination of the connections that exist between the capitalist order and the nation-state. He pursues this analysis across a long-term historical period, from early modernism to the late twentieth century.

THE COUNTRY AND THE WORLD

Williams began *The Country and the City* by looking at the practice of country house writing as it was inaugurated during the Elizabethan period. The cultural practice at work was one where poets and artisans were commissioned to produce specific pieces of work for specific landed patrons – usually aristocratic men. Within the context of Elizabethan England, and its nascent morality of virtue and improvement, to eulogize the country house was also taken somehow as eulogizing the master. The house was well kept because the master was a shrewd manager. The dinner hall was a place of great feasting and hospitality because the master was generous and giving. The parks and estates were beautifully maintained because the master was understood to be a kind of minor god, carefully controlling the natural order of his own little Eden. According to Williams, 'what we find . . . [in the poetry] is an idealisation of feudal and immediately post-feudal values: of an order based on settled and reciprocal social and economic relations of an avowedly total kind'.[1]

It is a practice of mystification: the servants, labourers and outcasts on whom the entire system depends are entirely written out of the poems so that the only people who appear to matter are the aristocratic lords of the manor. This social order is related by the country house and estate metaphor to the natural landscape and is thus presented as time-less, unchanging, natural. It is a mystification at work in the interest of the ruling landed class. As Williams says, 'it is then important that the poems coincide, in time, with a period in which another order – that of capitalist agriculture – was being successfully pioneered' (*CC*, p. 35). The best-known examples Williams gives of these poems are Ben Jonson's 'To Penshurst', Thomas Carew's 'To Saxham', and Andrew Marvell's 'Upon Appleton House'. Social and moral economy are mystified within these poems in order to ratify and support the class structure of the patrons.

The second stage of Williams's analysis in *The Country and the City* is to explore the connection between a mystified social capitalist order and an equally mystified concept of national identity and national interest. During the period Williams analysed in *The Country and the City*, the mystifying of the social order was achieved in part by the entrenched tradition of country house writing. The poems were power-ful primarily because the landlords who commissioned them were powerful figures, commanding the capacity to dictate literary tastes along with more direct rules on how to govern the estates. At the same time, that power was also in part derived from the idealization per-formed in the poetry.

The magnificence of the country estates was taken to be a measure of the virtue and morality of the landowners, and by a final extension, of the virtue and morality of the nation itself. As Peter de Bolla has written of

The Country and the City, it shows the enlightenment and imperial attempt to create 'a specifically national heritage' through appeal to the virtue and morality of the system and associated invocation of a supposedly natural order.[2] A growing interest in the English landscape was accompanied by an emotive appeal to the supposedly common origins of those who peopled that landscape, in an eternal and immutable social order. This created a hegemonic sense of united national identity while also mystifying the profoundly disunited character of the nation.

If the literary texts analysed by Williams played a material part in augmenting the power of the country house system domestically, this became even more strongly the case during the period of empire. The third stage of analysis that Williams opens in *The Country and the City* draws attention to the relationship between domestic national culture in formation, and the role played by the colonies in the construction of national culture. He was struck by a congruence between the establishment of capitalist society in Britain and imperial practice overseas. In *The Country and the City* he notes that the process of land enclosure in rural eighteenth-century Britain was decisive in setting up a class system based on economic strength. This is also what he showed happened in the colonies. 'The inequalities of condition which the village contains and supports are profound, and nobody, by any exercise of sentiment, can convert it into a "rural democracy" or, absurdly, a commune', he writes of eighteenth-century rural capitalism in Britain (*CC*, p. 102). He goes on to make a similar point about the establishment of colonial exploitation in Nigeria as portrayed in Chinua Achebe's novel *Things Fall Apart*:

> What is impressive about *Things Fall Apart* is that, as in some English literature of rural change, as late as Hardy, the internal tensions of the society are made clear, so that we can understand the modes of the penetration which would in any case, in its process of expansion, have come . . . The strongest man, Okwonkwo, is destroyed in a very complicated process of internal contradictions and external invasion. (*CC*, p. 286)

The integration of Williams's thinking on capitalism, nation and imperialism is evident from his consistency of approach. He shows that territorial acquisition had enabled rural societies in Britain to be brought into a capitalist structure, just as territorial acquisition enabled the colonies to be governed and exploited. His understanding of those processes is derived mainly from the literature produced in the societies in question. He shows that the structure of domestic capitalist society resembled the structure whereby the resources of colonized societies were exploited by European colonizers. He also suggests that the literature produced in each society is comparable. As a result, he makes a favourable comparison between Thomas Hardy and Chinua Achebe.

An important feature of this comment is that it is literary-critical, understanding imperial history primarily from its reading artefacts. The profoundest comment Williams is able to make on the relationship between domestic culture, national identity and imperialism is undertaken exclusively with regard to the *literature* of the period:

> In *Wuthering Heights*, in *Great Expectations*, in *Alton Locke* and in many other novels of the period there is a way out from the struggle within English society to these distant lands; a way out that is not only the escape to a new land but as in some of the real history an acquisition of fortune to return and re-enter the struggle at a higher point . . . The lands of the Empire were an idyllic retreat, an escape from debt or shame, or an opportunity for making a fortune. (*CC*, p. 281)

In *The Country and the City* Williams draws attention to the tendency of nineteenth-century novelists to view the colonies as the training ground for a domestic culture in formation. The metaphor of empire as 'idyllic retreat' extends the country house metaphor Williams had already detected in the poetics of nation building. Williams suggests that throughout the eighteenth and nineteenth centuries, the imperial project was partly legitimized by its country house literature. His theoretical approach tells us that literary texts had a material part to play in the significant make-up of society.

Implicit in this approach is the idea that to produce and disseminate different kinds of texts is to take a step towards altering the structure of society. At the fourth stage of analysis in *The Country and the City*, Raymond Williams turns from national and imperial processes to postcolonial history. He is aware of the pressures towards political change inside late colonial societies, primarily as a result of his reading of the canonical late colonial authors: E. M. Forster, George Orwell and Joyce Cary (*CC*, p. 285). 'But', he writes, 'we have only to go across to the Indian and African and West Indian writers to get a different and necessary perspective' (*CC*, p. 285).

Williams suggests that this alternative perspective on colonial history can be gleaned in the work of writers such as Mulk Raj Anand, Wilson Harris, R. K. Narayan, Chinua Achebe, Han Suyin and Ngugi Wa Thiong'o. Such writers challenge the model of country house dominance over hinterland/colony. This is particularly clear in George Lamming's novel *In the Castle of My Skin* (1953) and V. S. Naipaul's *A House for Mr Biswas* (published in 1960, the same year as Williams's own novel, *Border Country*). Lamming and Naipaul render the metaphor of the country house all too literally, in dramatizing the historical struggles of colonized peoples to gain effective political control over their own estates.

In the chapter of *The Country and the City* entitled 'The New Metropolis', Williams extends the country house metaphor. During the period of nation building, the image of country house and estate had already been extended to the more encompassing model of city and countryside, where all the power was assumed to lie in the metropolitan city and all the labour on which this depended was carried out in the countryside. The political power of the country house becomes worked up into the political power of metropolitan cities. In a final extension of the metaphor, Williams suggests that the dominance of country house over sprawling estate, and of metropolitan city over hinterland, is comparable to the dominance exerted by the imperial nations over their colonies. This is true of both the colonial period, and the neocolonial stage that followed formal decolonization. Within the context of globalization and extreme inequality between nations and peoples, Williams notes that the myth of the elegant and gentrified country house has been extended to cover the entire developed capitalist world:

> The 'metropolitan' states, through a system of trade, but also through a complex of economic and political controls, draw food and, more critically, raw materials from these areas of supply, this effective hinterland, that is also the greater part of the earth's surface and that contains the great majority of its peoples. Thus a model of city and country, in economic and political relationships, has gone beyond the boundaries of the nation-state, and is seen but also challenged as a model of the world. (*CC*, p. 279)

Williams suggests that the western world has become something like an enormous country estate. It operates with grace and elegance while also blinding itself to the processes of work on which that operation depends. Just as the industrial and agricultural labour on which the country house depends is entirely written out of the country house writing, so too the industrial labour in the developing world on which the lifestyles of the prosperous nations depend is distanced, dissociated from daily life in the metropolis. In postcolonial and post-industrial Britain, industrial work is devolved upon the developing world, which is thus metaphorically assigned the status of hinterland, or enormous rural estate, providing provisions and sustenance for the country house/ first world.

Williams concludes that 'a model of city and country' is 'seen but also challenged' as a model of the world. The phrase 'seen but also challenged' is central to the theory and practice of cultural materialism. Williams has been criticized for limiting his analysis of postcolonial societies to the *literature* produced within them, and for failing thereby to pay more specific attention to the *political* processes involved.[3] Williams's cultural materialism suggests that literary texts themselves play an admittedly modest yet nevertheless tangible part in those same political processes. By challenging the metaphor of country house dominance *in* their literature, Lamming, Naipaul, Suyin, Anand and Ngugi all contribute in their various ways to making change happen *outside* it.

The Country and the City relates the process of nation building in the early modern period to that of empire building throughout the eighteenth and nineteenth centuries. The material role played by literature in imagining these communities into existence is comparable in each case. Likewise, the potential of literature to participate in changing those structures and reimagining the community is equally prevalent. The important conjunction Williams makes is between nation building and imperialism: 'As we gain perspective from the long history of the literature of country and city, we see how much, at different times and in different places, it is a connecting process, in what has to be seen ultimately as a common history' (*CC*, p. 288). If the history of the nation is related to the formation of empire then, in the last instance, the break-up of the empire may be related to the break-up of the nation.

ANTI-IMPERIALISM AND *THE VOLUNTEERS*

The congruence between formal decolonization overseas and political break-up domestically is explored in Raymond Williams's novel, *The Volunteers*. It was published in 1978, and set in a then futuristic late twentieth-century Britain, under the control of an extreme nationalist government. Lewis Redfern, an investigative journalist for the Insatel broadcasting corporation, is assigned to investigate the shooting and wounding of secretary of state for Wales, Edmund Buxton, during a state visit to the Welsh Folk Museum at Saint Fagan's, outside Cardiff. Buxton had been involved in a government decision taken only a few months earlier, to use military force to break a strike at a steel works in Pontyrhiw. This decision had directly resulted in the death of a worker, Gareth Powell, and thus provoked great resentment against Buxton.

The Volunteers brings into relief two distinct events and explores the relationship between them. The two events refuse to cohere neatly, just as Williams refuses to subscribe to the enforced overriding version of unitary British identity. Lewis Redfern's attempt to discover the relationship between the breaking of the strike and the shooting of Buxton forms the basis of the investigation plot.

The location of the attack on Buxton is significant. Benedict Anderson suggests in *Imagined Communities* that 'museums, and the museum-izing imagination, are both profoundly political'.[4] Anderson suggests that the concept of 'provincial' museums enabled the nineteenth-century colonial powers to delineate the borders of their empires culturally, as well as geographically. The work of collecting and classifying cultural and ethnographic treasures posited the imperial powers as owners of the objects in their collections, even when those objects included entire human communities. This is how early museums sprung up in India, Indonesia and French Indo-China. At the same time, such delineation also sowed the seeds of a unified anti-colonial imagination, and would ultimately play a part in the formation of liberation and nationalist movements *against* the great empires. The museum, as with other tools mobilized to augment the strength of nation-state and of empire, ultim-ately undermined what it was supposed to support.

As an example of how potent a symbol of anti-colonial nationalism a museum can be, Anderson references the murder in 1984 of Arnold Ap, the political leader of the West Papua New Guinean movement for autonomy from Indonesia. Anderson notes that when he was assassin-ated in 1984, Ap 'was curator of a state-built museum devoted to . . . provincial culture'.[5] Setting *The Volunteers* around the aftermath of a political shooting in the Welsh Folk Museum aligns Williams with a similar anti-colonial perspective on Welsh history.

Buxton is not killed in the attack, merely wounded in the legs. 'There was no danger to his life but he was crippled and in great pain.'[6] The wounding of his legs leaves Buxton immobilized, cut off from the country house world whose power he is supposed to embody, and hence strikes at the authority behind that figure. The attack itself is facilitated by a smoke bomb, which leaves the police guard temporarily 'cut off' from the official party (V, p. 17). The country house system is temporarily denuded of its power in this way.

As in *The Fight for Manod*, the investigation that ensues is 'superficially clear' (V, p. 10). The police have a distinct image of Buxton's assailant: 'orange cape, with dark glasses and a blue denim cap, and with long fair hair and beard and moustache' (V, p. 19). Moreover, the police quickly find the getaway car, and discover from the London rental company that it was used by a German student, J. Tiller, who had mentioned that he was 'especially looking forward to visiting Wales' (V, p. 62). Happily, there is a file about J. Marcus Tiller on the intelligence network database; he is known to be a German radical subversive. The suspect is identified and need only be found.

Lewis realizes at once that this is too simple, and launches an alternative investigation. Suspecting a connection between resentment against Buxton over the death of Gareth Powell at Pontyrhiw and the symbolic shooting at Saint Fagan's, he tries to trace anyone else present at both events. Media photographs enable him to trace Bill Chaney, Rosa Brant and a younger woman called Lucy (V, p. 53). Rosa Brant turns out to be the sister of Sarah Brant, the young second wife of a politician, Mark Evans. Evans had previously served in the same cabinet as Buxton and is trying to make a populist political come back as an opponent of the repressive Buxton government. Finally it transpires that Evans has been recruited to join the same radical organization, the Volunteers, as Rosa.

Lewis discovers that Rosa's supposed alibi for the Buxton shooting, a camping trip to Ireland, has been manufactured (V, p. 104). He discovers also that Mark Evans's son, David, has joined the Volunteers, to try and resist the compromised sell-out of the political class. Marcus Tiller does not come into the equation. Rosa and her lover Bill Chaney were the ones who shot and wounded Buxton, aided by David Evans. They simply used the pretty girl Lucy to seduce Marcus Tiller, and thus manoeuvre him into a position whence the police will suspect him of the shooting.

What is striking about Lewis's alternative investigation is that it is no less simple than that of the police. The mystery itself rapidly becomes redundant, bankrupt, empty of suspense because effortlessly solved. The police easily come up with the name of Marcus Tiller. Lewis equally effortlessly comes to the opposite conclusion: that Tiller is not involved. In each investigation, there are no twists, no complications and no obstacles. And yet two irreconcilable conclusions are reached. How can Williams think himself out of this impasse? As in *The Fight for Manod* and *Loyalties*, Williams uses the investigation plot to launch all sorts of wider and more complex questions that outflank the basic mystery plot altogether.

For the question that most continually obtrudes into our reading is not: Who shot Buxton? Rather, it is: Who is Lewis? Although this character is the first-person narrator of the novel, we know surprisingly little about him. As his sympathy for the Welsh working classes and for the subversive organization the Volunteers deepens, we are bound to ask ourselves why this should be. Indeed, the novel insists on this question: 'For what, in the end, did I care about the Trust . . .?', muses Lewis (*V*, p. 142). 'What is it you want?', Gareth Powell's widow asks him when he comes asking questions. When Lewis finally learns that Mark Evans is working for the Volunteers and struggles to decide whether his loyalties lie with the capitalist establishment or this group of radical opponents, he asks Evans: 'Why should I [help the Volunteers?]' (*V*, p. 178).

There is an answer to this question, but unlike the surface mystery plot, Williams does not provide it easily. The clues are not blatant, like the bright orange cape discovered by the police. Neither are they discovered in any logical sequence. In fact, the details about Lewis's personal interest in the Buxton shooting are rendered piecemeal, fragmented and dispersed, so that our attempt at understanding is continually hampered.

As Lewis Redfern's investigation gathers momentum, there are hints that final understanding will be directly related to his personal affiliations. The whole dilemma facing him is that as an employee of Insatel, his job is to expose the Volunteers. His employer Friedmann is explicit about this. The Buxton affair ceases to be an interesting news story within a couple of days, he explains, 'but the Volunteers now, that's business' (*V*, p. 144). Moreover, the possibility that former cabinet minister Mark Evans might be involved with the Volunteers seems like the biggest media coup of all. Hence Friedmann's instructions:'You zoom in on Evans. You go all out to break him.' (*V*, p. 145)

On the other hand, having discovered that Evans is working for a political cause with which Lewis too sympathizes, Lewis himself is reluctant to carry out this breaking. If Lewis is really to endanger his career in this way (and, after all, he does end up resigning from Insatel), we feel certain he must have a bigger reason for sympathizing with Mark Evans.

The first hint of this comes when he interviews Evans's wife, Sarah. She is reluctant to provide any information that will cause legal trouble for Mark. He responds by pointing out that he is a journalist, not a police officer. She breaks down this distinction, arguing that, as a journalist, he will publish what he finds, so that 'when you tell the public about it, you are actually telling the police' (*V*, pp. 116–17). Then again, Lewis responds, he will not necessarily publish his findings, 'for legal reasons, or for my own reasons' (*V*, p. 117).

What could those reasons be? His personal affiliation is pointed up, but not explained. What possible motive could Lewis have for holding back the information he has spent an entire novel bringing to light? This, and not the political shooting, is the real mystery of *The Volunteers*. Indeed, when Lewis finally realizes that Mark Evans's political affiliations mirror his own, he tells Evans that although he knows about the Volunteers, 'I shan't be reporting it' (*V*, p. 161). Evans finds this almost beyond belief – as we must, if we are to take seriously the whole plot up to this point.

Evans provides the next clue as to why Lewis might withhold rather than publish. Lewis accuses him of involvement with the Volunteers and in the Buxton shooting. Evans seems unperturbed by this. He does not deny involvement because he does not regret it. He believes in the rightness of striking out against the oppressive nationalist state. This constitutes something of an anticlimax to Lewis Redfern's investigation. Moreover, Williams throws the real mystery back onto Lewis himself. The ostensibly guilty Evans fires a particular parting shot at Lewis:

> 'Just one thing before you go,' he said as we walked down the stairs. 'You research a lot of people. At least it's called research. It's an interesting process. We even tried it on you.'
> 'Don't rely on my past,' I said, irritably.

'No,' he said, laughing. 'There was never any danger of that. But it's interesting. It's especially interesting when the present connects.'
We had got to the door.
'I'm not the problem,' I said stubbornly. (*V*, pp. 163–4)

The idea that Lewis could have a reliable past is presented as laughable. This seems ironic, given that it is Evans and not Lewis who has been shown to be a member of a terrorist organization. Williams disadvantages the reader here. For though it is clear that Evans and Lewis are meant to understand each other, we as readers do not know what they are talking about. We cannot know what it is in Lewis's past that Evans is referring to – or how it connects to the present. Had the Volunteers considered Lewis a possible ally? A possible enemy? A possible target? There is an appearance of knowledge and answers, but this is continually frustrated. Lewis's personal involvement with the matter under investigation is both pointed up and continually deferred. Despite his assertion that 'I am not the problem', for us as readers, Lewis *has* become the real object of the mystery, rather than the terrorist he is investigating.

At Lewis's final meeting with Evans, Evans explains to him his reasons for working with the Volunteers. The reasons are simple: the current military-industrial complex of capitalist society is failing and needs to be changed. 'We are rotten with failure, all of us rotten. You must know this. You particularly.' (*V*, p. 176) Nothing in the novel so far has prepared us to feel that there is anything particular in Lewis that might cause him to turn against the establishment. Why does it seem so to Evans?

With the question of who shot Buxton and the discovery of the Volunteers in effect concluded, this becomes the real question. What is it in Lewis's past that will enable us to understand his present? Who is he? Why does he suddenly begin to sympathize with a radically subversive political organization, to the extent of endangering his own career? As in the earlier Williams novels, the mystery plot opens up all sorts of broader questions.

The counter-research which the Volunteers have carried out on Lewis offers some conclusions. Lewis finally decides to help the Volunteers, first by not publishing his research and then by presenting anonymous documents at the Ponytrhiw inquiry, demonstrating Buxton's direct involvement in the killing of Gareth Powell. This makes him the Volunteers' 'comrade' (*V*, p. 192), and they his. As a result, David Evans offers to help smuggle him out of the country, to protect him from the 'dirty' tricks (*V*, p. 194) that will otherwise be played to 'discredit' his testimony at the inquiry (*V*, p. 206). David suggests:

> 'Get out of the community. You've got a wife in Canada, haven't you?'
> 'There's no use. We've split.'
> 'Since you worked for Insatel?'
> 'Since I worked for Insatel. Since I got this political assignment.'
> 'Yes, that's what I'd heard. Since you'd become their creep.'
> 'You know nothing about it.'
> 'It's what she said, Lewis.'
> I jerked involuntarily. It was a moment of total surprise, total shock. (*V*, p. 194)

Lewis's reaction to this is shared by us as readers. Yet his shock is different from ours. We are surprised at Lewis's having a wife. This information has not previously been forthcoming. Lewis's surprise is different: he is shocked that David Evans has traced this estranged wife to Canada, and actually spoken to her. He is shocked that he, the investigator, has in effect become the investigated.

This holds the key to the whole mystery of Lewis's affiliation and identity. He cannot go and stay with his wife, Megan, because their break-up was not an amicable one. David knows this already – he has actually spoken to Megan. She apparently has informed David that the reason for the break-up of their marriage was ideological: Lewis had once worked in 'radical journalism' (*V*, p. 194). When he started working for the establishment broadcasting company, Insatel, Megan perceived Lewis to have betrayed his earlier political ideals and become, in David's word, 'their creep'. Megan seems to have found this intolerable. Moreover, David reports, Megan has also told him 'other things':

> 'More than that, Lewis. Your father was killed as a soldier in Kenya. As a national service soldier. But in one of the very worst of the last colonial wars.'
> I didn't answer for some moments. I avoided looking at him.
> 'He had no choice where he was sent.'
> 'Of course, Lewis. Imperialism killed him, whichever uniform he happened to be wearing. But you didn't think so. You told no one but Megan. You seemed bitterly ashamed.'
> 'Angry.'

'No, anger is public. You told none of your comrades. You wanted none of them to know. You let it fester under your exceptional activism. You divided yourself.' (*V*, p. 195)

The clues click into place at last. Why does Lewis side with the Volunteers against the Buxton government? He hates the entire military-industrial construction of society for which that government stands. He hates it because it killed his father in Kenya. Yet he is also deeply ashamed by it, for his father died, fighting needlessly on its behalf. The Mau Mau uprising against British rule in Kenya in the 1950s was one of the most violent guerrilla wars of the whole colonial period. The imperial order tried to dig in and hold onto its own power and authority in the face of global dissolution, and Lewis's father was part of the digging. Lewis had earlier been a student radical, working against imperialism and social injustice. The death of his father fighting on behalf of that system seems to have made Lewis's own position untenable. As a defence mechanism he has 'divided' himself, becoming part radical investigator, part establishment lackey. That is why he has sympathized with the Volunteers all along, while at the same time working for an organization hell-bent on their annihilation.

As stated above, one of the anti-colonial writers whom Raymond Williams most positively evaluates in *The Country and the City* is Kenyan novelist Ngugi Wa Thiong'o. Ngugi's political activities in opposition to continuing imperial oppression, the contribution of his novels to that activism and his refusal to separate his activities into the demarcated spheres of *politics* and *letters* distinctly parallel Williams's own work. It is interesting then to go to the work of Ngugi to see this process of colonial split-subject formation at work.

Ngugi has written of his education and development in colonial Kenya in the 1940s. He was educated in an English colonial school, by a teacher who had been discharged from the Royal Air Force. The reading material he was given included the imperial 'boy's own' adventures of *Captain Biggles* – a childhood hero of Ngugi's. Yet a crisis of loyalties occurred for Ngugi when the Mau Mau uprising against colonial rule broke out – and when his brother joined the revolutionaries. The Mau Mau fighters were defeated by the Royal Air Force, dropping bombs on the mountain strongholds of the revolutionaries. Ngugi's own brother and comrades were being bombed by people like his teacher and like his boyhood hero Captain Biggles. Thus, Ngugi concludes, his education in late colonial Kenya was 'a drama of contradictions', which rendered his unquestioning obeisance to the imperial order impossible.[7]

Raymond Williams's positive valuation of Ngugi's work is twofold. First, Williams thinks that Ngugi's work enables us to dispute the official metropolitan account of colonial history. Secondly, this in turn teaches us something about our own society. The colonial split subjectivity that Williams portrays in Lewis Redfern in *The Volunteers*, and that Ngugi recalls from his boyhood, enables us to open this post-imperial perspective on Britain itself. This is done by suggesting a comparability between colonial processes at home and abroad. In *The Country and the City* Williams makes this conjunction more explicitly:

> In Britain itself, within the home islands, the colonial process itself is so far back that it is in effect unrecorded, though there are late consequences of it in the rural literature of Scotland and Wales and especially of Ireland. It has become part of the long settlement which is idealised as Old England or the natural economy: the product of centuries of successive penetration and domination. What is important in this modern literature of the colonial peoples is that we can see the history happening, see it being made, from the base of an England which, within our own literature, has been so differently described. (*CC*, p. 285)

These are the two elements of Williams's positive evaluation of anti-colonial literature. It gives us a perspective on colonial history that would otherwise be completely unrecorded – even in the liberal but nevertheless metropolitan writing of E. M. Forster, George Orwell or Graham Greene. It then enables us to relate the construction of the British state to the construction of the British empire, in such a way as to question the political make-up of both.

The Country and the City illuminates the climax of *The Volunteers* by making these conjunctions. During the final section of *The Country and the City*, Williams extends his metaphor of the country house dominating its impoverished hinterland to describe the relations between Europe and its colonies, first world and third. He then goes on to discuss resistance to the colonial system in the decolonizing world:

> Out of these country areas there eventually came, through blood and struggle, movements for political independence. At various stages, to protect such an order, young officers from the country-houses led other

Englishmen, and the expropriated Irish and Scots and Welsh, to the colonial battles in which so many died. It is a strange fate. (*CC*, p. 283)

Out of the country houses of ruling-class England, imperial military officers were sent to police the imperial order overseas, with some dying in the process. This is exactly the fate of Lewis's father in *The Volunteers*. Out of a disjointed series of clues as to Lewis's identity, suddenly there is coherence. His distrust of country estate-owning Mark Evans and his interest in the shooting of Buxton inside the grounds of a country house/seat of power, can both be traced to this filial relation to the imperial system.

This understanding retrospectively underwrites the whole plot of *The Volunteers*, showing it to be a profoundly anti-imperialist work. Williams is in no doubt that the Welsh and Scots and Irish who died fighting on behalf of the imperial system were 'expropriated', subtly pressured into fighting. His novel thus implicitly questions that whole enforced kind of nationalism, and instead puts that unitary identity in question.

The Country and the City helps us to understand *The Volunteers* by illuminating the implicit parallel between political violence as it was used domestically and in the colonies. As a result of this, it is tempting to see *The Country and the City* as an important work of postcolonial history.

There are a number of important conceptual issues to be addressed here. First, it is clear that *The Country and the City* cannot be considered as a postcolonial text from a simple historical perspective, as it was published in 1973, long before self-rule in Wales. Moreover, despite the incidental references to expropriated Scots, Welsh and Irish, the majority of the anti-colonial writers whom Williams discusses are those who might somewhat paradoxically be described as the canonical postcolonial writers. Lamming, Ngugi and Naipaul are all demonstrably anti-colonial writers, writing about political struggles in their own colonies. *The Country and the City* says nothing about Welsh writers or the specifics of Welsh political struggles in history. There are hints as to the unequal power relations that exist between England, Scotland, Ireland and Wales, yet political struggles in those places are marginalized relative to the work of overseas activists.

The Country and the City is not a postcolonial study in any straightforward manner. It can be read as a study that carries a number of important and illuminating implications about the relationship between the break-up of the empire and the break-up of the British state, without ever following those implications to their full conclusion in detail. Extrapolating these implications makes it possible to read Williams's *Country and the City* as a postcolonial account of the history and culture of Britain in general, and Wales in particular. This is so because how we read the text, and its descriptions of the centralistic state apparatus, will inevitably be different if we are reading during a historical period when that unitary apparatus has begun to break up, rather than if we were reading before such a period. In other words, the values and meanings that we can derive from the text change over time. This enables us retrospectively to read *The Country and the City* as a postcolonial text, even though it was published well before political devolution in Wales. By writing it, Williams made a significant contribution to exploring issues of British nationhood, decolonization and political devolution in Scotland and Wales.

When *The Country and the City* is used in this way to illustrate *The Volunteers*, the latter is a profoundly predictive novel. For when we re-read those scenes about the Buxton shooting retrospectively, armed with the knowledge of Lewis's hatred of the colonial system, what shines through is the way in which Wales itself is governed in unequal relation by a muscular London government. The significance of Buxton is explained in the following way:

> Since the Welsh senate was established, in the initial devolution of powers under the second coalition government, the Financial Commission had been the political storm-centre. For what the devolution said, in effect, was this: you can govern yourselves, on this range of issues, within the limits of the money we are prepared to allocate to you . . . It became apparent, above all, in the figure of the Financial Commission's Secretary of State (Wales). He was supposed to be an impartial figure . . . But of course, he was political, and through his office flowed all the fierce currents of political conflict between an impatient people and a constrained, fatigued and impoverished administration. (*V*, p. 11)

By imagining a Wales ruled by a devolved government of its own as early as 1978, Williams attempted to raise the levels of Welsh self-consciousness to a sufficiently high level for self-rule to become a reality in the 1979 devolution referendum. The 'no' vote in 1979 followed by the eventual 'yes' in 1997 shows that, all the time, this critical consciousness was on the rise. Tom Nairn has warned that devolution in Scotland and Wales will be meaningless if it is implemented simply as a minimal concession, denying any real self-determination to the people of Scotland and Wales while also allaying the demand for further political change.[8] This is the scenario that Williams too seems to warn against in *The Volunteers*.

The conjunction Williams makes in *The Volunteers* is between the decolonizing process overseas and the gradual break-up of the British Union itself. Although there are complications and differences, Williams implies that these processes are somehow related. In the novel, after Lewis gives testimony at the Pontyrhiw tribunal, he drives to the steel works where Gareth Powell was shot, and sees bullet marks still on the walls:

> We stopped and looked at the gate of the depot. It was still shut. The fading chalk bullet-marks were still on the walls along the street. A street in Pontyrhiw. A dirt road in Kenya. I must have gone silent looking at them . . . (*V*, p. 207)

Imperial violence in Kenya is juxtaposed directly with radical authoritarian violence back in Wales. This extraordinary and moving moment retrospectively informs the whole construction of *The Volunteers*. As in the previous novels by Williams, the investigation plot provides not answers, but questions. For at this moment, we have left the Buxton–Powell mystery behind altogether. We are invited to ask much bigger questions: What is identity? What is nationality? What is loyalty? Williams's opposition to the imperial order reveals the break-up of the empire and the break-up of the union to be part of the same process.

DEVOLVING *FRANKENSTEIN*

Raymond Williams was aware that all nations are at root imagined communities. The implication of this is that the break-up of the nation is also largely an imagined event – hence the utility of considering that event through a fully historical reading of the literature which imagines it. This can be seen in relation to self-rule in Scotland and Wales. Recent literature from these nations has emphasized a lack of united Britishness. Indeed, in many cases, such as Alasdair Gray's novel *Poor Things* (1992), the literature imagined the break-up into being long before the actual moment of devolution.

Poor Things is an explicit rewrite of the Gothic classic, *Frankenstein*, set in Victorian Glasgow. Interestingly, around the moment of devolution, we also find a reworked Welsh *Frankenstein*, appearing in Malcolm Pryce's 2003 novel, *Last Tango in Aberystwyth*. Gray and Pryce have submitted *Frankenstein* to a process of devolution. Historically, this would have been more difficult at an earlier date, because the literary consciousness of Scotland and Wales (expressed in English, as distinct from Welsh, where an anti-colonial sensibility was already well established before the end of the nineteenth century) was for the most part too deeply submerged within the British mainstream. With the steady rise of Scottish and Welsh consciousness came a complicating of the ways in which the literature produced within those nations related to the British whole because the ways in which the nations themselves related were changing.

Since 1997, English literature has been devolved just as much as political power and representation has been devolved from Westminster to Edinburgh and Cardiff.[9] What many recent writers in Scotland and Wales have in common is that their historic imagination is able to subvert the imagined harmony of an earlier period. This in turn can be read in tandem with the process of undoing to which the United Kingdom has more recently become subject. Since devolution has to be understood as an ongoing process rather than an accomplished fact, it can be said that the writing plays a part in the continuing process.

One of the techniques employed in the post-Frankenstein novels of Gray and Pryce is that of the mystery plot. By posing the process of scientific creation of human life as a mystery that can be solved, these writers are able to use the literary progeny of their imaginary scientists to question the structure of the society into which they are created. This is the most innovative variation brought into the *Frankenstein* mould by Gray and Pryce. They do not imagine the progeny as a monster or a threat. Rather, the offspring of their scientists' endeavours are posed as children and outsiders; people who cannot understand the workings of the world around them and so question them. It is a technique which, as Dorothy McMillan puts it, 'gives monstrosity a good name'.[10]

At the end of the first novel in Pryce's Aberystwyth series, *Aberystwyth Mon Amour*, master villain Dai Brainbocs had fled to South America with beautiful singer Myfanwy Montez. His assistants Mrs Llantrisant and Dai Custard Pie were imprisoned respectively on an island off the Aberystwyth coast and in a cell thirty metres below Aberystwyth castle. Herod Jenkins was presumed dead, after falling from a plane.

The assumption is wrong. Herod has survived, living wild in the woods around Aberystwyth. He is taken in by the mysterious 'Philanthropist' who runs the Ysbyty Ystwyth project. Detective Louie Knight learns from the crime reporter Meirion that this hospital is home to a military- scientific project in memory control and identity grafting.

The philanthropist is Dai Brainbocs. He has used Herod Jenkins as a guinea pig in legislated memory experiments. He claims to have invented a machine to graft new identities onto existing human subjects. Herod Jenkins is only a trial, converted from school games teacher and part-time gangster to wild man of the woods. What Dai Brainbocs really wants to do is graft a new identity onto Myfanwy Montez, make her 'forget' that she is in love with Louie and 'remember' that she is in love with Dai himself.

Unlike Shelley's *Frankenstein*, there are two progenies here rather than one. Readers do not sympathize with the fate of Herod Jenkins, as he is known to be a bully, who in his days as a school sports teacher had sent Louie's friend Marty out for a cross country run in a blizzard – to his death. Also unlike Shelley's novel, Myfanwy is not in fact created by the Frankenstein figure, Dai Brainbocs. The machine is an elaborate ruse to deceive Louie into thinking that Myfanwy is lost to him forever. When Louie calls Dai's bluff and unplugs the equipment supposedly keeping her alive, he discovers Myfanwy herself – mind and body – still very much alive in another room in the house. The attributing of human emotion to the monster which we find in Shelley is not operative here, since Myfanwy is not the monster to Dai's Frankenstein. In this way, Pryce switches attention from the individual version of identity and directs our focus onto the social and collective process of its formation. Myfanwy is not simply created by Dai. She is a fully historical subject.

Thus, unlike Mary Shelley, Pryce is able to suggest that the creating has not really been carried out by the crazed scientist at all. From this point attention is switched to the social and historical factors that have made Herod, Myfanwy, Louie and Dai the people they are. At the conclusion of *Last Tango in Aberystwyth*, Louie discovers the reason for Herod Jenkins's habit of bullying schoolchildren: he had lost his own child years earlier and spent his subsequent career venting repressed emotion through violence. Louie wonders, '[c]ould I blame him? Could any of us really be blamed for becoming what we had no power to avoid becoming? . . . But is it enough to blame the Furies? It was hard to know.'[11]

As with Raymond Williams's novel, *The Volunteers*, the investigation leads to a point where further questions can only be asked, not answered. Like Williams, Pryce uses the investigation plot to open up these bigger questions about identity. Also like *The Volunteers*, one of the important stages of Louie Knight's investigation is to seek answers at a folk museum. In other words, *Last Tango in Aberystwyth* implicitly accesses the anti-colonial imagination in the ways described by Benedict Anderson. It is produced from within a gradually emerging post-imperial society, and is written as a conscious modification of the English literary tradition of which *Frankenstein* is a part.

This is also the case in Alasdair Gray's 1992 novel *Poor Things*. Gray transplants *Frankenstein* into a late nineteenth-century Glaswegian setting. His scientist, Godwin Baxter (or 'God'), has been working on finding ways of preserving life in the bodies of people drowned in the city's canal – by inserting alternative brains into them. The result is Bella Caledonia: the daughter of Scotland. She is recreated from the body of Lady Victoria Blessinton, who had drowned herself in the weir to escape the cruelty of her husband, Sir Aubrey de la Pole Blessinton. At the time of the drowning, she was carrying a child, and it is the brain of this unborn child which Godwin Baxter transplants into her head to make a new life – Bella.

The important facts about the progeny of this scientist compared to Shelley's hideous progeny are that Bella is both a woman and a child – in the strongly patriarchal world of Victorian Britain. As a result of being both a grown woman *and* a child, Bella is able to see the world as adults see it, but without the learned inherited prejudices of adults.

The technique of centring a novel on a naive narrator who is freed from the conventions of the society in which (s)he is trapped has deep roots in postcolonial literatures. Tony Tanner has drawn attention to the 'voice of the outlaw' in early nineteenth-century American fiction.[12] He relates this outlaw voice, or voice of unofficial culture, to that process whereby the cultural and literary aesthetics of a dominant culture are called into question by a subordinate one in the process of discovering itself. Ngugi Wa Thiong'o has more succinctly described it as the 'liberation of the mind'.[13]

In order to complete Bella's education, God takes her on a world tour. Upon her return, she falls in love with God's student Archibald McCandless. This frustrates God, who, as with Brainbocs in the Pryce novel, was planning to marry his creation himself. Before Bella marries McCandless, she goes on another world tour with a brief lover, Duncan Wedderburn. They spend some time on a yacht with an English aristocrat, Harry Astley, and an American missionary, Dr Hooker. Bella's confused dialogues with these figures form the biggest part of her section of the multi-textual novel.

Over the course of several conversations, Bella questions Astley and Hooker about why there is poverty and inequality in the world. In other words, Gray uses the voice of outsider Bella Caledonia to ask fundamental questions of social justice. Hooker and Astley respond with a series of classic imperialist assumptions: that inequality is inevitable; that it is the European man's burden to civilize Africa and Asia; that the 'natives' of these places are godless, corrupt and dirty; and that Bella, a mere woman, should not worry her head with these matters.

As the ship nears the end of its voyage, Bella summarizes her lessons from Astley under a series of neat notebook headings: Women; Education; History; Benefits of War; Unemployment; Freedom; Free Trade; Empire; Self-Government and World-Improvers. They each recapitulate the central theme of the European civilizing mission. The entry on education may be regarded as typical:

> Very poor children learn to beg, lie and steal from their parents – they would hardly survive otherwise. Prosperous parents tell their children that nobody should lie, steal or kill, and that idleness and gambling are vices. They then send them to schools where they suffer if they do not disguise their thoughts and feelings and are taught to admire killers and stealers like Achilles and Ulysses, William the Conqueror and Henry the Eighth. This prepares them for life in a land where rich people use acts of parliament to deprive the poor of homes and livelihoods, where unearned incomes are increased by stock-exchange gambling, where those who own most property work least and amuse themselves by hunting, horse-racing and leading their country into battle. You find the world horrifying, Bell, because you have not been warped to fit it by a proper education.[14]

The education Bella receives about the imperial world order recalls Benedict Anderson's notion of the 'reassuring use of fratricide'. That is, the ways in which official narratives of a nation are used to mystify the violence on which they are founded, by invocation of heroic mythical or historical figures. Gray, like Raymond Williams, subtly suggests that there is a tie-in between class division and capitalism, on the one hand, and state building and imperialism on the other. Gray, a committed campaigner for Scottish self-government, seems to make this comparison in order to suggest that the break-up of the empire might also be related to the break-up of the unitary British state.

THE BREAK-UP OF BRITAIN

The break-up of the empire and the break-up of the unitary state can be seen as related processes. The precise utility of understanding those processes through a reading of their literature is this: the literature does not merely passively reflect the social changes in question. Rather, it imagines new forms of relation into existence and therefore anticipates the changes in advance of their occurrence. The Gray novel demonstrates this quite clearly: published in 1992, it imagines devolution into existence five years before the event.

There is a wide overlap between Benedict Anderson's notion of the *imagined community* and Raymond Williams's practice of cultural materialism. Anderson tells us that the development of print media was critical in enabling a disseminated sense of nationhood. Williams tells us that literary texts, as well as political pamphlets and factual accounts such as newspapers, participate in the process of imagining the nation into existence. In an important late essay entitled 'The culture of nations', Williams supplements Anderson's notion of imagined community with an accompanying sense of *who* is doing the imagining: 'the building of states at whatever level is intrinsically a ruling-class operation'.[15] Williams explores the correlation between imagined versions of the nation and the ruling sector of it:

> When children start going to school they often learn for the first time that they are English or British or what may be. The pleasure of learning is attached to the song of a monarch or a flag. The sense of friends and neighbours is attached to a distant and commanding organisation: in Britain, now, that which ought to be spelled as it so barbarously sounds – the

United Kingdom, the 'Yookay'. Selective versions of the history underlying this impressed identity are regularly presented, at every level from
simple images and anecdotes to apparently serious textbook histories.
The powerful feelings of wanting to belong to a society are then in a
majority of cases bonded to these large definitions. ('Culture of nations,'
p. 182)

This passage recapitulates the argument presented in chapter 3 above.
Education on a top-down model fulfils the needs of the dominant sector
to divide people into separate, functionally necessary classes through a
selective process of advancement. This can be combined with the students'
powerful aspiration for success to ratify the competitive system. There
is thus an important emotive or emotional dimension at work in the
sphere of education. Feelings of kinship or comradeship in the wider
community of the nation-state are offered as a pay-off for acquiescence
in the dominance of that state.

It is an under-recognized feature of Raymond Williams's work that
he was interested in distinguishing between different kinds of emotional
experience. He emphasized again and again the need for socialist change
to occur in the historic *imagination* quite as much as in political and
material *reality*. As he had already written in 1975, 'the task of a successful socialist movement will be one of feeling and imagination quite as
much as one of fact and organisation' (*RH*, p. 76).

Williams knew that it was important to be able to imagine alternative versions of identity inside the mind, before change could occur
on the outside. This is the advantage of considering the literature which
imagines the change into being. At the same time, since the task of
imagining and renegotiating national communities is self-evidently a
large one, it is clear that the novels of Gray and Pryce do not stand
alone. They instantiate a much broader historical process, that could be
found occurring in a whole seam of literature from the period
surrounding devolution in Scotland and Wales.[16] Although full
analysis is not possible here, it seems reasonable to suggest that
writers such as Janice Galloway, A. L. Kennedy, Agnes Owens and
Irvine Welsh (in Scotland), and Trezza Azzopardi, Niall Griffiths,
Christopher Meredith and Catherine Merriman (in Wales) could all
be seen as examples of the same process.[17]

Raymond Williams advocated the movement for self-rule in Wales,
and showed that writing had a part to play in enabling that movement

to gain momentum. It is important to emphasize that he advocated this kind of nationalism not out of abstract chauvinism or ethnic pride, but out of a strong sense of the need for democracy. Williams was interested in finding the means by which people can direct their own lives. The question has then to be seen less as a matter of how English imperial institutions frustrate national aspirations in the peripheral areas of Scotland and Wales, and more as a matter of how the ruling-class version of nationhood hinders effective democracy at every level, including within England itself. Williams himself draws attention to the problem – and a potential solution:

> A friend from the north of England said to me recently that the Welsh and Scots were lucky to have these available national self-definitions, to help them find their way out of the dominance of English ruling-class minority culture. In the north, he said, we who are English are in the same sense denied; what the world knows as English is not our life and feelings, and yet we don't, like the Welsh or the Scots, have this simple thing, this national difference, to pit against it. (*WSW*, p. 10)[18]

Williams becomes aware of a problem faced by certain English people, wanting the same democratic institutions as the nationalist movements in Scotland and Wales, yet lacking the easy definition of nationhood. He suggests that this lack of national element should free those regions from an emotional burden, and allow them to get more directly to the heart of the real problems. The emotional pull of nationhood can be a barrier to the deeper issues of social class, and an unequal social order. Lacking the national element, then, the English regions should be able to address these problems more – rather than less – directly than in Scotland and Wales. As Williams puts it in another essay entitled 'Are we becoming more divided?', 'this means, among other things, that a nationalist movement isn't the only way, often isn't the way at all, to work for these things' (*WSW*, p. 189).

The great advantage of considering the renegotiation of British identity that occurs in contemporary and postmodern fiction is that it gives us a sense of some of the different specific and variable means by which people can explore their identity. Thus postmodernist fiction throws up an opportunity for explorations of the concept of Englishness quite as much as it offers the post-devolution nations of Britain an opportunity to develop their own voices.[19] There is an exploration of outdated class-bound notions of Englishness in Graham Swift's 1995 novel, *Last Orders*, and a parody of the stereotypical cultural artefacts of England in Julian Barnes's *England, England* (1998).[20]

The imaginative break-up of the British union that can be traced in fiction is not simply a literary history of devolution in Scotland and Wales. It also registers the break-down of national consensus and belonging along several other sets of coordinates. These include Celtic difference but are not limited to it. Other examples of such terrains include regional identity, feminism and racial difference. These terrains of renegotiation can all be explored in the fiction that implicitly puts deeper questions to the unitary state.

In 1978 – the same year as Raymond Williams's *Volunteers* – A. S. Byatt published her novel *The Virgin in the Garden*. It is a parody of events that took place in 1952 to mark the coronation of Queen Elizabeth II. Yorkshire country house Long Royston Hall is the venue for a play written by Alexander Wedderburn about the life of Elizabeth I. One glorious Elizabethan age is juxtaposed with another. Yet Byatt's novel is no simple celebration of the poetics of nation building. On the contrary, it is a sharp parody of that whole process. From the beginning, the association of the play with the fate of the nation is undercut:

> In 1952 history took a grip on the world of Alexander Wedderburn's imagination. When the King died Alexander's play was in fact largely finished, although later he had perpetual difficulty in establishing, in other people's minds, the true chronological order of his own choice of themes and the accident of death. His play was frequently misinterpreted as a Pageant, commissioned for the Festival which celebrated the handing-over of Long Royston Hall to the still insubstantial new North Yorkshire University. The Festival itself was certainly timed to coincide with the spontaneous outbursts of national cultural fervour in parks and gardens all over the country in celebration of the Coronation.[21]

The opening of Byatt's novel both cultivates an imaginative association between Wedderburn's play and events of national-historic importance, and severs that association. It is as though an official, or state-sponsored, account of a particular moment in history is being held up to ironic interrogation and critique from members of the population of that nation. Throughout *The Virgin in the Garden* an attempt to resuscitate versions of a prior golden age is deliberately flawed by an incompatible alienation from it. This alienation in turn arises from Byatt's sense that an understanding of the fate of the nation cannot be gleaned simply from the pageantry of power. Her narrative of the staging of such a pageant employs a strong convention of parody in order to raise the political consciousness of the reader/audience. *The Virgin* of the title refers both to Queen Elizabeth I and to the schoolgirl, Frederica Potter, who plays her in the pageant. The narrative is then far more concerned with Frederica's amorous pursuits of playwright Wedderburn and actor Edmund Wilkie than it is with the celebrations of nationhood that might otherwise inhere in the pageant form.

Byatt's point is less that contemporary Britain is a travesty of its supposedly heroic earlier golden age than that she thinks it entirely inappropriate to measure the fate of the nation in these limited terms. The reality of the play utterly conflicts with the lofty mythopoeic aspirations of its author, Wedderburn, yet the sharp parody to which those aspirations are subjected makes it impossible for us as readers to share them. When Wedderburn watches the play, he feels that his lofty ideals have been sullied – and worse:

> [D]eeper than his sense of some dilapidation of his imagined gorgeous palace ran the sense that he had meant to state his passion for the past, to provide pipes, timbrels, wild ecstasy, Tempe, and the Vale of Arcady. What they had made was not immortals stalking under Hesperidean boughs but sex in sundresses, sandwiches in gilded papier-mâché helmets, the extravagances of Edmund Wilkie's Bottle Chorus.[22]

The Virgin in the Garden combines intense poetic imagination with farcical physical realization. Her women are unruly and troublesome. They will not allow themselves to be controlled by Wedderburn, whose pretensions they actively mock. By this means, Byatt rejects the exclusive association of cultural authority with men. Byatt, like Raymond Williams, wishes to show that culture is ordinary. Her feminist parody of the pageantry of monarchic culture is one way of performing this demonstration.

During the course of his career, Williams was notoriously unable to conceptualize the work of radical, political feminism or to address it in his own work. This failure can be seen like something of a missed chance for Williams. The concerns raised by women writers like Byatt in *The Virgin in the Garden* offer a sophisticated development of the ways in which Williams otherwise understood and worked for the re-negotiation of cultural and political relationships in Britain. This missed chance gives rise to Morag Shiach's comment that feminists are likely to find many things of interest in the work of Raymond Williams, but that they cannot find many women.[23]

Byatt's parodic disavowal of the pageantry of monarchy invites readers to contemplate a different kind of nation and a different kind of political relationship. Byatt uses the feminist satire of monarchic culture to open up these issues, and this reveals the extent to which feminism is one of the most important conceptual terrains on which the unitary British identity has begun to be renegotiated.

A similar exploration can be found in Andrea Levy's 2004 novel, *Small Island*. It takes the form of a new mythology of an important moment in modern British history – the Second World War. The heroism is undercut by a plot that is distinctly unheroic. It is about conscripted fighter pilots from British colonies in the Caribbean, their love affairs in London and their subsequent abandonment by the British state. It is not clear if the small island of the title refers to Britain, or to Jamaica. Certainly, the novel is set during a period when Britain's relative stature on the world stage was in decline, and examines the implications of that decline for how we understand the make-up of the nation.

Small Island hints at another important way in which the British identity has been renegotiated in postmodern fiction – through the lens of specific ethnic communities. Francis Mulhern has accused Raymond Williams of paying too little regard to the institutionalized racism experienced on a daily basis by members of Britain's ethnic subcultures.[24] In 'The culture of nations' Williams draws attention to a deeper theoretical problem:

> [T]he most active legal (and communal) defence of dislocated and exposed groups and minorities is essential. But it is a serious mis-understanding, when full social relations are in question, to suppose that the problems of social identity are resolved by formal definitions. For unevenly and at times precariously, but always through long experience substantially, an effective awareness of social identity depends on actual and sustained social relationships. To reduce social identity to formal legal definitions, at the level of the state, is to collude with the alienated super-ficialities of 'the nation' which are the limited functional terms of the modern ruling class. ('Culture of nations', p. 195)

In one sense Williams could be said to be too keen to overlook the hard-won recognition and legal equality gained by members of Britain's immigrant population in the years after 1945. Yet his point is not that such advances are not important. It is rather that a legal definition of identity alone is not enough to provide mature cultural expression and growth. The purely passport sense of Britishness is of vital legal importance in guaranteeing freedom and equality to members of Britain's ethnic minorities, but it is at the same time inadequate to answer any of the long hard questions about community.

The problem can be more intuitively seen in Salman Rushdie's 1988 novel, *The Satanic Verses*. It is a great irony of Rushdie's novel that the Islamic controversy which surrounded its publication has deflected attention away from the main thrust of its satire. *The Satanic Verses* is a committed satire on the lives and treatment of London's racial and ethnic communities during the Thatcher era, culminating in the Brixton race riots. The main protagonists, Saladin Chamcha and Gibreel Farishta, are Indian actors who have come to Britain because they admire its civilized culture – and reject their own. In other words, they are archetypal postcolonial split subjects – like Lewis Redfern in Raymond Williams's novel *The Volunteers*.

Allowing for the well-documented innovation of Rushdie's magical realism, there is a surprising congruence between Rushdie's novel and Williams's interests. Upon entry to Britain, Saladin is immediately seized by Inspector Stein's immigration police and beaten up. As Williams may have predicted, the discovery among the police that Saladin is in fact a British citizen and not an illegal immigrant does not solve his problems:

> Stein said: 'Better check him out.' Three and a half minutes later the Black Maria came to a halt and three immigration officers, five constables and one police driver held a crisis conference – *here's a pretty effing pickle* – and Chamcha noted that in their new mood all nine had begun to look alike, rendered equal and identical by their tension and fear. Nor was it long before he understood that the call to the Police National Computer, which had promptly identified him as a British citizen first class, had not improved his situation, but had placed him, if anything, in greater danger than before.[25]

A British passport is not the answer to Saladin's problems: it causes the police to fear recriminations for beating him. They thus beat him further and leave him abandoned. Again, as Raymond Williams may have foreseen, Saladin then seeks a more substantive identity than its merely passport version, by taking refuge at the Shaandaar Café, run by Mr and Mrs Sufyan, and home to a number of other racial outsiders in Margaret Thatcher's prosperous 1980s London. A subcultural community is formed in this way, with Mrs Sufyan as its matriarch. 'And what was it that made them a living in this Vilayet of her exile, this Yuké of her sex-obsessed husband's vindictiveness? What?'[26]

The answer to this rhetorical question is that it is the cooking of Mrs Sufyan that keeps the business going financially. Moreover, at a much deeper cultural level it is also the communion of preparing and consuming food together, in secret, that keeps the subcultural community together in the face of political disintegration. It is striking that Rushdie's 'Yuké' recalls Williams's 'Yookay'. *The Satanic Verses* performs in fiction what Williams attempted in *The Volunteers* and theorized in a more coherent way in 'The culture of nations' and 'Are we becoming more divided?' That is, a critique of the limiting and residually imperial construction of the Yookay, and a deeper exploration of precise local communities. Saladin, Gibreel, Mr and Mrs Sufyan, the characters who meet at the Hot Wax nightclub to burn effigies of their Nemesis Mrs Thatcher and the Brixton victims can all be identified as voices of unofficial culture.

Similar voices could also be found in such novels as Zadie Smith's *White Teeth* (1999) and Monica Ali's *Brick Lane* (2003), but one final detailed example must suffice here. Kazuo Ishiguro's *When We Were Orphans* (2000) is a sophisticated variation on the conventional detective story. Like *The Volunteers*, it turns the investigator into the ultimate mystery and thereby launches much deeper questions of identity. It is centred on a famous detective, Christopher Banks, who had grown up in 1930s Shanghai with a Japanese best friend. Professional success has never enabled him to solve the deepest mystery of his life: the disappearance of his parents when he was a child.

Unlike a conventional detective novel, Ishiguro does not dwell on the crimes which Banks investigates. They are mentioned as it were in passing. The early events of the novel, for example, take place 'barely a month after the conclusion of the Mannering case, and I was still on something of a cloud. Certainly, that period after my first public triumph was a heady one . . .'[27] Where an entire Sherlock Holmes story or Hercule Poirot novel would be centred on a case like this, in Ishiguro's novel it is incidental to his main plot.

It was not until my experience of such cases as the Roger Parker murder that it came home to me just how much it means to people – and not only those directly concerned, but the public at large – to be cleansed of such encroaching wickedness.[28]

Ishiguro establishes the credentials of his detective, Christopher Banks, without providing any of the details of the crimes that he has supposedly solved: 'It took me no more than a few days to unravel the mystery of Charles Emery's death.'[29] In this way, as in *The Volunteers*, investigation is posed as initially simple and straightforward – until the investigator runs into a more fundamental problem.

This is what happens to Christopher Banks. Following the disappearance of his parents, he 'returns' from his émigré Japanese friends in Shanghai to an England he has never known. This could be said to have happened to Ishiguro himself, in reverse, for the Japanese-born author seems to have found it deeply problematic to become identified as an English writer.[30] Ishiguro, like his detective Banks, is continually crossing borders in such a way as to render simplistic notions of belonging untenable.

Having launched his career as a detective vowing to find his parents, Banks finds himself in a conversation with local church minister Canon Moorly, on the gathering clouds of war:

'What I mean to say, forgive me, is that it's quite natural for some of these gentlemen here tonight to regard Europe as the centre of the present maelstrom. But you, Mr Banks. Of course, *you* know the truth. You know that the real heart of our present crisis lies further afield.'
I looked at him carefully, then said, 'I'm sorry, sir. But I'm not quite sure what you're getting at.'
'Oh come, come.' He was smiling knowingly. '*You* of all people.' (Emphasis in original)[31]

The extent to which this scene echoes an earlier passage from *The Volunteers* is striking. We are forced to ask why Banks in particular should have a deeper insight into these world affairs, just as we wondered what was hidden in Lewis Redfern's past that made him particularly involved with the Volunteers' work. The conjunction between militarism, imperialism and personal identity becomes more explicit as the conversation continues:

'You know better than anyone the eye of the storm is to be found not in Europe at all, but in the Far East. In Shanghai, to be exact.'

'Shanghai,' I said lamely. 'Yes, I suppose . . . I suppose there are some problems in that city.'

'Problems indeed. And what was once just a local problem has been allowed to fester and grow. To spread its poison over the years, even further across the world, right through our civilisation. But I hardly need remind *you* of this.'[32]

Why this emphasis on Banks's own knowledge? Ishiguro in effect posits the investigator as the mystery. Although the credentials of Christopher Banks as a first-class detective have been clearly established, he is unable to provide the answers sought by Canon Moorly. There is a hinted relationship between the disappearance of Christopher's parents and a deepening crisis in the world order. But Christopher cannot say what that relationship is. As with *The Volunteers*, the apparently simple structure of the crime genre opens up a space from which further questions can only be asked, not answered. This again elevates the quest for personal identity into a much broader interrogation of an opaque and distant imperial order.

The main shift is away from providing final answers and mastery, and towards an aesthetic of incompleteness, where the protagonists themselves are invariably shown to be the real object of the mystery. This forces us to ask: What is identity? What is belonging? It is a technique that was already at work in *The Volunteers*, but without the formal innovation that can be characterized as postmodernist and which only became possible under subsequent historical conditions.

The Satanic Verses and *When We Were Orphans* both resemble *The Volunteers* at a strictly thematic level. Both deploy narrative techniques that have been described as postmodern: parody, subversion, irony and a deep-rooted commitment to questioning different forms of identity politics. The fictional break-up of Britain affords a new opportunity, beyond the entrenched modes of the past, for an active reimagining of the present and the future.

Raymond Williams can be understood as an early postcolonial writer, in the very particular sense that he anticipated the moment of devolution and the political break-up of Britain, and set these processes in the context of the worldwide phenomenon of decolonization. His own novels have then to be understood as part of a much more general process of questioning the received unitary identity of Britain, which occurs along all sorts of other coordinates. The general movement of this chapter is therefore away from analysis of the cultural consciousness of *late* modern Britain, and the break-up of its empire. It is a movement towards analysis of *post*-modern Britain, and the break-up of the kingdom.

5

Williams, Film and the Break-Up of Britain

Raymond Williams's theoretical work in literary studies was the tool by which his critical practice opened onto a much wider political world. In his fiction, this was related to the process of imagining new forms of nationhood. Moreover, his historical study of drama in Scandinavia, Ireland and Wales revealed a deep underlying interest in the relationship between emergent forms of writing and emergent national identities.

The same can be said of Williams's interest in film. To him, the critical cultural analysis of film constituted a natural extension of his interest in drama. This is partly because Williams was interested in the relationship between technology and culture. It is also partly because film offered him a new kind of drama in which to explore his interest in the relationship between culture and society. Film studies gave Williams the chance to apply his theoretical insights in drama to a truly large-scale audience and hence bears very deeply on his sense of how national communities are constituted. At the same time, the cultural analysis of film throws up a series of new theoretical and methodological challenges, arising out of the precise technological properties of the medium.

Presentation of Williams as a film theorist depends quite strongly on the mobilization of his concept of *flow*. He used this term in *Television: Technology and Cultural Form* in 1974, and it has been associated almost exclusively with his analysis of television ever since.[1] This key concept in the Williams oeuvre was first used in his little-known book, *Preface to Film*, as early as 1954. His work of this time was theoretically sophisticated and analytically complex. His work on film and *flow* can be related to the subsequent development of the theory of the *gaze*, and its influence in much later film theory – especially in the academic film journal, *Screen*.

In other words, not only did Williams enter the field of film studies earlier than some subsequent and better-known film theorists, but also in an important sense he got there before himself. That is, his work on film is not a mere appendage to his work on cultural materialism. Rather, it is actually the place where he worked out in advance some of the central concepts of that work.

WILLIAMS, FILM AND FLOW

Raymond Williams opens *Preface to Film* (1954) with a succinct statement of his principles of dramatic criticism. The problem he sets out to address is *how* drama represents what it represents on stage. Or, to put it another way, the question is as to what kind of representation drama can achieve:

> Representation, for example, has strong naturalistic associations, as if the intention of drama were the 'lifelike representation' of actions and speech and emotions, by the methods familiar in the naturalist theatre. But clearly it is not, in the simplest sense, lifelike representation when an author writes, and an actor speaks or sings, in verse; nor is formal gesture or movement lifelike in this same sense. Yet such conventions are a major part of our known drama.[2]

'Representation' does not, and cannot, refer to the unproblematic re-creation of everyday life on stage. However a piece of drama represents reality, it does not do so by pretending to be real. The word Williams uses for such pretence is 'naturalism' – and he is rather disdainful of it.

The distinction Williams draws in *Preface to Film* is between a dramatic practice that consciously brings the members of the audience to an awareness of their own participation in an act of fantasy, and that which obscures its own fictive nature. It is an important distinction, for Williams argues that only the former kind of drama can allow the audience to relate onstage drama to outside life, thereby gaining from the drama a dynamic self of heightened consciousness in their own world. It is the kind of drama to which Bertolt Brecht referred as *epic theatre*.[3] Williams elsewhere refers to it as *subjunctive* drama, because it allows the audience to imagine their own world – differently.[4]

The whole argument that Williams states in the first half of *Preface to Film* is that drama, from fifth-century Athens onwards, must be understood as the prehistory to film. Film cannot then be understood separately from this history of drama. Williams suggests in *Preface to Film* that, with further work, it may become possible to analyse what is historically and culturally specific to different kinds of drama, 'to understand the relation of particular conventions to the life of the time in which they flourished' (*PF*, p. 21). He would later realize this in his own *Drama in Performance* (1968). In a sense, this early work on film can be identified as an important test-ground for the work that would later be identified as cultural materialism.

This point emerges even more strongly as *Preface to Film* turns to the specific technical properties of film itself, in a section co-written with Michael Orrom. In analysing a piece of drama within its cultural/historical specificity, Williams reaches for an understanding of what he calls 'a total expression' (*PF*, p. 31; p. 51). This emphasizes the integrated nature of filmic performance – combining acting, lighting, sound, dialogue and technical editing. This integrated combination is specific to film, enabling Williams to emphasize the dramatic prehistory on one hand, while examining certain precise properties of film on the other. It shows Williams already reaching forward to the concept of total *flow* that he developed later in the work on drama and television.

The section of *Preface to Film* about Pudovkin's film *The Mother* leads directly into a theoretical formulation of film as total flow. 'Film expression demands movement and flow. That is its nature' (*PF*, p. 83). Flow in this early formulation is not yet an analytic concept. Rather, it is a technical device employed by the filmmaker: 'The basis of the film is movement, so then the basis of the linkage must be movement, smooth movement, *flow*' (*PF*, p. 83, emphasis in original). As a technical practice, flow primarily consists of editing sequences smoothly together into a melodic whole. The musical metaphor is appropriate because Williams and Orrom argue that if the smooth sequences produced by filmic flow are to be compared to any other art, then it should be to music:

> In the method of music will be found the clue to the new method which must be used in film. To get 'flow', the new concept is introduced from within the expression of the old; it begins as a small part of the first and gradually eclipses it. But the new is presented from a reference point within the old. This is precisely the method which must be used in film to avoid the disturbing jerks of normal cutting. The new character, the new concept, must be introduced through a development in the existing image. By that means we get not only a complete and convincing sense of location, we also get a smooth and satisfying transition. (*PF*, p. 84)

In a musical symphony, one theme gives way to another during a smooth and gradual transition. The varying themes flow over each other, so that it is not easy to identify the precise moment at which one is replaced with another. This is how Williams and Orrom try to relate the concept of flow to film. Each scene, each section, must blend with those preceding and succeeding it, to create an integrated whole. At this first stage of Williams's development of the concept, *flow* is defined as a technical device aimed at cutting or editing the filmed sections into a smooth symphonic whole.

This early sense of the concept of flow exerted a deep influence over Williams's thinking for much of the early part of his career. It is ironic that in his 1968 study *Drama from Ibsen to Brecht*, Williams continued to use *flow* in this sense – the careful editing out of jerky disturbances to create a harmonious whole. This is despite the fact that flow so conceived appears to militate against the epic theatre for which Williams praised Brecht. Epic theatre depends on the continual suspension of smooth naturalistic representation, and its replacement with a series of uneasy juxtapositions which provide an oblique commentary on the dramatic action. Williams's early definition of *flow* does not seem to sit well with such a practice.

The second stage in the development of the concept of flow, as developed in the 1968 book, is very much akin to the 1954 version. Flow remains a technical method employed by the *dramatist* to create smooth (naturalistic) drama. It has not yet been developed as an analytic concept to be used by the analyst. For example, Williams used this version

of flow in *Drama from Ibsen to Brecht* to describe the dramatic method
of Strindberg:

> If the scenic imagery is taken within the read work, the whole becomes a
> drama of rich and controlled complexity. But of course that was the problem:
> the practical integration of word and scene. What was available in the theatre
> was their *association*, but this is very different. It was the true sequence,
> the *flow* in one medium of scene and word, which Strindberg wanted and
> imagined, but which . . . he could not then get. Once again, he was writing
> well ahead of his time, imagining a single word-and-scene medium – in effect
> the patterned control of film – which did not yet exist. (*DIB*, p. 93,
> emphasis added)

Williams suggests that Strindberg's drama anticipated technical developments in television and film. It is interesting then that Williams's study
of Strindberg's drama anticipated his own later study of television.
That is why Williams uses the same term, flow, in each case.

This emphasis on avoiding 'disturbing jerks' in the editing would
not remain the main point of Williams's interest in flow throughout his
work. Indeed, flow would come to seem rather pernicious. Epic theatre
requires that the naturalistic representation of drama be continually
suspended, and a series of ideological questions be inserted into the
dramatic action itself. As a dramatic practice dedicated to achieving a
smooth melodic whole, flow does not enable this epic theatre to be
realized.

In 1968, Williams was still using total *flow* to refer to a method of
combining the different elements that make up dramatic form. Thereafter, an important complication of the original concept of flow came
into his thinking. This development saw Williams cease to use flow as
a technical method employed by the dramatist/ filmmaker, and mobilize
it instead as an *analytic* concept employed by the critic or analyst.

The third stage in the genesis of *flow* as an analytic concept was
signalled in *Television: Technology and Cultural Form* in 1974. By now,
Williams has become less uncritically enthusiastic for the makers of
film and television drama. He has become more aware of the need to
adopt a stance of scepticism towards these things. Accordingly, he ceases
to use *flow* as a term for registering his approval for the process of film-
making. Instead, he begins to use it as a rather pejorative term, capable
of directing attention towards the more insidious effects of film and
television.

The contribution to television studies for which Williams has become rightly known was in this area of *flow*. He uses the term to describe the deliberate planned sequences in which television programmes – and advertisements and intermissions – are broadcast. He realized that television could not be adequately understood through the analysis of individual programmes. Since these are broadcast in an orchestrated sequence, it is as a sequence that they must be considered.

Williams announces this important methodological breakthrough when he writes:

> there has been a significant shift from the concept of sequence as *programming* to the concept of sequence as *flow*. Yet this is difficult to see because the older concept of programming – the temporal sequence within which mix and proportion and balance operate – is still active and still to some extent real.'[5]

The shift Williams achieved in television studies was from an analytic practice of considering individual programmes in isolation to considering the programmes and advertisements alongside each other, as a continual sequence. This is his third definition of *flow*:

> The flow offered can also, and perhaps more fundamentally, be related to the television experience itself. Two common observations bear on this. As has already been noted, most of us say, in describing the experience, 'watching television', rather than that we have watched 'the news' or 'a play' or 'the football' *on television* . . . Then again, it is a widely if often ruefully admitted experience that many of us find television very difficult to switch off; that again and again, even when we have switched on for a particular 'programme', we find ourselves watching the one after it and the one after that. The way in which flow is now organised, without definite intervals, in any case encourages this. (*T*, p. 94, emphasis in original)

The positive concept of flow as being the technical means of ironing out annoying jerky interruptions has now been replaced by this idea of flow as something much more insidious. Flow defined in this way is not so much what we look at. Rather, it is what looks *at* us. The flow, in other words, is located outside the viewer. It has power over the viewer, whom it can 'capture' (*T*, p. 91) for a period of time. This period of time itself is referred to technically as 'an evening's viewing' (*T*, p. 93).

Yet again, this term, *viewing* is not used to refer to the act carried out by the viewer. It refers to what is viewed. As such it is a kind of mystification. It is enabled by the medium of the external flow, located outside the individual viewer's control. *Viewing* then refers not to the act of watching television, but to the act of being confronted by tele-visual flow. The flow, that is, reaches out to us, rather than we to it.

By this third stage, then, the concept of flow has a much more complex meaning than that which was used in the earlier work on film and drama. Yet we can see retrospectively that it was in that work that Williams was beginning to develop the concept itself. When looked at in this light, the interest in film is not simply an interesting add-on to Williams's practice of cultural materialism. It is a positively central component of it. If we were then to apply the later, more sophisticated version of flow retroactively to the areas of film and drama in which it was first developed in a simple way, what would be the result?

The version of *flow* that has emerged from this third stage of Williams's career has the potential to be mobilized in film study. His definition of *flow* has much in common with the Lacanian concept of the *gaze* that was by this stage beginning to be developed in film studies – particularly in the journal, *Screen*. This brings us to a stage where Raymond Williams can be presented as a complex film theorist in his own right. His work then converges with the much broader *Screen* school of analysis in fruitful and important ways.

SCREEN THEORY

Jacques Lacan understood the *gaze* as an analytic concept rather than any physically accessible piece of sensory equipment. This strikingly parallels Raymond Williams's distinction between flow and act of viewing. Lacan states the distinction concisely: 'The world is all-seeing, but it is not exhibitionistic – it does not provoke our gaze.'[6] It is not the eye that commands the gaze. Rather, the gaze is located in the object beheld by the eye.

To Lacan, this theoretical insight bears on the process of subjectivity formation. A united sense of self has to be performed in order to exist. This is enabled by the gaze which, by virtue of being located outside the self, enables the subject to imagine its own unified identity. The gaze is a way of imagining the self looking at itself from a point outside it. As Lacan puts it, 'the gaze "I" see is a gaze imagined by me in the field of the Other'.[7]

The externally located gaze is redefined in film study as the *fourth look*.[8] It comes after the three cinematic looks of audience to screen; character to character; and actor to camera. The fourth look is then the illusion of being caught in the act of looking at others looking at others looking at others. It is again only an illusion, a concept, rather than any physical act of looking that takes place. It bears deeply on Lacan's notion of the means by which the gaze enables subjectivity formation by overcoming the divisions within the restlessly searching ego, and by presenting a unified self for presentation in the imaginary fourth look. As Lacan puts it, the gaze enables the individual subject to acquire a full subjectivity by providing the illusion of 'seeing oneself see oneself'.[9]

A landmark moment in the history of film studies was the publication in *Screen* in 1975 of Laura Mulvey's paper, 'Visual pleasure and narrative cinema'. Emerging out of the women's movement, Mulvey employed the Lacanian notion of the *gaze* to critique what she saw as the tendency in mainstream cinema to pose women as fetish objects. She proposed the three cinematic looks of viewer to screen; character to character; and actor to camera. Yet she noted that the mystique of the cinema serves to conceal the first and third, thus naturalizing the presented relationship between characters. This in turn naturalized a scenario where women were fixed as passive objects of male desire. Their role in film was to provide a fantasy of wish fulfilment for the actively desiring male viewer. This could take the form of sexual desire and its wished-for fulfilment, or it could take *desire* as a more generalized principle of subjectivity formation.

Mulvey's analysis depends strongly on a notion of *scopophilia*, or the sexual gaze. She suggests that the conditions of cinema itself support such a gaze. We know from Lacan that the gaze I see is a gaze imagined by me in the field of the Other. In the darkness, it is hard to imagine being looked at by the Other and therefore hard to imagine a united sense of self identity. In cinematic conditions, the exhibitionism of the viewer, the desire to be looked at, is projected onto the performer, and so enables the individual viewer to imagine being looked at by others. This provides a unified self identity for the viewing subject and gives rise to a level of visual pleasure which Mulvey calls *identification* with the main actor. The main actor is not the viewing subject, only an imagined ideal version of the subject. Identification thus depends on an interplay between similarity and misrecognition. The filmic gaze depends on likeness and difference or, as Mulvey writes, 'the glamorous [star] impersonates the ordinary [viewer].'[10]

As with Lacan's work on gaze and Raymond Williams's idea of flow, this suggests a contradiction in the gaze. Film is *diegetic*: it uses both spectacle and narrative. When the action is moving on, we 'look' through identification with the main male characters. However, Mulvey argues that the woman as object suspends this. When we look at a woman in a film, the narrative is frozen. We look just at a woman, not at part of a narrative. If the woman becomes active as part of the narrative, rather than existing simply as an object, this level of satisfaction is denied. The tendency of women to enter the narrative gives rise to a castration fantasy – a fear of womanly power. The two dominant filmic solutions to this are punishment/containment of the woman; or transfer of anxiety to a fetish object so that the source of anxiety loses its threat. Mulvey gives Sternberg's film *Morocco* as an example of a film which is emplotted in such a way as to *contain* the possibility of female power by restoring women to the status of objects. She cites another Sternberg film, *Dishonoured*, as an example of the latter strategy – where anxiety is transferred from woman to fetish object. Mulvey concludes:

In *reality* the phantasy world of the screen is subject to the law which produces it. Sexual instincts and identification processes have a meaning within the symbolic order which articulates desire. Desire, born with language, allows the possibility of transcending the instinctual and the imaginary, but its point of reference continually returns to the traumatic moment of its birth: the castration complex. Hence the look, pleasurable in its form, can be threatening in its content, and it is woman as representation/ image that crystallises this paradox.[11]

The gaze poses women as fetish objects for the satisfaction of the male viewer. If women on screen are allowed to move and form part of the narrative, this satisfaction is short-circuited. This cannot be allowed and so womanly power is eliminated by the returning of female bodies to stasis. It must be noted that this perhaps simple binary opposition between active male/passive female has attracted considerable critique since the article was published in 1975.[12]

The significant conclusion that Mulvey proposes is the theoretical relation between *gaze* and *phantasy*, or symbolic wish fulfilment. The contradictory nature of the gaze gives rise to a need to distinguish between different kinds of phantasy. Twenty-one years earlier, in *Preface to Film*, Raymond Williams had made just such a distinction. Like Mulvey, he drew attention to the conditions of cinematic viewing, and explored how those conditions bear on the viewing experience:

> It is an immensely powerful medium, and in the darkened auditorium the dominating scene, with its very large, moving figures, its very loud sound, its simultaneous appeal to eye and ear can, it seems obvious, exercise a kind of 'hypnotic' effect which very readily promotes phantasy and easy emotional indulgence. (*PF*, p. 13)

In order to imagine a self identity, the viewer needs to imagine being looked at by the Other. The darkened auditorium enables this exhibitionism to be projected onto the actor. Cinema thus offers to resolve the viewer's need to imagine being looked at from a point outside the self. The desire of the viewer for a united sense of self is projected onto the screen where it is organized for presentation to the audience. *Phantasy* is the term used to refer to the viewer's desire for unified self identity and to the tendency of cinema to offer resolution to this desire. The ways in which the cinematic gaze organizes unconscious phantasy in this way has important implications for the construction of dominant versions of society.

Later in *Preface to Film*, Williams refers to *fantasy* (with an 'f') as an example of a more conscious generic mode, rather than the organization of unconscious desire. Addressing the concept of naturalism in the cinema, he writes: 'we find it applied indiscriminately, in new plays, to orthodox religious drama, to melodramas of an essentially nineteenth-century type, to *fantasies*, and even . . . to farce' (*PF*, p. 39, emphasis added).

Implicit in Williams's critique of naturalism is something quite different from unconscious *phantasy*. The tendency of naturalism was simply to reproduce 'real life' on the screen. This fails to draw attention to the fact that any film is not reality, it is only representation. It is not self-conscious, and in Williams's sense it is thus undramatic. This point bears on the distinction between *phantasy* and *fantasy*.

Implicit in the critique of naturalism is an idea that it supports a static and unchanging world-view, supported by the mobilization in film drama of unconscious phantastic desires which support that view. For example, as Mulvey later argued, a cinematic gaze which appropriates women as objects of possession implicitly supports a world-view where this is also the case outside the cinema, by harnessing an unconscious phantasy of male domination over women.

The separate use Williams makes of the term *fantasy* suggests that not all desire is unconscious. Implicitly, then, if fantasy is a conscious phenomenon, it is harder for the filmic gaze to manipulate. The ability of the analyst to *disbelieve* or *contest* the film's reality becomes as a result much stronger.

This point is only implicit in Williams. He does not clearly define what he means by the different terms *phantasy* and *fantasy*. However, that a writer so scrupulously careful in verbal precision should employ such a distinction at all implies an important conceptual difference. This difference can be teased out by looking at another article published in *Screen*, almost thirty years later, by Lesley Stern.

In 'The body as evidence', published in 1982, Stern draws attention to a need for conceptual clarity in the different ways in which the terms *phantasy* and *fantasy* are used:

> The understanding of 'phantasy' used in this theoretical work is fairly broad, and indeed capitalises on a lack of clarity in Freud's own work. Freud uses the term in three ways: first to denote conscious imaginings or daydreams (in less specialised writings this is often spelt 'fantasy'); second, to denote unconscious phantasies which have a similar structure to dreams in that their origin lies in repressed material – analysis of the manifest content should reveal the way in which the prohibition is present in the actual formation of the wish that motivates the dream or the phantasy; and third to denote primal phantasies, fundamental unconscious structures which transcend individual experience.[13]

Stern refers to the need for conceptual clarity between the different uses of the term, *phantasy*. This need for clarity drives her towards the distinction between *phantasy* and *fantasy* that Williams had implicitly made in *Preface to Film*. Moreover, Stern's insight here recalls Williams's critique of dramatic naturalism. Williams had argued that in simply recreating everyday life on stage or on camera, naturalism in effect ratified a static series of relations outside the theatre. In other words, mainstream naturalist film drama is deeply conservative, for it leaves no room for effective critique of the social order. This is also the effect of films that privilege realist narrative and its logical progress towards wish-fulfilment and closure.

Lesley Stern advocates a viewing strategy that resists such closure, by viewing the film against the grain. This generates a degree of conscious agency for the viewing subject, who is thereby able to resist acquiescence in the imagined order of the filmic gaze. This is the point Stern tries to draw out of the phantasy/fantasy distinction thirty years after Williams:

> At a certain level it seems useful to make a distinction between, on the one hand, *fantasy* as conscious imaginings, daydreams, inventions, make-believe, reverie; and on the other hand, the various other senses in which *phantasy* is used. This is not to make a strict demarcation between the conscious on one hand and the unconscious on the other, for clearly daydreams can tell us about the unconscious and are indeed structured by psychic mechanisms. However, the functioning of different kinds of phantasy needs to be distinguished.[14]

Stern renders explicit what had been latent in Williams's *Preface to Film*. In cinema, *fantasy* is taken to be congruent with conscious desire. It is not defined as an unconscious process of identity formation, and this unconscious process is what Stern calls *phantasy*. Fantasy as conscious desire can be used to interrupt the organization of un-conscious wish-fulfilment and hence throw the tendency of the filmic gaze to posit a stable subject into sharp relief. Stern continues:

> Realism and narrative have been privileged sites for the return of the repressed, and breaks with them have been advocated as ways of fracturing the false unity of the viewing subject, provoking a more self-conscious and active subject. What has been glaringly absent from much of this discourse is a conceptualisation of fiction. Fiction is most often collapsed into narrative or seen as shaped by and subordinate to realism: even when we know that we are watching something unreal we are structured into 'belief' through the strategies of realism. But it might be important to explore the way in which *disbelief* operates in film viewing.[15]

Stern's emphasis on the fictional nature of conscious fantasy takes us all the way back to Williams's early concept of *convention*. In films and drama where the dramatic conventions are functioning successfully, the viewer is not asked to collude in an affirmation of some mystified sense of exterior reality. Rather, he or she is asked to participate consciously in an act of make-believe that opens onto the exterior world in such a way as to throw that construct into question.

FILM HISTORY AND NATIONAL TRADITION

Raymond Williams's first strategy for using film to question the dominant ideology in society was to reject entirely the idea of a single unified object – 'film'. This rejection was based on terms that recall his contemporary rejection of 'literature' in favour of the more open-ended 'writing'. The rejection of 'film' as a category does not imply rejection of the study of actual filmic products. Rather, it represents Williams's clearing the ground of any preconceived notion of what we might mean by 'film'. Just as a preconceived notion of the *literary* disqualified in advance interesting forms of writing such as diaries, letters and journalism, in favour of the supposedly literary forms of the novel and poetry, so too a reified notion of film excludes certain forms such as drama adaptation, documentary or reportage, again in favour of certain imaginative forms, as if these and these alone are worthy of attention. Williams explored these conceptual issues in his paper, 'Film history', in 1983:

> To write a critical history of 'film' which is actually going to exclude, on such grounds, those films which were really only 'theatrical or literary bastards' is a procedure so astonishing that it could only ever be undertaken in the same spirit of misplaced confidence that is shown in similar histories of Literature (excluding not only all 'non-imaginative' writing, but also most actual novels and poems which fall below the proper standard of 'literature') or Theatre (restricting drama to one of its places of performance – the theatre – and to work of certain types, while excluding other places of performance and rejecting all other types as 'popular entertainment'). What we really find, in each case, is a categorical argument, based on what, if it were not categorical, could be openly offered as a justified opinion, which manages to reduce the actual diversity of its real subject and to offer its highly selective version as the whole real history of its now necessarily hard- line area.[16]

Williams's approach takes the form of a negation of a negation. He rejects the dominant institutional rejection of some kinds of writing as non-literary. He rejects too the dominant rejection of some kinds of film as not worthy of study. By rejecting this unitary object, 'film', Williams opens up the discipline to more precise analysis. Rather than a single category, 'film', we are then in a position to pay attention to different kinds of production in different scenarios. Like the shift from 'Literature' to 'Writing', we might say that the death of 'Film' gives rise to the birth of 'film'.

This leads Williams on to an important second rejection. Associated with a preconceived notion of the literary is a historical tradition of literary idealism, or of viewing the literary text as if it were entirely separate from daily life. When Williams rejects one tendency, he also attacks the other. This is again his approach to film just as much as to literature:

> temporary and provisional indications of attention and emphasis – of 'subjects' – can never be mistaken for independent and isolated processes and products. For they are at best provisional intellectual identifications of significant areas of a common life. At worst, and frequently, they draw hard lines around certain areas, cutting off the practical relations with other 'areas' (which are indeed then seen only as 'areas' – 'the economy', 'the family', 'literature') which are in fact necessary if we are to understand the 'outward' relations – how 'the economy' affected 'the cinema' – but also the 'internal' relations and compositions, the supposed fixed properties of 'cinema' or 'film' which can often be clarified if the specific processes are seen in the context of much more general processes. ('Film history', p. 133)

Williams's mention of 'temporary and provisional indications of attention and emphasis' is a reference to the dominant habit of dividing all areas of life and work up into separate areas or specializations. Because he knows this autonomy of spheres to be an illusion, Williams rejects the idea of film as a discrete field of study that cannot be related to other fields – like drama, or economics. Implicitly, he advocates a practice of analysing film production as it occurs in its historic and institutional milieu. As a result, he cannot see film as an idealist realm. On the contrary, it is thoroughly materialist, deeply involved in much wider social, cultural, political and economic formations which have themselves to be factored into our understanding of the films.

Williams calls for a methodological self-consciousness, whereby the analyst will not mystify the item under scrutiny as an example of a timeless generalized category, 'Film'. Critical self-consciousness will enable the analyst to realize that these classifications are themselves highly provisional, amenable to much discussion and change.

> Lines have indeed to be drawn, to make any account possible, but it is always necessary to see ourselves as drawing them, and willing to redraw them rather than to suppose that the marks on this one of many maps are hard features, of similar content and isolation, on the ground. ('Film history', p. 133)

Williams wants to transcend disciplinary maps. This is a suggestive metaphor, for it opens onto the national context. It is not surprising that in film, as in literature, Raymond Williams makes a third crucial rejection, that of the idea of national tradition. He notes in the essay 'Film history' that, at a comparatively early stage in the development of cinema, certain films began to be assimilated to a putative national tradition – which then also excluded certain other films. This of course was happening not only in film, but also in literature, in history and in all sorts of other areas. Thus, Williams writes, 'national traditions are identified within the more general phases: a form of history which can then be developed into a form of criticism' ('Film history', p. 132). As with literature, films that could be made to conform to an externally constructed sense of what the nation stood for were accepted into the tradition. Films that did not so conform were overlooked. What Williams never manages to pinpoint is *which* nation is being referred to. The implication is that he is discussing a unitary *British* film history. But there were always different traditions in Scotland and Wales, as we shall see.

Williams's response to the metropolitan history of film is ambiguous. He was rather disdainful of the metropolitan preference which emerged relatively early in the history of cinema. The drama for which he was most enthusiastic was that of the emerging nations of Scandinavia and Ireland. Moreover, earlier in this chapter we saw that Williams understood that drama was the prehistory of film. In other words, the pre-emergent stage of important radical cinema was not located in the metropolitan centres of London or Paris at all. Williams's positive evaluation of the work of Synge, O'Casey, Ibsen and Strindberg leaps from every page of *Drama from Ibsen to Brecht* and *Drama in Performance*. The most important work in early film, and what we might call 'late pre-film drama', was being carried out in these newly self-conscious and distinctly subordinate nations.[17] Thus Williams suggests that the metropolitan bias was 'inherently false' ('Film history', p. 141).

On the other hand, Williams points out that historically there followed a kind of parasitism, whereby new kinds of centralization took place according to where money was available to fund films. 'Within capitalist and state-capitalist economies, it came to seem natural that this led, by a familiar financial logic, to an extreme concentration and relative monopoly of production: massive production costs made more affordable by a controlled system of mass distribution' ('Film history', p. 144). In Britain, this centralization gave rise to the idea of a national tradition, centred on the fashionable London studios of Ealing and Pinewood. It had the effect of making seem natural what was really a historically produced phenomenon: the concentration of cultural authority in a few metropolitan centres. Williams can see how this situation might seem natural, but warns us off such an approach: 'the material factor itself could, within different general relations, lead as easily to more diverse centres of production, beyond the old metropolitan fixed points, and to a radically extended and more diverse distribution of this wider range' ('Film history', pp. 144–5).

Williams knows that cinematic production remains overwhelmingly metropolitan in form and that it mystifies critical consciousness as a result. He knows too that attempts to resist this centralization have been brave, but have rarely succeeded for long. 'The tendencies to monopoly, to incorporation and to agency or outpost production in terms of the dominant centre have been so strong that only relatively brief periods of fully independent production, and then more often than not in "national" terms, have escaped them' ('Film history', p. 145).

This at last hints at a problem Williams had earlier failed to address: namely, in discussing the national tradition, *which* nation does he mean? By referring briefly here to independent cinematic production which is nevertheless carried out in 'national terms', Williams is surely referring to alternative national traditions in Scotland and Wales. It is perhaps no coincidence that when London's National Film Theatre held a screening of films selected in tribute to Williams shortly after his death in 1988, Dai Smith chose Karl Francis's Welsh film, *Ms Rhymney Valley 1985*, as an appropriate tribute.[18]

In other words, there have always been independent centres of production which the metropolitan mainstream tends to overlook. Although, as Williams points out, these outposts have normally taken the form of alternative nationalisms in Scotland and Wales, this is not necessarily the case. Williams himself wrote with great enthusiasm in the journal *Screen* on the film *The Big Flame*, written by Jim Allen and directed by socialist documentary filmmaker Ken Loach (*WCS*, pp. 226–39). *The Big Flame* was set in the Liverpool docks which Allen understood more immediately than he would have understood similar situations in Scotland and Wales. The film is as fully committed to resisting the metropolitan bias as anything produced in Scotland or Wales.

This points to a problem to which Williams himself had earlier drawn attention: that it is apparently easier for artists in Scotland and Wales to pit national difference against the conflated English/British mainstream than it is for English artists who nevertheless are not represented by metropolitan forms. What we have to remember, then, is Williams's suggestion that the national difference can be an emotional obstacle, and that writers like Allen, free from such a burden, should be able to get through to the real problems more – rather than less – easily than in Scotland and Wales. Accordingly, Williams concludes his essay on 'Film history' by averring that 'it has been almost wholly in these comparatively independent centres that work of real value has been done' ('Film history', p. 145). It is a note of cautious optimism. He asserts that work from the periphery rather than the centre has been really valuable. He then concludes with the telling words 'break up': 'the old economy of the cinema is beginning to break up' and this will allow the unitary history of the national tradition to be 'reinterpreted by being changed' ('Film history', p. 146).

HUGH GRANT'S ENGLISH BUFFOON

These issues can be explored in relation to the mainstream films produced in Britain during the period surrounding political break-up of the union. For example, in a number of interrelated films, the actor Hugh Grant created a persona as a charming middle-class English buffoon. The films *Love Actually* (2003), *Notting Hill* (1999) and *Four Weddings and a Funeral* (1994) were not explicitly created as part of a series. Yet there are sufficient thematic similarities between them for them usefully to be considered in relation to each other. These similarities, coupled with the ubiquitous figure of Hugh Grant's middle-class English buffoon, bring the films into an interesting relation with each other in a way that allows a final extension of Williams's concept of flow.

As we have seen, the cinematic gaze offers to satisfy the need of the viewer to imagine being looked at from the position of the Other. In this way, film provides a united identity for the viewing subject, by enabling the viewer to imagine what it is like to be looked at from a point outside the self. Cinema promotes a phantasy geared towards securing the unity of the viewing subject.

In the series of films featuring the middle-class English buffoon, this unity of the viewing subject is then worked up onto collective lines, in order to offer a second phantasy of a unified national identity. This can be called a *compensatory phantasy*, for it aims at securing a stable unified collective ego, a national ego we might say, during a historical period when the unity of the United Kingdom has been very much more in doubt than at an earlier period. The potential of film to create a collective ego in this way bears strongly on Benedict Anderson's notion of the imagined community. It is notable that, according to Lacan, the gaze which enables films to carry out this kind of work is *imagined* by the subject in the field of the Other, just as, to Anderson, the national community itself is imagined into being.

Richard Curtis's 2003 film, *Love Actually*, opens with a frame narrative spoken by actor Hugh Grant. This frame narrative sets the scene for the film. It occurs before the title music and therefore also before the dramatic action proper has got under way. In other words, Hugh Grant at this stage has not been ascribed to any particular character. He is a disembodied voice: the accumulation of all of his previous film roles speaking simultaneously.

> Whenever I get gloomy with the state of the world, I think about the arrivals gate at Heathrow airport. General opinion is starting to make out that we live in a world of hatred and greed, but I don't see that. It seems to me that love is everywhere.[19]

The frame narrative is simple. Grant tells us that love is more prevalent in daily life than is popularly acknowledged in a media society where the news is always terrible. This simple message is also couched in a precise social and historical context. The Hugh Grant figure goes on:

When the planes hit the twin towers, as far as I know, none of the phone calls from the people on board were messages of hate or revenge. They were all messages of love. If you look for it, I've got a sneaking feeling you'll find that love actually is all around.[20]

The historical reference to the attacks in New York in 2001 appears to date the film in the immediate aftermath of that event – an aftermath characterized by American militarism. In other words, the film is located in a historical period in which British military power and global importance had diminished, relative to the new militarism of the United States of America. This is the situation that the film aims to redress. It sets out to provide a compensatory phantasy, where the relegation of Britain to junior partner in a larger military alliance can be symbolically conjured away, and where a strong sense of British unity can be perpetuated.

The quested-for unified national ego opens directly onto larger questions of global power and politics. These issues are crystallized in the figure of Hugh Grant, whose character, we soon discover, is the newly elected prime minister. The frame narrative's reference to the 'twin towers' anticipates a later scene, where the new prime minister holds his first Cabinet meeting. He is warned by a colleague that there is a strong feeling in the country that the previous government had failed to stand up to brash American power in global affairs, and that the new government should take a more positive role in doing so. It is the vacuum created by this relative loss of power on the world stage that *Love Actually* aims to redress:

Prime minister: 'Okay, what's next?'
Colleague: 'The president's visit.'
Prime minister: 'Ah yes, yes. I fear this is going to be a difficult one to play. Alex?'
Alex: 'There's a very strong feeling in the party, we mustn't allow ourselves to be bullied from pillar to post like the last government.'
All: 'Hear, hear.'[21]

The historical context which was generated by the 'twin towers' reference suggests that the 'last government' referred to here is Tony Blair's administration of the turn of the century. It was the same government which in 1997 had let the cat out of the devolution bag, granting some measure of self-rule to Northern Ireland, Scotland and Wales,

and therefore placing the unity of the ego-collective in jeopardy. The
film makes an implicit conjunction between loss of an unified sense of
nationhood and loss of global power, and sets out to provide symbolic
compensation for these losses. As Lesley Stern says, the filmic text
works 'towards wish fulfilment by providing satisfaction, a happy
ending; but also . . . working towards unification, securing identity
and resolution, both of the film and of the viewing subject'.[22] In other
words, it offers to provide resolution to the ego of the individual viewing
subject, and to work this up into a collective audience.

Love Actually asserts a spurious version of a unified British ego-
collective. This is encapsulated in the contest Hugh Grant's prime
minister enters into with the visiting American president to win the
affection of a working-class girl, Natalie. The prime minister initially
tells his cabinet colleagues that he has no intention of acting 'like a
petulant child' when he welcomes the leader of 'the most powerful
country in the world'.[23] It is only when the prime minister interrupts
the president stealing a kiss from Natalie that he appears to harden in
his attitude towards the president.

Laura Mulvey's argument about the male identity of the filmic gaze
is that women in film do not act. Rather they suspend narrative and
become objects of the scopophilic gaze. Female action represents a
tangible threat to the ideological closure of the narrative. This threat
must be contained by the flow of the film – hence the suspension of the
narrative when Natalie is on camera. *Love Actually* offers to provide a
new ego-collective for Britain. To threaten narrative closure is to threaten
that unified identity, and the film cannot allow this. Accordingly, Natalie
is converted into a fetish object, where the threat posed by her suspension of the narrative can be overcome by posing her as the object of the
narrative itself.

The film cuts to the scene of a press conference at the end of the
president's visit. The president informs reporters that he has had a very
satisfactory visit, and that the 'special relationship' between the two
countries remains strong and close. Keeping in mind the prime
minister's chagrin over the president's advances towards Natalie, the
word 'relationship' also operates in another dimension here, that of
the romantic. The prime minister tells reporters:

I love that word, relationship. Covers all manner of sins, doesn't it? I fear
that this has become a bad relationship. A relationship based on the

president taking exactly what he wants and casually ignoring all those things that really matter to Britain.

We may be a small country, but we are a great one too. The country of Shakespeare. Churchill. The Beatles. Sean Connery. Harry Potter. David Beckham's right foot. David Beckham's left foot, come to that.

A friend who bullies us is no longer a friend. And since bullies only respond to strength, from now onward, I will be prepared to be much stronger, and the president should be prepared for that.[24]

Romantic envy over the president's perceived relationship with Natalie prompts the prime minister to revoke the 'special relationship' between the countries, reverse his earlier policy and strengthen Britain's position with regard to America. In other words, the film uses the figure of the woman, Natalie, to allegorize a mythical restitution of British power. The film thus modulates between provision of finished subjectivity within the individual viewer and ideological closure of the collective viewing community. Benedict Anderson expresses this modern tendency to use individuals as metonymic expressions of national identity, at the conclusion of *Imagined Communities*, when he writes: 'as with modern persons, so it is with nations.'[25]

The main scenes of the film are intercut with scenes from around the country, where people are following the fortunes of the prime minister. The film invites viewers to cultivate a sense of simultaneous communion in the same viewing experience, through reference to the same signifiers, which thereby have the effect of reasserting the unity of the United Kingdom. As Raymond Williams had earlier put it,

the sense of friends and neighbours is attached to a distant and commanding organisation: in Britain, now, that which ought to be spelled as it so barbarously sounds – the United Kingdom, the 'Yookay' . . . The powerful feelings of wanting to belong to a society are then in a majority of cases bonded to these large definitions. (*T2000*, p. 182)

It is notable that none of the scenes from around the nation are in any way place-specific – except for London. The political institutions of Downing Street and Westminster are unmistakeable. Yet none of the scenes supposedly showing people around the country following the media reports of the prime minister are anchored in this place-specific way. Similarly, the appearance of precise historical dating generated by the 'twin towers' reference proves elusive and evaporates upon closer inspection, leaving the film floating outside history. The version of the Yookay perpetuated by *Love Actually* can then be said to be everywhere by being nowhere, to express everyone by expressing no one.[26]

It is striking how often films featuring Hugh Grant's middle-class English buffoon persona follow this pattern. A generic British identity is affirmed through the representation of a middle-class hero, portrayed by Hugh Grant. In each case the fate of this hero becomes tied up with that of the nation. This embodiment of a putative British national identity is created: 1) by suspending any threat to the narration of that identity which would be posed by figures from the different nations of Northern Ireland, Scotland and Wales; and 2) in contradistinction to an American outsider – usually a woman. The films follow a linear narrative working towards ideological closure. This takes the form of modulation, between securing a unified ego for the individual viewing subject and his/her resolution within the similarly unified viewing community, the ego-collective. This modulation can, following Raymond Williams, be described as a kind of flow.

In other words, flow in Williams's sense is important as an analytic concept because it modulates between two properties. These are the twin tendencies of a film to work towards ideological closure *both* within the ego of the viewing subject *and* within the ego-collective of the viewing community. It is possible to make a theoretical extension of Williams's use of the term *flow* to draw attention to the capacity of films to modulate between the subjective and collective egos in this way. This modulation brings the films into a relation with each other, and that relation itself can be expressed by the term *flow*.

In each of the films featuring Hugh Grant's middle-class English buffoon, the buffoon is a kind of modulator, or mediator, figure. The mediation of collective identity that occurs in *Love Actually* had already been operative in the earlier film, *Notting Hill* (1999). American actress Anna Scott (played by Julia Roberts) comes to London to promote a film. A chance encounter results in her meeting Hugh Grant's character, the bookshop owner William Thacker. The film simply follows the path of their unfolding relationship.

It is another compensatory phantasy. The American actress earns $14m per film, in stark contrast to the struggling Thacker. The film seems to suggest that no matter how powerful the USA might become relative to Britain, the British middle-class hero is still able to get the American girl. This is a clear example of the theoretical phenomenon explored by Laura Mulvey: the figure of the woman is used to crystallize male desire and anxiety.

Notting Hill enacts a kind of wish-fulfilment: recapitulating Britain's lost strength and unity relative to America. It is interesting that in *Notting Hill* the achievement of this goal is placed in jeopardy by the character of Thacker's uncouth lodger, Spike – who is Welsh. It is Spike's casual and unreliable attitude that almost results in Thacker not receiving a message from Anna and so threatens to hijack the film's satisfactory denouement. It is as though Welsh difference must be overcome, and be seen to be overcome, if the symbolic unity and power of this imaginary Yookay is to be recapitulated. Once the threat posed by Spike is overcome, he is simply left behind in the busy traffic of a London street. He is allowed to play no meaningful part in the film's conclusion.

The threat posed to the narration of British identity, in other words, is held in place by the final suspension of Spike's actions. This is akin to the treatment Laura Mulvey associates with the containment of female power in mainstream cinema. In Mulvey's account, the gaze is always male in the sense that it is a means by which men look at women, suspend feminine power in time and space and so forestall the threat of female strength. Spike suffers in the same way, and yet Spike is a man. How can we explain the contradiction?

In an important rejoinder to Mulvey, published in *Screen* in 1980, Steve Neale questioned the assumption that only female bodies are used as fetish objects in securing a film's ideological conclusion.[27] In Neale's account, the gaze is still identified as male. This time, however, *male* refers less to the process of individual men securing an ideological place for women, and more to the means by which the symbolic order – comprising both men and women – is constructed. In *Notting Hill* the symbolic order is synonymous with the maintenance of a unified collective ego for the United Kingdom. Welsh differential identity would threaten this and is thus frozen by the gaze of the film. The gaze is thus male in Neale's sense that it augments the symbolic order, rather than in Mulvey's sense of men looking at women.

Meanwhile, the threat of Scottish otherness to symbolic unity had already been contained in the even earlier film, *Four Weddings and a Funeral* (1994). Here the main character Charles's Scottish friend Gareth dies and is shut up in a coffin. This symbolically contains the menace that assertion of Scottish otherness would present to the ego-collective of the renascent Yookay, and again allows Hugh Grant's character Charles to go ahead and get the American girl, Carrie. Significantly, the Scottish friend is also a gay man. Again, we can argue that the filmic gaze is male in the sense that it secures resolution for the symbolic order of the ego-collective, and not simply in the sense that it sets up a binary opposition between active men and passive women. The symbolic order of the unitary British state can be characterized as *male* for similar analytic purposes. Although it comprises both men and women, it is male in the sense that it provides resolution to the ego-collective and hence achieves ideological containment of any forces threatening that resolution. The flow of these films modulates between individual subject and collective audience, offering a phantasy of a unified national identity to compensate for the fact that the films were produced during a period when the united nature of the United Kingdom has begun to be called into question.

FRACTURING THE FLOW

In each of these cases, the cinematic gaze is a kind of lure. This can also be said about filmic flow. The mediator figure expressed by Hugh Grant's character calls out to an imagined viewer, inviting him or her to feel *direct* personal identification with the metropolitan version of the nation presented by the films. Yet, as Stephen Heath points out, the ideal spectator whom the film purports to address is inevitably never the same as the actually spectating individual.[28]

This point can be made strongly by quoting Raymond Williams again, this time on Dickens's novel *Hard Times*. *Hard Times* was written during a period of rapid social change, which had thrown up huge social divisions within society. It explores those divisions by exploring social relations in the allegorical industrial city of Coketown. In his path-breaking analysis of the novel, Raymond Williams argued that Dickens posed every inhabitant of Coketown as identical, so that an imaginative appeal to symbolic unity can be put in place by the novel: 'there is . . . a Coketowner, who is ideally present before the effective individual versions are introduced' (*WS*, p. 172). The ideal Coketowner offers to conjure away the social divisions thrown up in society by the industrial revolution. The novel offers to express everyone by expressing no one.

Hard Times posits an imaginary set of characters to populate its world. In directly addressing his audience, Dickens also posits an ideal imaginary *reader*. Williams finds in *Hard Times* a blurring of the boundary between inside and outside the fiction, by modulating between ideal reader and ideal inhabitant, between subjective ego and collective resolution. Williams says: 'the reader can move, at many critical points, *within* the composed general response of indignation and sympathy. What he should *do* . . . is left undefined, within the composed response, since specifications would fracture his ideal unity.' (*WS*, p. 174) In other words, *Hard Times* posits the kind of imagined community relating those inside to those outside the fiction that Benedict Anderson considered symptomatic of the way in which national self-imagining occurs.

This is the effect of Hugh Grant's mediator figure and of filmic flow. The flow offers to transcend all differences in the creation of an ideal unity, despite the precisely located and different positions of each viewer. Williams draws attention to this much more general process of distilling and diluting difference when he asks, 'Who knows what is Welsh or Wales when all is U.K. or Yookay? Will there be Yookayans yet?' (*WSW*? p. 67)

Williams is suspicious of the 'ideal Coketowner', because he knows that the ideal reader whom the text purports to address is never the same as any individual reader. Each reader is materially situated and approaches the text differently – despite the text's attempt at overriding all difference. Similarly, there is no ideal *Yookayan*. Rather, the range of cultural identities within the British whole is far more diverse than consideration of these films would suggest.

After *Love Actually*, *Notting Hill* and *Four Weddings and a Funeral*, it is something of a surprise to come to Chris Monger's 1995 film, *The Englishman Who Went Up a Hill but Came Down a Mountain*. Outwardly, there is great similarity between Hugh Grant's character here and his mediator figure in the other films. Grant plays Reginald Anson, a government cartographer, sent to a small Welsh borders community in 1917 to map the terrain. As with the other films, romance is sparked into life between Anson and his landlady, Elizabeth. This romance is threatened by the wider forces in which the characters are involved, but finally blossoms.

Unlike the other films, however, there is no outside interloper. Or rather, Hugh Grant's middle-class English buffoon is now the interloper in a Welsh nonconformist society. Consequently, the threat of Welsh difference is not suspended from the film's narrative, as we find in *Love Actually* and *Notting Hill*. The buffoon figure is used in this instance not to repress and override difference, but as a creative tool whereby difference itself can be explored. The flow whereby Hugh Grant's mediator figure modulates between subjective ego and ideal collective is thereby suspended. It is important to explore the reasons for this varying impact of an outwardly similar character.

In *Preface to Film*, Williams combined an early theory of flow with his interest in the history of drama. Arising out of that history, Williams was aware that the whole concept of *character* has a varying history. He says that it 'has acquired certain particular associations, which are the result of historical change rather than anything essential in the dramatic process' (*PF*, p. 9). As an example of this historic variation, Williams points out how the figures of ancient Greek drama cannot really be understood as characters in the same way that those in modern naturalistic drama can. They are more like carnival figures than rounded human beings. Or, again, the allegorical figures of medieval morality plays do not function in the same way as the characters in a Shakespeare play. In medieval allegory, the 'characters' express only the virtue or vice after which they are named. They do not have a biography or a private life. The achievement of Shakespeare, by contrast, was to create characters expressing attributes appropriate to their station in life, who were also able to express individual human identities. The nurse in *Romeo and Juliet* is famous for being both a typical nurse and a precise individual human subject. This would have been impossible in Greek or medieval drama.

If we apply this sense of how the concept of character varies historically to the figure of the charming buffoon, we can see that this figure too undergoes variation with time. Fredric Jameson has noted the temptation to trace the buffoon character across five centuries of European literature, as a continuous symbolic function. He argues that we must resist the temptation to emphasize only continuity, for to do so is to enter into what he calls a *positive hermeneutic*, where the possibility to imagine variation and change would be cancelled. Jameson goes on:

> A negative hermeneutic, then, would on the contrary wish to use the narrative raw material shared by myth and 'historical' literatures to sharpen our sense of historical difference, and to stimulate an increasingly vivid

apprehension of what happens when plot falls into history, so to speak, and enters the force fields of the modern societies.[29]

Jameson is interested in a dialectical historical approach. He suggests that as a given society undergoes historical variation, the comic figure produced in its literature does not simply recur, but undergoes important modifications. This implies that a consideration of historical change is necessary to tell us why these deviations in function occur. *The Englishman Who Went Up a Hill but Came Down a Mountain* deploys the mediating figure of Hugh Grant's charming buffoon. Yet it does not manage the same ideological closure as the other films; it cannot imagine a unified Britain into being. What then is the history into which the plot of this film has fallen, to create such a variation?

The historical context of the film is very much akin to that of the post-devolution Welsh and Scottish novels analysed in chapter 4. It is a film that was produced roughly at the moment of devolution, of self-rule in Scotland and Wales, and of what Raymond Williams finally calls 'the break-up of the United Kingdom' (*WSW*, p. 186). Rather than conjuring away Welsh identity, or treating it as an obstacle to be overcome in the reaffirmation of an ideal united British ego-collective, *The Englishman Who Went Up a Hill but Came Down a Mountain* maintains a sense of the encounter between England and Wales, without allowing one to collapse into the other. This is no doubt partly because it was produced in a Welsh society that was in the process of rediscovering its own confident sense of itself. Or, again, rather than using the figure of a woman to allegorize mythical restitution of Britain's lost unity and global power, the film sidesteps these constructs.

The Englishman Who Went Up a Hill but Came Down a Mountain may seem like a strange choice of film to be invested with qualities of political dissonance and dissent. The quaint tone of rural nostalgia could hardly be said to drive the film towards a strongly oppositional stance with regard to mainstream cinema. It may be the case that whatever oppositional qualities the film does mobilize can only be glimpsed by viewing the film comparatively, alongside the other Hugh Grant English buffoon films, to reveal a fracture in the narrative logic of those filmic flows. In order to see this implicitly oppositional work occurring more explicitly, we have to turn to other films.

If all nations are imagined communities, then the break-up of the nation is also an imagined process. Since the task of fashioning a nation is a large one, it is necessary to present this argument historically, by considering the broadest possible number of texts that participate in this process. Thus the 'devolved Frankensteins' written by Malcolm Pryce (in Wales) and Alasdair Gray (in Scotland) can be located in the context of a whole seam of contemporary Welsh and Scottish writing, where the voice of the outsider is used to question the make-up of official culture. A similar point can be made with regard to the films of the same period.

Kevin Allen's *Twin Town* (1997) and Justin Kerrigan's *Human Traffic* (1999) are both worlds away from the valleys nostalgia of *The English-man Who Went Up a Hill but Came Down a Mountain*. These films present a Welsh culture that is urban as opposed to rural; youthful as opposed to stagnant; and cosmopolitan as opposed to inward looking. By departing from stock notions of Welsh culture in this way, these films participate in the process of exploring Welsh identity as an open-ended question, rather than as an already concluded answer.

Meanwhile, Steve Blandford points out that another Welsh film, Amma Asante's *A Way of Life* (2004), usefully raises the question of 'what constitutes a Welsh film at all'.[30] Asante was raised in London by parents who had emigrated to Britain from West Africa in the 1960s. *A Way of Life* is centred on the murder of a Turkish immigrant to the Welsh valleys. Again, the film departs from stock notions of Welsh identity and does so in a way that complicates any simplistic notion of national identity.

The films of Allen, Kerrigan and Asante all undercut outdated notions of Welshness. This can also be found happening in a series of commercially – and critically – successful films produced in Scotland during the years surrounding devolution. Danny Boyle's *Shallow Grave* (1994), Peter Mullan's *Orphans* (1997) and Lynne Ramsay's *Ratcatcher* (1999) all reject outdated notions of Scottish culture and identity by providing an ironic critique of those very notions. The cultural material-ist point that is then worth making is that these films do not only reflect the gathering cultural self-confidence in Scotland during the period in question. They also contribute to that increase in cultural confidence.

Moreover, since the break-up of Britain is not restricted to the process of devolution in Scotland and Wales, there are several other kinds of film to undertake this kind of ironic critique. Thus *The Full Monty* (Peter Cattaneo, 1997) and *Billy Elliot* (Stephen Daldry, 2000) assert distinctive regional cultures and identities in contradistinction to the metropolitan culture of England's capital city, while Derek Jarman's 1988 film *The Last of England* is a sombre meditation on the ways in which advanced capitalism has destroyed vital communities within the metropolis itself.

Similarly, films produced from within specific ethnic and immigrant communities carry out a radical exploration of the meaning of British identity for British Asian populations. Steve Blandford suggests that Gurhinder Chadra's films *Bhaji on the Beach* (1993), *Bend it Like Beckham* (2002) and *Bride and Prejudice* (2004) 'have all taken totemic icons of Englishness and used them as the basis for a comic exploration of their meaning for British Asian identity'.[31] The 2002 film, *Dirty Pretty Things*, directed by Stephen Frears, tells the story of a group of illegal immigrants in London, and thereby opens up the cinematic record to a group of people who officially do not exist, yet without whom the British economy, the lynchpin on which metropolitan and imperial British culture had been founded, could not operate.

All of these films, on their different terrains, carry out a renegotiation of British identity, and contribute to the imaginative break-up of the British union. The filmic flow of an imagined ideal viewing community is fractured by the making and viewing of these films, which all put deeper questions to the unitary British state. In British film of the 1990s, there is thus a conflict between a mediated reaffirmation of unified identity in the mainstream cinema and valuable oppositional work from these alternative centres of production. As we know from Raymond Williams, this alternative production takes place partly in the name of alternative national traditions in Scotland and Wales. But we also know that it is a much more general process, occurring on a number of other conceptual grounds.

The films of the devolution period were produced after Raymond Williams's death in 1988. By this time, he had already shown significant insight into the processes of symbolic and political break-up that were beginning to accelerate in Britain. Williams developed a critique of the idea of a national tradition in the cinema as part of his general interest in superseding constructions of national identity and national interest at metropolitan level. Tracing the development of Williams's concept of filmic flow enables us to explore how film participates in the ongoing contest over Britain's self-imagining. In other words, Raymond Williams's work can be used to help us to understand the relationship between contemporary film and the break-up of Britain.

Williams's theoretical concept of filmic flow shows us how main-stream cinema offers to conjure away the challenges presented by alternative cinematic production to the unitary British imagination. At the same time, his critique of a single national cinematic tradition also enables us to see that those challenges are not so easily silenced. Rather than being simply concluded, the contest between a unified British identity and the break-up of that image remains open and ongoing. It is a contest that can be seen in the different kinds of film now being produced, and is also a contest taking place outside the cinema, in the society.

A Reconsidered Conclusion: Post-British Williams?

BRITAIN, EMPIRE AND ENGLISH LITERATURE

The foreword to this new edition of *After Raymond Williams* surveyed some of the important recent research into the relationship between the construction of Britain following the 1707 Act of Union, and the foundation of the discipline of English literature during the same period. The principal finding of that research was that the idea of Britain was cultivated by the political and patrician classes through recourse to myth making and the popularization of 'national' narratives of all kinds. During the period of nascent imperialism, the national identity of a greater Britain was cultivated among the people of England, Scotland, Wales and Ireland through the foundation of the discipline of English literature in order to provide a coherent vehicle for the imperialism that would be propounded in the name of that Britain. In other words, the discipline subsequently known as English literature itself has its origins in a British imperialist cultural agenda dating back to the eighteenth century. Implicitly, to enter a post-imperial phase of British history is to enter also a phase of literary history in which the structuring imperial dynamic of the discipline is no longer operative so that it requires redefinition. For this reason, Gayatri Spivak has recently referred to the death of the discipline of English literature as such.[1] Michael Gardiner suggests that since it was an imperialist construct during the period of *British* imperialism, the redefinition of a post-imperial literary culture in England will free contemporary

English writers from the imperial prerogative of the British past, allowing England to develop a healthy, civic, democratic sense of its national culture just as is being attempted in Scotland and Wales.[2]

Although he frequently referred to 'our literature' and 'our history', Raymond Williams was never fully explicit about whether he was referring to a British 'we' or an English or Welsh 'we'. This underlines the extent to which the discipline of English literature offered historically to provide a sense of cohesion across the whole of Britain, and to drive the culture of imperialism on its behalf. After the period of British imperialism has become obsolescent, the British discipline of English literature no longer has access to the same ideological reference point, enabling Scotland, Wales and England to redefine and reassess their literatures and national cultures.

Consistent with his occasional inability to think through the historical conflation of Britain with its constituent nations, the argument presented by the final chapter was that Williams was equally unclear when talking about a national film tradition which nation he was referring to: Britain, England or Wales? Possibly this is because in Britain there has not been as strong a sense of national tradition in film as there is in literature. Possibly again one reason for this is that by the time of the development of the technologies of cinema, the discipline of English literature was already fully established and already performing the ideological and hegemonic work of the imperial period, so that another national cultural tradition was unnecessary. By contrast, the single nation that has the clearest and strongest sense of ownership of a national cinematic tradition is the USA – whose imperialism unfolded at a much later date than Britain's and coincided more closely with the technological developments of the cinema. This suggestion that Britain's national cinematic tradition is comparatively weak should not be taken as a claim that there are not fine filmmakers in Britain; rather that they have not been associated with the cultural and ideological work of imperialism, in the way that the literary tradition has. In this sense, the looseness of a national tradition can be seen as freeing and liberating, and perhaps provides a model for the kind of literary redefinitions that are necessary in the post-union and post-imperial nations of Britain, which are in the process of moving away from that imperialist agenda and trying to develop new cultural forms expressing new, and democratic, national identities.

WILLIAMS AND THE SPECTACLE OF BRITAIN

Like 'the novel' or 'the author', it seems as though 'English literature' is a category that many are eager to declare dead. To some extent, the same is true of the United Kingdom itself. Tom Nairn in *The Break-Up of Britain* and *After Britain* takes the dissolution of the United Kingdom state for granted, suggesting that the spectacles of 1997, when Hong Kong was returned to Chinese rule and Princess Diana was given a large public funeral, represented the last performances on the world stage of a Britsish imperial culture that would evaporate following home rule for Scotland and Wales and hence the break-up of the unitary state.[3] Michael Gardiner makes a similar point about the brief popular cultural movement referred to as 'Brit Pop' during the 1990s, and the establishment of the Millennium Dome.[4]

In the accounts provided by Nairn and Gardiner, the Diana funeral, the return of Hong Kong, Brit Pop and the Millennium Dome are all afforded the status of spectacles of a British imperial culture soon to be rendered obsolete. Raymond Williams situated the last throw of British culture's imperial dice almost twenty years earlier, in the Falklands War of 1982. It was at this historical moment that several of the general trends in his thinking began to line up together: the relationship between culture and technology; a critical literacy with regard to the consumption of media images; and the emergence of a new global political and economic order.

To Williams, the Falklands/Malvinas War had the ontological status of a media-managed spectacle. It was covered in detail on television, radio and in print media. This had the effect of reducing the violence and danger of conflict to a series of carefully orchestrated images that were depthless, and behind which the viewer/reader could not hope to look. The conflict itself was distanced to the other side of the globe and media coverage of the event therefore rendered it strangely unreal, reduced to the status of a game, with surprisingly little sense of urgency or danger. The signals being given off by the political machinery of government were contradictory, overloaded, difficult to interpret. For example, the Thatcher government had spent the first two or three years of its administration bombarding Britain with what Williams calls an 'anti-state rhetoric' in matters of social welfare and public spending. This was suddenly combined with an aggressive 'pro-state rhetoric' in the sphere of policing at home and military sanction overseas (*T2000*,

p. 191). Perplexed by the combination of pro-state rhetoric in military aggression with anti-state rhetoric in matters of social welfare, Williams could not reconcile the versions of British identity he saw perpetuated in media reports during the Falklands episode with his understanding of the British people. In an article entitled 'Problems of the coming period', subsequently collected in *Resources of Hope*, he addresses this difficulty:

> It is not because the British people are excessively nationalist and self-confident that you got the absurd jingoism of the Falklands episode . . . The kind of spectacular consumerist militarism which that episode was – with all the guns going off eight thousand miles away, thus with war reduced, for all but the unfortunate people who were sent there, to television screens, rhetoric, flags and so on – simply cannot be identified with other versions of nationalism, let alone of national identity. It is in absence and distance that this kind of artificial and superficial image of the nation can be generated and temporarily adopted. (*RH*, p. 164).

Williams makes a distinction between the British people and the imperialist warfare prosecuted in their name while travestying their ideals. Such a distinction pre-empts Arthur Aughey's more recent concept of the *constitutional people*. It was argued in the foreword to this new edition of *After Raymond Williams* that Aughey's constitutional people are re-defined as civic citizens rather than imperial subjects during the historical transition away from imperialism. Moreover, in Aughey's sense imperial subjects are also defined historically as British subjects, whereas during the later period the constitutional people are understood more precisely as English citizens, Scottish citizens, Welsh citizens and Northern Irish citizens. That is to say, implicit in Aughey's account of the historical transition from imperial subjecthood to constitutional people there is also an account of the civic rediscovery of different post-British national identities. Williams's distinction between the people and a travestied version of their interests can be seen as an embryonic form of Aughey's later extrapolation of the constitutional people in the civic sense, without quite making the connection to the post-British sense. In other words, Aughey renders explicit what was already implicit to some extent in Williams's distinction – that Britishness was associated with the imperial agenda of the past so that consciously sloughing off the unitary identity of imperial Britishness restores a commitment to constitutional democracy to the people of each of the nations. Writing since devolution, Aughey elucidates much more fully than Williams was able to the need to define the constitutional peoples of each nation. Writing before devolution, Williams was unable to make that definition in theory because the historical circumstances did not yet allow the step from *Britain* to post-British *nations* to be made. Only retrospectively can Williams be said to have been attempting to take that step. In other words, Williams saw in the spectacle of the Falklands War in 1982 the last act of Britain's imperial drama on the world stage – a last act that Nairn associates with events in Hong Kong in 1997 and Gardiner with the Millennium Dome in 2000.

Stemming from these and other ascriptions, it has become something of a tradition to declare the last of Britain. Robert Hewison argued in *The Heritage Industry*, for example, that among the largest barriers to a confident contemporary culture in Britain are those institutions that present an idealized version of Britiain's cultural past, converting contemporary Britain into an island museum with the effect of inhibiting cultural growth.[5] Contra those proclamations of the end of Britain, Arthur Aughey has argued that despite the relish with which some commentators declare the twilight of the British state, the United Kingdom has not yet fallen into the dissolution that Nairn thought was inevitable. Fully fifteen years after the Diana affair, Hong Kong, Brit Pop and the Millennium Dome, therefore, British culture was again paraded for another 'last' outing on the world stage in the guise of the London 2012 Olympic Games.

That the opening ceremony of London 2012 was directed by a film director, Danny Boyle, is highly significant because – it has been suggested here – Britain's tradition in film, if there is one at all, has not been associated with the period and ideology of British imperialism – as have the traditions of literature and theatre. Boyle's opening ceremony was highly filmic in style, portraying the history of the Industrial Revolution from the perspective of the workers who drove those industries; the history of gender equality in Britain from the perspective of the suffragettes; the history of the welfare state from the perspective of the doctors and nurses who worked for it; and the history of multicultural Britain from the perspective of first, second and third generation immigrants. In other words, Boyle portrayed the contribution made by the constitutional people to the effective civic functioning of Britain's political state, rather than portraying its imperialist culture that really belongs to an earlier period.

On the other hand, and as with Raymond Williams, it was not quite clear in Boyle's opening ceremony which people were being celebrated: British or English. The performances were non-verbal, making literal interpretations of the history that was being staged difficult to extrapolate. This was true not only of the opening ceremony but also of the games themselves. There was significant unease over the question of whether it was appropriate for Great Britain to enter a football team, whereas normally the nations of Britain have separate, individual national teams. The British cycling team achieved considerable success, which was attributed in part to the excellent training facilities available to them at the national velodrome in Manchester. But there is also a 'national' velodrome in Newport, south Wales, which the British team had frequently used in preparation for the previous Olympics in Beijing in 2008. Thus the tricky question that was unanswered by the non-verbal nature of the opening ceremony rippled through the performance of the teams and the competitors throughout the games. Is there a British nation in football terms? Is the Manchester cycling centre an English national centre or a British one? Was the host nation Britain or England?

How one perceives the answers to these questions will say much about how to interpret London 2012 as a whole. If it is seen as primarily a British festival, it will necessarily take its place in the line of 'last' performances of British public culture on the world stage – with the lowering of the Olympic flag during the closing ceremony of London in 2012 perhaps recalling and repeating the lowering of the imperial flag in Hong Kong in 1997. If, on the other hand, the ceremony and the games are primarily seen as a celebration of the contribution made specifically by the people of England to a specifically English populist, political, national culture, then London 2012 will not be seen as yet another last outing for a British imperial culture on the world stage, but rather as the first articulation of an English, and in this sense post-British, cultural consciousness. Is there any reason, given that such a consciousness is precisely what the nationalist movements in the other nations of Britain have been trying to articulate for themselves since before devolution, that they should shy away from such an interpretation of the London Olympics or from this new sense of Englishness?

ENGLISHNESS AND DEVOLUTION

It has been argued here that Raymond Williams actively worked to establish self-governance in Wales and hence to bring about the break-up of the British union. His novels imagined that break-up into existence at least eighteen years before self-government for Scotland and Wales was realised in 1997. He foresaw that, as a process, devolution would be complex and lengthy rather than established once and for all time. Indeed, the process itself is still only gradually being worked out and Williams remains a significant figure in our understanding of the different contemporary postcolonial cultures within Britain – including England.

In his late essay 'Are we becoming more divided?', Williams drew attention to two possible kinds of English reaction to the nationalist movements in Scotland and Wales. The first of these was what Williams referred to as the 'unity backlash', in which, Williams explained, the Thatcherite government and its spokesmen would seek to forestall and prevent other groups of people from gaining control of their own resources at local level (*WSW*, p. 189). The 'unity backlash' would, Williams warned, be carried out in the name of British unity, and was likely to combine powerful emotional appeal with economic and political rhetoric in the dissemination of a broader national interest that would be inflicted on the people rather than generated by them.

There was, however, a second possible English response to the nationalist movements in Scotland and Wales, and Williams referred to this second reaction as the 'why not us?' backlash (*WSW*, p. 189). Williams used the term 'why not us?' to draw attention to the latent fact that what many of the things nationalist political groups in Scotland and Wales were aiming to achieve were also real material aims for diverse and under-represented sections of the English population. He used the rhetorical question, 'why not us?' to suggest that if new attempts at gaining real political control could be made in Scotland and Wales, despite the attempts made to forestall that attempt through the conflation of British *national* with specialized *class* interest, then the same oppositional work could also be carried out within England itself. In other words, 'why not us?' is a response to devolution that should not really be seen as a 'backlash' – with all the negative connotations implied by that term – at all. Rather, 'why not us?' is a position that sees the increase of self-government in Scotland and Wales as an opportunity to interrogate forms of cultural and political representation in England. Because 'why not us?' is a response to the nationalisms of Scotland and Wales that identifies an opportunity for redefining an effective, civic, popular, political nationalism in England, and hence offers to contribute to a democratic renewal across Britain, Williams stated that it is a response that 'every genuine nationalist would welcome' (*WSW*, p. 189).

Of the two potential backlashes in England against self-rule in Scotland and Wales that Williams discussed, the second, that is, the 'Why not us?' response, can be identified as the one that sees devolution as an opportunity for creating new forms of representation – both in England and of the English. It is a response that sees devolution as causally belated from an English standpoint in the sense that a positive English reaction to Scottish and Welsh self-government would be to try to work for the same access to rights of decision and legal and political processes that are becoming available in those nations. In literary terms, this book has argued that literature and culture play a complex role in helping people to form values and judgements that are political as well as cultural, and hence that the distinctive literary cultures of Scotland and Wales have helped to contribute to the growing national political consciousness of each nation. It was argued in chapter 2 that the Library of Wales represented a major development in Welsh cultural reclamation. As we have seen, the overall concept of 'English literature' has residual implications of British imperial ideology. To develop a literature of England as distinct from the overall British canon of English literature would be to emulate in England the process of literary and cultural rediscovery that has already started in Scotland and Wales. In other words, the challenge for English writers laid down by the process of devolution is to try to separate precise literary practices in England from the overall canon of English literature – a canon that, for historical reasons, has been inculcated with a British nationalist ideology and an imperial prerogative. In addressing this challenge to historical construction and imperial ideology, English writers are entering a new phase of cultural catch-up, specifically in the now well-established post-imperial practice of 'writing back'.

'Writing back' is a cultural practice that originated in decolonizing and postcolonial societies in the early decades of postcolonial history. Typically, a postcolonial writer interested in the cultural tactic of 'writing back' would start off with a canonical text of European literature from the period of empire and seek opportunities for the insertion of previously marginalized, outcast or neglected voices – in other words, for the insertion of the voice of the colonial 'Other'. 'Writing back' was a technique that challenged European readers to see the world in a new way, from the perspective of this oppressed or neglected 'Other'. At the same time, it created opportunities for readers in the newly decolonized societies to reimagine their own relationship to the former imperial centre and hence re-inscribed a new and radical anti-colonial consciousness. Bill Ashcroft describes 'writing back' as a 'project of post-colonial writing' that aimed to 'interrogate European discourse and discursive strategies from its position within and between two worlds; to investigate the means by which Europe imposed and maintained its codes in its colonial domination of so much of the rest of the world.'[6] That is to say, European literature from the period of empire implicitly assumed and at times explicitly portrayed a series of global hierarchical relationships in which the power of the metro-politan centre and the subordination of people at the periphery became entrenched and reinforced through repeated assertion of the dominant ideology. To approach the canonical works of that period in a new way and to create in those works a perspective capable of questioning the assumed superiority of empire was to engage in a cultural practice that was also a political orientation. Ashcroft suggests that 'the re-reading and the rewriting of the European historical and fictional record' was 'a vital and inescapable task at the heart of the post-colonial enterprise,' because it was a cultural practice that challenged political structures and thereby offered to change them.[7]

Jean Rhys's *Wide Sargasso Sea*, Derek Walcott's *Omeros* and Peter Carey's *Jack Maggs* are all examples of 'writing back'. In each case, a well-known text of European culture is taken apart and reconstructed from the viewpoint of a colonial 'Other', enabling the establishment of a new narrative of identity, in contradistinction to the imperial assump-tions that permeate the foundational texts. The dates of these now-established works of postcolonial literature are particularly instructive: *Wide Sargasso Sea* was published in 1966, *Omeros* in 1990, and *Jack Maggs* in 1997. These dates indicate that 'writing back' was a cultural practice that was already well established in the former colonies by the time of the second devolution referenda in Scotland and Wales in 1997. Moreover, in keeping with the general tendency among Scottish and Welsh writers to see their own nations and cultures as postcolonial cultures, 'writing back' had also become common in the works of writers from those nations by the time of the opening of the new Scottish Parliament and Welsh National Assembly in 1999.[8] Hence it was argued in chapter 4 that by 'writing back' to *Frankenstein*, Alasdair Gray's *Poor Things* and Malcolm Pryce's *Last Tango in Aberystwyth* reversed the tight association that has been made in the early imperial period between English literature and cultural Britishness from their specific post-British positions in Scotland and Wales. By contrast, during the 1990s the writers of England had not yet started to see their own literary culture as post-British, and had not yet started to 'write back' to the British canon.

It was further argued in chapter 4 that writers in Scotland and Wales both before and during the process of devolution generated literary practices not amenable to incorporation within the dominant mainstream of British 'English literature' and used those practices to explore and assert cultural difference. In England, the 'why not us?' reaction to a growing sense of nationhood in Scotland and Wales is one that identifies those cultural nationalisms as ones to emulate in a causally belated manner. In this sense, the cultural workers of a post-devolution England could seek to catch up with the cultural work of 'writing back' that had already developed in the former colonies and in the other nations of Britain. For this reason, 'writing back' has already become a historical practice in certain postcolonial societies, but is a more recent practice for writers in England. Seeking to undo the conflation of 'English literature' with 'Britishness' will enable the development of new literary practices that depart from the older imperial assumptions and in this sense catch up with the cultural opportunities presented by devolution.

It was also suggested in chapter 4 that Graham Swift's 1996 novel *Last Orders* is an example of the causally belated 'writing back' that started to develop in England at approximately the same time as devolution in Britain – a generation after it had already been developed in decolonizing societies. *Last Orders* narrates a journey undertaken by four friends of the deceased butcher Jack Dodds to Margate in Kent to scatter his ashes from the pier there. The text is narrated in the form of a series of monologues spoken by the four protagonists Ray, Lenny, Vince and Vic. From these monologues, readers learn about the complex and precarious relationships that each man had with Jack before his death. Each monologue is also interrupted by sections named after the particular places that the pilgrims are passing through: Blackheath, Gravesend, Chatham, Canterbury. In other words, just as Jean Rhys's *Wide Sargasso Sea* 'writes back' to Charlotte Brontë's *Jane Eyre* and Peter Carey's *Jack Maggs* 'writes back' to Dickens's *Great Expectations*, so too Graham Swift's *Last Orders* 'writes back' to Geoffrey Chaucer's *Canterbury Tales*. Though they visit Canterbury Cathedral, however, Swift's protagonists do not 'end' their journey there because they are 'going on' to Margate.[9] In other words, Swift hints from the beginning that the journey undertaken by his travellers will be physically longer than that of Chaucer's, as if Swift is interested in enlarging our understanding of the myriad lives involved in it.

The Canterbury Tales are notable, by the standards of a medieval text, for the astonishing social range that they depict. The same is almost certainly not true, however, of the relationships in which the text itself was produced: a network of courtly patronage creating and promulgating work for an educated, patrician and privileged reader-ship. Chaucer's pilgrims travel to Canterbury to visit the shrine of Thomas Beckett so that the journey conveys an overt memorial function in which the murder of the outspoken bishop becomes converted into a moment of narrative origin for the medieval court. The *Tales* them-selves were retrospectively assimilated to the British canon of English literature, which at times they have even been seen as having instigated.

Last Orders also enacts the cultural work of memory and remem-brance, but this time without the imbrication of narrative function with a British canon of works. That Swift puts into the mouths of each of his characters their own monologues creates the effect of a private relation-ship between speaker and reader, where the reader is now re-imagined by the text as a listener or confidant. In other words, Chaucer's pilgrims tell tales about other people, and the tales they tell become part of the texture of their narrative and its collective self-imagining. Swift's travellers, by contrast, tell their 'own' stories in a private relationship between speaker and listener that is not laid down for public utility and which serves as a kind of history from below.

By 'writing back' to *The Canterbury Tales*, Swift in *Last Orders* hints at the possibility of making a distinction between 'English literature' as defined along British canonical lines and the diverse experience of working-class communities previously under-represented in the canon. Swift's portrayal of working-class lives, and of the close association that exists between memory, identity and location, suggests a new political topology that moves towards an enlarged understanding of the cultural politics of place. In this sense, Swift embraces the opportunity both necessitated and enabled by transition away from British Empire and British union to examine and regenerate diverse narratives of English identity – just as has been happening in the other post-British nations during the same period.

The political process of devolution has created an opportunity to carry out such work by creating the possibility that members of different communities in England could work for many of the same things that were being worked for by the nationalist movements in Scotland and Wales: local control of resources, and immediate access to decision-making processes. For this reason, the political process of devolution included the 2003 Regional Assemblies Bill, which laid down a timetable for holding similar referenda to those of Scotland and Wales in the North West, the North East and Yorkshire.

In the elections of Autumn 2004, the campaign for a North East Assembly was heavily defeated, with the result that the assembly that was eventually created there was a relatively loose, informal and short-lived congeries of local government councils in the region, and was abolished altogether in 2009. The South West Regional Assembly followed a similar trajectory: it was established without referendum in 2000 with a mandate to promote the economic, social and environmental wellbeing of the South West region and those who live and work there. It too was a relatively informal grouping of members from the 51 different local government authorities in the South West region, meeting no more than three times per year. In practice, it was primarily concerned with issues of planning, housing and transportation, although the first two of these roles were revoked by the Conservative-Liberal Democrat coalition government following the 2010 general election, by which time the South West Regional Assembly itself was already defunct.

The fate of the South West Regional Assembly and of the region's planning and housing roles under the management of the first Conservative government to take office since devolution is a clear example of what Raymond Williams called the 'unity' backlash. Access to decision-making processes and powers of control over resources at local level were forestalled in the name of a putative economic national interest. This contrasts sharply with the 'why not us?' reaction, which, as Williams defined it, would unlock specific regional needs at local level from the economic interest of one sector. He showed that the single interests of the corporate sector had been substituted for the diverse needs of the various people of the wider nation in the name of 'national' interest or 'unity', and suggested that a more democratic response to devolution would be to try to separate those things.

In a sense, 'Why not us?' is the question rhetorically asked of working-class communities in the South West of England by Alan Kent's 2005 novel, *Proper Job, Charlie Curnow!* The novel challenges dominant images of Cornwall as a wealthy, privileged and Edenic part of the country and attempts to bring onto the literary record a kind of working-class experience. Kent attempts to articulate through Charlie's musical dreams a new cultural confidence on the part of the southern English working class and hence to give the English people an idea of themselves as a confident and functioning nation. This is envisaged as distinct from the earlier sense of British identity that, as Tom Nairn showed, was really based on class exclusion and on lack of cultural confidence among the English working class due to the lack of available models of a confident English people. The 'selective' version can be seen in the character Beverley's highly romanticized idea of Charlie's Cornish identity: 'In another age he'd have been inventing steam engines, or discovering lodes of copper, or smuggling whisky in from the coast. Now, he was making modern rock music an' after world domination of the album charts. She hadn't met anyone like him.'[10]

Kent depicts Charlie and his band aspiring to use their music to transform external images of Cornwall because the working people of Cornwall have been subjected to a highly selective and distorting version of who they are and therefore of what their economic interests represent. The received, romantic imagery of Cornwall as a land of railway engineers such as Richard Trevithick, or of miners or smugglers, creates an impression of a landscape of opportunity and of a people full of unbridled frontier spirit. It is an image that contrasts with the economic conditions, educational availability and professional un-fulfillment that Charlie represents and which Kent wishes his readers to see as a different version of contemporary relationships in Cornwall. In this sense, the title character is highly symbolic: the name Charlie Curnow, or Charles Cornwall, appears to suggest an ironic contrast between members of the urban working-class people of the peninsula, and that other Charles, Prince Charles of the Duchy of Cornwall. Just as Swift rejects the 'King's List' version of English history in *Last*

Orders, so too Kent rejects the 'King's List' version of contemporary cultural nationhood and tries to foster an articulate, populist idea of the English people on which a new and confident English nationalism might be based, and which, arguably, was celebrated in Danny Boyle's opening ceremony for the London 2012 Olympic Games. Kent, like Swift, starts with a series of received ideas about regional identity and regional interest and tries in his fiction to enlarge his readers' understanding of both these things. His fiction moves from the 'unity' backlash against regional political and economic control towards the 'why not us?' reaction by challenging the unitary identities and interests of an earlier period.

THE QUESTION OF BRITAIN

Proper Job, Charlie Kurnow! was published eight years after the successful referenda in Scotland and Wales. Reading it in the context of other English works of the post-devolutionary period reveals a gradual shift in emphasis both in political structures and cultural practices. In other words, a contextual reading of English writing since devolution points to devolution itself as an ongoing process rather than a stable product.

In the light of this fluid sense of political and cultural processes, this reconsidered conclusion has argued that Raymond Williams's practice of cultural materialism can be used to inform our understanding of the process of devolution across Britain. Much of Williams's writing was produced for specific occasions. The period leading up to the first referendum on self-rule for Wales and Scotland in the 1970s provided the context in which Williams developed some of the best-known concepts in his thinking: the relationship between *dominant, emergent* and *residual* cultural forms, and the notion of how historical change is initially generated through the gradual build up of *pre-emergent* practices. This critical vocabulary for the sophisticated analysis of culture was developed in 1977–8, at the time of the campaign for Welsh self-government in which Williams was involved. Thus, not only do those concepts help us understand the recent political history of Wales; but it is also true that that history of Wales helps us understand how Williams developed the concepts. This underlines the dialectical relationship between kinds of writing and historical processes by which Williams characterizes cultural materialism and which is particularly evident in post-devolution literature in Scotland and Wales. There has been a change in the quantity and kind of literary production in those nations, reflecting their increased cultural confidence. At the same time, the increased cultural confidence of those nations is itself partly generated by the literary production.

This reconsidered conclusion to the second edition of *After Raymond Williams* has stressed that to explore the relationship between political changes in the United Kingdom's state structure and contemporary literary and cultural production in Britain is not simply to chart a literary history of devolution in Scotland and Wales. It has argued that because the United Kingdom was at least in part an imperial construct, and because the fusion of English, Scottish, Welsh and Irish people into British subjects coincided with imperialism, the people of those same nations will only be able to free themselves from a residual commitment to imperial culture by adjusting their perspective towards a new post-British and therefore necessarily post-imperial orientation.

Just as devolution has created an opportunity for writers in Scotland and Wales to interrogate or re-negotiate their own positioning with regard to a British mainstream of 'English literature' that is in the process of becoming obsolescent, so too the same opportunity is available for English writers to depart from the unitary, nationalist and imperial cultural monoliths that characterized an earlier historical period. In other words, the unfolding of devolution is simultaneously a political process and a cultural process. It both necessitates and enables a new cultural politics in each of the nations of Britain, decoupling contemporary writers from a canonical, unitary and hegemonic English literature and hence indicating a subtle shift in understanding, from 'writers of English literature' to 'writers who are English' or 'writers who are Welsh' and so on. Whether the people in those nations continue to see themselves as 'British and English', 'British and Scottish', 'British and Welsh' or 'British and Northern Irish' or whether they increasingly express their national identities as '*not* British *but* English' or '*not* British *but* Welsh' will depend on a series of political structures that do not yet exist.

Williams was unable to foresee precisely how those structures would develop and at the start of 2013 the future of the unitary British state remains an open question. As we have seen, the break-up of the political state is still by no means a done deal, whatever other writers might have urged. One thing that Williams was certain about in the 1970s, however, was that some change was necessary in the political forms available in late twentieth-century Britain. The need to move beyond a residually imperial unitary British political culture and embrace instead a range of different forms of representation was a topic for which he reserved some of his strongest arguments. Thus on the subject of nationalist movements in Scotland and Wales, he wrote in 'Are we becoming more divided?' that the imposition of a central political system on the diverse peoples of Britain was in fact a barrier to any real potential cooperation between them and hence should be replaced by a range of different political bodies in the different nations and regions:

> Unless in one way or another people can get effective positive control of their own places and their own lives, this complex industrial society will smash itself up, with increasing hatred and bitterness, not in spite of but because of the imposed and artificial unity which the existing system is fighting to maintain . . . Once you are not controlled, in advance and systematically, by others, you soon discover the kinds of co-operation, between nations, between regions, between communities, on which any full life depends. But it is then your willing and not your enforced co-operation. That is why I, with many others, now want and work to divide, as a way of declaring our own interests, certainly, but also as a way of finding new and willing forms of co-operation: the only kind of co-operation that any free people can call unity. (*WSW*, pp. 189–90)

Williams did not go as far as Tom Nairn and suggest that the break-up of Britain's political state was inevitable. On the other hand, he did believe that the unitary system in existence when he was writing had become outmoded, historically obsolete, and in need of reform, providing self-rule for the people of Britain at every available level, from the local to the national – where national refers to the individual nations rather than to the United Kingdom as a whole. Whether that self-governance need inevitably imply absolute political separatism between some or all of the nations is far from proven. Whether the nations themselves might gain increasing political autonomy while also continuing to function in tandem in a loose confederation of autonomous states has as yet barely been questioned. What the political forms that would create such a confederation might look like has also not really been substantiated.

Williams himself seemed to come down on the side of 'British and Welsh' or 'British and English' rather than 'not British but Welsh' or 'not British but English.' The proposals he made in *Resources of Hope* and *Towards 2000* for the establishment of autonomous bodies in Scotland, Wales and different English regions appear to have been proposals for a re-defined – as opposed to entirely abolished – political union. In this sense his work is committed to a break-up of the singularity of political unit in Britain, without necessarily proposing a breakaway.

NOTES

Introduction

[1] Williams mentions Hechter's work in his 1983 essay 'Wales and England,' recently reprinted in the anthology *Who Speaks for Wales?*, ed. Daniel Williams (Cardiff: University of Wales Press, 2003), p. 25. Cited hereafter as *WSW*.

[2] Williams refers to *The Break-Up of Britain* in *Politics and Letters: Interviews with New Left Review* (London: New Left Books, 1979), p. 381. Cited hereafter as *PL*.

[3] Patrick Brantlinger, *Crusoe's Footprints: Cultural Studies in Britain and America* (London: Routledge, 1990), p. 36.

[4] Andrew Milner, *Cultural Materialism* (Melbourne: University of Melbourne Press, 1993), p. 48, and Anthony Easthope, *Literary into Cultural Studies* (London: Routledge, 1991), p. 67.

[5] Raymond Williams, *Resources of Hope*, ed. Robin Gable (London: Verso, 1988), p. 111. Cited hereafter as *RH*.

[6] Eric Hobsbawm, ed., *The Invention of Tradition* (Cambridge: Cambridge University Press, 1985), pp. 1–14.

[7] Linda Colley, *Britons: Forging the Nation 1707–1837* (London: Yale University Press, 2005).

[8] Raymond Williams, *What I Came to Say* (London: Radius, 1990), p. 124. Cited hereafter as *WCS*.

[9] Raymond Williams, *The Long Revolution* (Harmondsworth: Penguin, 1965), p. 190. Cited hereafter as *LR*.

[10] Benedict Anderson, *Imagined Communities: Reflections on the Origins and Spread of Nationalism* (London: Verso, 1991), pp. 6–7.

[11] Ibid., p. 36.

[12] Ibid., p. 29.

[13] Ibid., p. 30. Emphasis in original.

[14] Quoted in Raymond Williams, *WSW*, p. 35.

[15] Anderson, *Imagined Communities*, p. 34.

[16] Ibid., p. 35.

[17] Ibid., p. 194.

[18] Quoted in ibid., p. 200.

[19] Ibid., pp. 199–201.

[20] Ibid., p. 206.

[21] Tom Nairn, *The Break-Up of Britain* (London: Verso, 1981), p. 15.

[22] Ibid., p. 17.

[23] Williams, *The Politics of Modernism* (London: Verso, 1989), p. 31. Cited hereafter as *PM*.

[24] Nairn, *The Break-Up of Britain*, pp. 64–5.

[25] Ibid., p. 41.

[26] Ibid., p. 73.

[27] Ibid.

[28] Homi Bhabha, *Nation and Narration* (London: Routledge, 1990), pp. 3–4 and 305.

[29] Homi Bhabha, *The Location of Culture* (London: Routledge, 1994), ch. 9.

[30] Raymond Williams, *Marxism and Literature* (Oxford: Oxford Paperbacks, 1977), p. 121. Cited hereafter as *ML*.

1: Towards a Materialism of Culture

[1] Wilson declares in his introduction that his approach to cultural materialism is 'to interrogate materialism by introducing the psychoanalytic notion of the real . . . in Jacques Lacan'. See Scott Wilson, *Cultural Materialism* (Oxford: Blackwell, 1995), p. ix.

[2] Brannigan argues that the two founding texts of cultural materialism are Raymond Williams's *Marxism and Literature* and Michel Foucault's *The History of Sexuality*. Alan Sinfield combines the work of Williams and Lacan in his analysis of Shakespeare's *Othello* and *Macbeth*. See John Brannigan, *New Historicism and Cultural Materialism* (London: Macmillan, 1998), pp. 49–53; and Alan Sinfield, *Faultlines: Cultural Materialism and the Politics of Dissident Reading* (Oxford: Clarendon, 1992), pp. 52–79.

[3] Williams says in his autobiographical interviews, published as *Politics and Letters* in 1979, 'I have never felt that Freud and Marx could be combined in that way. There can be no useful compromise between a description of basic realities as ahistorical and universal and a description of them as diversely created or modified by a changing human history' (*PL*, pp. 183–4).

[4] Alan Sinfield discusses 'the importance of Raymond Williams' in the introduction to *Faultlines*. Scott Wilson similarly describes 'the work of Raymond Williams' as 'seminal', while Brannigan accords Williams 'key theorist' status in discussing the origins of cultural materialism. See Sinfield, *Faultlines*, p. 9; Wilson, *Cultural Materialism, p.* ix; and Brannigan, *New Historicism and Cultural Materialism*, pp. 31–3.

5 The best-known of these studies are E. M. W. Tillyard, *The Elizabethan World Picture* (1943; London: Pimlico, 1998) and *Shakespeare's History Plays* (1944; Harmondsworth: Penguin, 1991).

6 F. R. Leavis, *The Great Tradition* (1948; London, 1979), p. 7. Emphasis in original.

7 Williams clarifies this in *PL*, p. 190.

8 Raymond Williams, *Drama from Ibsen to Eliot* (London: Chatto and Windus, 1952), p. 12. Cited hereafter as *DIE*.

9 T. S. Eliot, *The Sacred Wood: Essays on Poetry and Criticism* (London: Faber and Faber, 1997), p. 48.

10 The rapprochement with Leavis is discussed by Andrew Milner in his *Literature, Culture and Society* (London: University College Press, 1996), p. 34.

11 For an account of Williams's eventual break with Leavis see R. P. Bilan, 'Raymond Williams: From Leavis to Marx', in *Queens Quarterly*, 87 (1980).

12 Raymond Williams, *Culture and Society* (1958; Harmondsworth: Penguin, 1963), p. 289. Cited hereafter as *CS*.

13 The foundation of this approach is generally held to be Marx's 'Preface' to *A Contribution to the Critique of Political Economy*. See Karl Marx, *The Marx–Engels Reader*, ed. Robert C. Tucker (London: Norton, 1975), p. 5.

14 Though Williams's own definitions here seem vague, Patrick Brantlinger suggests that vagueness was the price he paid for a 'remarkable openness to history and diversity'. See Patrick Brantlinger, *Crusoe's Footprints: Cultural Studies in Britain and America* (London: Routledge, 1990), p. 58.

15 However, Williams himself was somewhat guilty of neglecting the system of nurture, and this has provoked considerable critique, especially from feminists. Morag Shiach suggests that Williams understood 'nurture' as a metaphor for 'women in general'. She concludes that, as a result, feminists may find many useful ideas in the work of Williams, but are unlikely to 'find many women'. Morag Shiach, 'A Gendered History of Cultural Categories', in Christopher Prendergast (ed.), *Cultural Materialism: On Raymond Williams* (Minneapolis: University of Minnesota Press, 1995), p. 51.

16 Louis Althusser, *For Marx*, trans. Ben Brewster (New York: Pantheon, 1969), p. 111.

17 Raymond Williams, *Writing in Society* (London: Verso, 1984), pp. 142–9 and 158–60. Cited hereafter as *WS*.

18 Stuart Hall, 'Politics and letters', in Terry Eagleton (ed.), *Raymond Williams: Critical Perspectives* (Cambridge: Polity, 1989), p. 64.

19 Raymond Williams, 'Social environment and theatrical environment: the case of English naturalism', in *Problems in Materialism and Culture* (London: Verso, 1980), p. 134. Cited hereafter as *PMC*.

20 Raymond Williams, *Drama from Ibsen to Brecht* (London: Hogarth, 1987), p. 90. Cited hereafter as *DIB*.

21 *Purposive rationality* is a term coined by the German rationalist Jürgen Habermas to draw attention to the ways in which the nation-state, the capitalist economy and modern legal systems operate without regard to human subjectivity. See Jürgen Habermas, *Theory of Communicative Action, Volume*

One: Reason and the Rationalization of Society, trans. Thomas McCarthy (London: Heinemann, 1984), pp. 217–21.

22 This is certainly how Terry Eagleton describes it, in his *Raymond Williams: Critical Perspectives* (Cambridge: Polity, 1989), pp. 6–8.

23 Williams mentions Rossi-Landi and Chomsky in *PL* pp. 182 and 341 respectively. On Williams and Benveniste, see Michael Moriarty, 'The Longest Cultural Journey: Raymond Williams and French Theory', in Christopher Prendergast (ed.), *Cultural Materialism: On Raymond Williams* (Minneapolis: University of Minnesota Press, 1995), pp. 95–6.

24 Julia Kristeva, *Revolution in Poetic Language*, trans. Margaret Waller (New York: Columbia University Press, 1984), p. 16.

25 Ibid., p. 83.

26 Edward Said provides a fuller argument for understanding Freud as a modern *writer* in his *Beginnings: Intention and Method* (London: Granta, 1997), pp. 161–74.

27 Fred Inglis discusses this affair in his biography, *Raymond Williams* (London: Routledge, 1995), pp. 278–84.

28 Raymond Williams, *Keywords: A Vocabulary of Culture and Society*, 2nd edn (Glasgow: Fontana, 1983).

29 Georg Lukács, 'Narrate or Describe?', in his *Writer and Critic*, trans. Arthur Kahn (London: Merlin, 1978), pp. 111–47. Tony Pinkney discusses the distinction in relation to Williams in his *Raymond Williams* (Bridgend: Seren, 1991), p. 72.

2: *The Welsh Identity of Raymond Williams*

1 Raymond Williams, 'Working-class, proletarian, socialist: problems in some Welsh novels', in H. Gustav Klaus (ed.), *The Socialist Novel in Britain* (Brighton: Harvester, 1982), pp. 110–21. Reprinted in Raymond Williams, *Who Speaks for Wales?* (Cardiff: University of Wales Press, 2003). Hereafter cited as 'Working-class, proletarian, socialist'; page numbers refer to the later edition.

2 Raymond Williams, 'The Welsh industrial novel', in *Who Speaks for Wales?* (Cardiff: University of Wales Press, 2003), p. 103. Cited hereafter as 'Welsh industrial novel.'

3 Williams, 'Working-class, proletarian, socialist', p. 152.

4 Dai Smith has analysed the relationship of industrialisation to new kinds of writing produced in Wales in his 'Relating to Wales', in Terry Eagleton (ed.), *Raymond Williams: Critical Perspectives* (Cambridge: Polity, 1989), pp. 34–53.

5 Raymond Williams, *The Country and the City* (1973; London: Hogarth, 1985), p. 189. Cited hereafter as *CC*.

6 Raymond Williams, *Culture* (Glasgow: Fontana, 1981), pp. 74–83.

7 Raymond Williams, *Border Country* (Harmondsworth: Penguin, 1964), p. 271. Cited hereafter as *BC*.

8 Raymond Williams, *The Fight for Manod* (London: Chatto and Windus, 1979), p. 28. Cited hereafter as *FM*.

9   Raymond Williams, *Loyalties* (London: Hogarth, 1989), pp. 242–3. Cited here-
     after as *L*.
10   One of the few commentaries on Williams's drama is Bernard Sharrat, 'In Whose
     Voice? The Drama of Raymond Williams', in Terry Eagleton (ed.), *Raymond
     Williams: Critical Perspectives* (Cambridge: Polity, 1989), pp. 130–49.
11   Prys Morgan provided seminal analysis of the retrospective creation of an
     ideologically motivated Welsh tradition in his 'From a view to a death: the
     hunt for the Welsh past in the romantic period', in Eric Hobsbawm (ed.),
     The Invention of Tradition (Cambridge: Cambridge University Press, 1983).
12   Jasmine Donahaye analyses the process of selecting material for the Library
     of Wales in her 'Is there anybody out there?', *New Welsh Review* 77, Autumn
     2007.
13   Tom Nairn, *After Britain* (London: Granta, 2001), p. 82.
14   Williams left Plaid Cymru in the 1970s only because he found it difficult to
     'discharge his obligations living at a distance from Wales' (*WSW*, p. 206).
15   Tom Nairn notes that 'intimations of United Kingdom mortality' include the
     end of empire, self-rule in Scotland and Wales and 'stirrings of republicanism'.
     See Nairn, *After Britain: New Labour and the Return of Scotland* (London:
     Granta, 2001), p. 42.
16   Raymond Williams, 'The tenses of imagination', in *Writing in Society* pp. 260–1.
17   Some of the Welsh literature, music and film from the period is discussed by
     Jane Aaron and Wynn Thomas in 'Pulling you through changes: Welsh writing
     in English before, between and after two referenda', in M. Wynn Thomas
     (ed.), *Welsh Writing in English* (Cardiff: University of Wales Press, 2003),
     pp. 278–309.

3: Universities – Hard and Soft

1   Bill Readings, *The University in Ruins* (Cambridge, Massachusetts: Harvard
     University Press, 1996), p. 65.
2   Raymond Williams, 'Cambridge English, Past and Present', in *Writing in Society*
     (London: Verso, 1984); p. 180. Cited hereafter as 'Cambridge English'.
3   Terry Eagleton, *Literary Theory* (Oxford: Blackwell, 1985), pp. 28–30.
4   Tom Nairn, *The Break-Up of Britain* (London: Verso, 1981), p. 100.
5   Eric Hobsbawm, *The Invention of Tradition* (Cambridge: Cambridge University
     Press, 1984), pp. 1–14.
6   Gauri Viswanathan, *Masks of Conquest: Literary Study and British Rule in India*
     (London: Faber and Faber, 1990), p. 23.
7   Benedict Anderson, *Imagined Communities* (London: Verso, 1991), p. 90.
8   Quoted in Anderson, *Imagined Communities*, p. 91.
9   Viswanathan, *Masks of Conquest*, p. 6.
10   Ibid., p. 153; p. 113.

[11]   Ibid., p. 147.

[12]   Ibid.

[13]   Ibid., p. 113.

[14]   Chinua Achebe, *Morning Yet on Creation Day* (London: Heinemann, 1975), p. 72.

[15]   Readings, *The University in Ruins*, p. 19.

[16]   Paulo Freire, *The Paulo Freire Reader*, ed. Ana Maria Araújo Freire, trans. Donaldo Macedo (New York: Continuum, 2000), pp. 67–8.

[17]   Raymond Williams, 'Figures and shadows', *The Highway*, February 1954, 169–72.

[18]   Freire, *The Paulo Freire Reader*, p. 71.

[19]   Fazal Rizvi, 'Williams on democracy and the governance of education', in Dennis L. Dworkin and Leslie G. Roman (eds), *Views Beyond the Border Country: Raymond Williams and Cultural Politics* (New York: Routledge, 1993), pp. 146–7.

[20]   Freire, *The Paulo Freire Reader*, p. 74.

[21]   Raymond Williams, *The Volunteers* (1978; London: Hogarth, 1985), p. 130. Cited hereafter as *V*.

[22]   Louis Althusser, *Lenin and Philosophy and Other Essays*, trans. Ben Brewster (New York: Monthly Review Press, 1971), p. 145.

[23]   See, for example, Raymond Williams, *PM*, pp. 156–7; or *T2000*, p. 151.

[24]   Tony Pinkney, *Raymond Williams* (Bridgend: Seren, 1991), p. 89.

[25]   Raymond Williams, *Communications* (Harmondsworth: Penguin, 1976), p. 149.

[26]   See also Raymond Williams, *Orwell* (Glasgow: Fontana, 1971), p. 87; and *Raymond Williams on Television* (London: Routledge, 1989), p. 104.

[27]   Kingsley Amis, 'Definitions of culture', *New Statesman*, 2 June 1961, p. 880.

[28]   Ibid.

[29]   Raymond Williams, 'Definitions of culture', *New Statesman*, 2 June 1961, p. 882.

[30]   Ibid.

[31]   Kingsley Amis, *Lucky Jim* (Harmondsworth: Penguin, 1961), pp. 28–9.

[32]   Ibid., p. 169.

[33]   Ibid., p. 213.

[34]   Raymond Williams, *The English Novel from Dickens to Lawrence* (1970; London: Hogarth, 1984), pp. 98–9. Cited hereafter as *EN*.

[35]   Kingsley Amis, *The Alteration* (London: Jonathan Cape, 1976), p. 28; p. 136.

[36]   Ibid., p. 55.

[37]   Ibid., p. 162.

[38]   Ibid., pp. 200 and 206.

[39]   Williams, 'Definitions of culture', p. 882.

[40]   Williams, *Second Generation* (London: Chatto and Windus, 1964), p. 253. Cited hereafter as *SG*.

[41]   Edward Lobb, 'The dead father: notes on literary influence', *Studies in the Humanities*, 13 (2), 1986, pp. 67–80.

[42]   J. P. Kenyon, 'The business of university novels', *Encounter*, June 1980, pp. 81–4.

[43]   John Wain, *The Contenders* (Harmondsworth: Penguin, 1962), p. 7.

[44]   Ibid., p. 263.

4: Postcolonial Britain

1   Raymond Williams, *The Country and the City* (1973; London: Hogarth, 1985), p. 35. Cited hereafter as *CC*.

2   Peter de Bolla, 'Antipictorialism in the English landscape tradition: a second look at *The Country and the City*', in Christopher Prendergast (ed.), *Cultural Materialism: On Raymond Williams* (Minneapolis: University of Minnesota Press, 1995), p. 182.

3   See Aijaz Ahmad, *In Theory: Classes, Nations, Literatures* (Oxford: Oxford Paperbacks, 1992), pp. 282–3.

4   Benedict Anderson, *Imagined Communities* (London: Verso, 1991), p. 178.

5   Anderson, *Imagined Communities*, p. 178.

6   Raymond Williams, *The Volunteers* (1978; London: Hogarth, 1985), p. 19. Cited hereafter as *V*.

7   Ngugi Wa Thiong'o, *Moving the Centre: The Struggle for Cultural Freedoms* (London: Heinemann, 1993), pp. 136–41 (p. 138).

8   Tom Nairn, *After Britain* (London: Granta, 2001), p. 43.

9   I have taken this idea from Robert Crawford's *Devolving English Literature* (Edinburgh: Edinburgh University Press, 2000).

10 Dorothy McMillan, 'Constructed out of bewilderment: stories of Scotland', in Ian A. Bell (ed.), *Peripheral Visions: Images of Nationhood in Contemporary British Fiction* (Cardiff: University of Wales Press, 1995), p. 87.

11 Malcolm Pryce, *Last Tango in Aberystwyth* (London: Bloomsbury, 2003), p. 249.

12 Tony Tanner, *The Reign of Wonder: Naivety and Reality in American Literature* (Cambridge: University of Cambridge Press, 1977), p. 127.

13 Ngugi Wa Thion'o, *De-Colonising the Mind: The Politics of Language in African Literature* (London: Heinemann, 1994), *passim*.

14 Alasdair Gray, *Poor Things* (London: Bloomsbury, 1992), pp. 155–6.

15 Raymond Williams, 'The culture of nations', in *T2000*, p. 181. Cited hereafter as 'Culture of nations'.

16 For a detailed analysis of the Welsh writing in question, see Jane Aaron and M. Wynn Thomas, 'Pulling you through changes: Welsh writing in English before, between and after two referenda', in M. Wynn Thomas (ed.), *Welsh Writing in English* (Cardiff: University of Wales Press, 2003), pp. 278–309.

17 My attention was drawn to the Scottish writers mentioned here by Ian Bell in the Introduction to his *Peripheral Visions: Images of Nationhood in Contemporary British Fiction* (Cardiff: University of Wales Press, 1995), p. 3. Clearly the list is not intended to be exhaustive.

18 This friend is Fred Inglis, who recounts the same incident in his biography, *Raymond Williams* (London: Routledge, 1995), p. 258.

19 Paul Gilroy discusses the need for the political break-up of the British state to be accompanied by a new definition of Englishness in his *After Empire* (London: Routledge, 2004), p. 105.

[20] On Swift's ironic critique of outmoded versions of Englishness, see Emma Parker, 'No man's land: masculinity and Englishness in Graham Swift's *Last Orders*', in Berthold Schoene (ed.), *Posting the Male: Masculinities in Post-War and Contemporary British Literature* (Amsterdam: Rodopi, 2000), pp. 90–103. Tom Nairn discusses the Julian Barnes novel in *After Britain*, p. 85.

[21] A. S. Byatt, *The Virgin in the Garden* (Harmondsworth: Penguin, 1981), p. 17.

[22] Ibid., pp. 315–16.

[23] Morag Shiach, 'A gendered history of cultural categories' in Christopher Prendergast (ed.), *Cultural Materialism: On Raymond Williams* (Minneapolis: University of Minnesota Press, 1995), p. 51.

[24] Francis Mulhern, '*Towards 2000*, or news from You-Know-Where' in Terry Eagleton (ed.), *Raymond Williams: Critical Perspectives* (Cambridge: Polity, 1989), pp. 87–90.

[25] Salman Rushdie, *The Satanic Verses* (London: Vintage, 1998), pp. 163–4.

[26] Ibid., p. 248.

[27] Kazuo Ishiguro, *When We Were Orphans* (London: Faber and Faber, 2000), p. 19.

[28] Ibid., p. 30.

[29] Ibid., p. 36.

[30] Barry Lewis notes that Ishiguro suffers 'through comparison with well-known Japanese writers' such as Mishima, Tanizaki and Oe. See his *Kazuo Ishiguro* (Manchester: Manchester University Press, 2000), p. 10.

[31] Ishiguro, *When We Were Orphans*, p. 137.

[32] Ibid., p. 138.

5: *Williams, Film and the Break-Up of Britain*

[1] See for example Shaun Moores, 'Television, geography and mobile privatisation', *European Journal of Communication*, 8, 3 (1993), 365–79, and Stuart Laing, 'Raymond Williams and the cultural analysis of television', *Media, Culture and Society*, 13, 2 (1991), 153–67.

[2] Raymond Williams and Michael Orrom, *Preface to Film* (London: Film Drama Ltd, 1954), p. 7. Cited hereafter as *PF*.

[3] On Williams and Brecht, see Bernard Sharrat, 'In whose voice? The drama of Raymond Williams', in Terry Eagleton (ed.), *Raymond Williams: Critical Perspectives* (Cambridge: Polity, 1989), pp. 130–49.

[4] This concept is discussed by Loren Kruger. See her 'Placing the occasion: Raymond Williams and performing culture', in Dennis L. Dworkin and Leslie G. Roman (eds), *Views Beyond the Border Country* (New York: Routledge, 1993), p. 56.

[5] Raymond Williams, *Television: Technology and Cultural Form* (1974; London: Routledge, 2003), p. 89. Cited hereafter as *T*.

[6] Jacques Lacan, *The Four Fundamental Concepts of Psychoanalysis*, trans. Alan Sheridan (Harmondsworth: Penguin, 1979), p. 75.

7 Lacan, *The Four Fundamental Concepts of Psychoanalysis*, p. 84.

8 I have taken this term from Paul Willemen. See his 'Letter to John', in John Caughie and Annette Kuhn (eds), *The Sexual Subject: A* Screen *Reader in Sexuality* (London: Routledge, 1992), p. 174.

9 Lacan, *The Four Fundamental Concepts of Psychoanalysis*, p. 83.

10 Laura Mulvey, 'Visual pleasure and narrative cinema', in Caughie and Kuhn (eds), *The Sexual Subject*, p. 26.

11 Ibid.

12 Articles in *Screen* to dispute this binary reading include Mary Ann Doane, 'Film and the masquerade: theorizing the female spectator' and Steve Neale, 'Masculinity as spectacle', both in Caughie and Kuhn (eds), *The Sexual Subject*. Doane's article, first published in *Screen* in 1982, attempts to theorize a position where the female viewer is more empowered than Mulvey's analysis suggested. Neale's article, of 1980, questions the assumption that only female bodies are used as fetish objects.

13 Lesley Stern, 'The body as evidence', in Caughie and Kuhn (eds), *The Sexual Subject*, p. 213.

14 Ibid., p. 214.

15 Ibid.

16 Raymond Williams, 'Film history', in *WCS*, p. 134. Cited hereafter as 'Film history'.

17 We could also add Australia to the list. Andrew Milner points out that the first feature-length film ever made was Australian, *The Story of the Kelly Gang*. See Andrew Milner, *Literature, Culture and Society* (London: University College Press, 1996), p. 75.

18 Smith writes about his reasons for this selection in the volume printed to accompany the screenings. See Dai Smith, 'Miss Rhymney Valley 1985', in David Lusted (ed.), *Raymond Williams: Film, TV, Culture* (London: BFI, 1989), pp. 35–41.

19 Richard Curtis (director), *Love Actually* (2003), scene 1.

20 *Love Actually*, scene 1.

21 *Love Actually*, scene 4.

22 Stern, 'The body as evidence', p. 214.

23 *Love Actually*, scene 4.

24 *Love Actually*, scene 7.

25 Benedict Anderson, *Imagined Communities* (London: Verso, 1991), p. 205.

26 I have paraphrased John Barrell here. See his 'Sir Joshua Reynolds and the Englishness of English art', in Homi K. Bhabha (ed.), *Nation and Narration* (London: Routledge, 1990), p. 163.

27 Steve Neale, 'Masculinity as spectacle', in Caughie and Kuhn (eds), *The Sexual Subject*, pp. 277–87.

28 Stephen Heath, 'Difference', in Caughie and Kuhn (eds), *The Sexual Subject*, pp. 93–4.

29 Fredric Jameson, *The Political Unconscious* (London: Routledge, 2002), p. 117.

30 Steve Blandford, *Film, Drama and the Break-Up of Britain* (Pontypridd: University of Glamorgan, 2005), p. 36.
31 Ibid., p. 39.

Post-British Williams?

1 Gayatri Spivak, *Death of a Discipline* (Chichester: University of Columbia Press, 2003).
2 Michael Gardiner, *The Cultural Roots of British Devolution* (Edinburgh: Edinburgh University Press, 2004).
3 Tom Nairn, *After Britain* (London: Granta, 2000), p. 56.
4 Gardiner, *The Cultural Roots of British Devolution*, p. 107.
5 Robert Hewison, *The Heritage Industry: Britain in a Climate of Decline* (London: Methuen, 1987).
6 Bill Ashcroft, *The Empire Writes Back: Theory and Practice in Post-Colonial Literatures* (London: Routledge, 1989), p. 196.
7 Ibid.
8 In Wales, for example, Diane Green's recent study *Emyr Humphreys: A Post-colonial Novelist* (Cardiff: University of Wales Press, 2009) argued in part that Humphreys's whole career can be seen as a process of 'writing back' to the canon of English literature.
9 Graham Swift, *Last Orders* (London: Picador, 1996), p. 192.
10 Alan Kent, *Proper Job, Charlie Curnow!* (Tiverton: Halsgrove, 2005), p. 100.

BIBLIOGRAPHY

Aaron, Jane; Betts, Sandra; Rees, Teresa and Vincentelli, Moira (eds), *Our Sisters' Land: The Changing Identity of Women in Wales* (Cardiff: University of Wales Press, 1994).

Aaron, Jane and Thomas, M. Wynn. 'Pulling you through changes: Welsh writing in English before, between and after two referenda', in M. Wynn Thomas (ed.), *Welsh Writing in English* (Cardiff: University of Wales Press, 2003).

Achebe, Chinua, *Morning Yet on Creation Day* (London: Heinemann, 1975).

Ahmad, Aijaz, *In Theory: Classes, Nations, Literatures* (Oxford: Oxford University Press, 1992).

Albert, Lauren, 'From structure to process', *Found Object*, spring 1995.

Allan, Stuart, 'Raymond Williams and the culture of televisual flow', in Jeff Wallace, Rod Jones and Sophie Nield (eds), *Raymond Williams Now: Knowledge, Limits and the Future* (London: Macmillan, 1997).

Althusser, Louis, *For Marx*, trans. Ben Brewster (New York: Pantheon, 1969).

—— *Lenin and Philosophy and Other Essays*, trans. Ben Brewster (New York: Monthly Review Press, 1971).

Althusser, Louis and Balibar, Etienne, *Reading Capital*, trans. Ben Brewster (London: New Left Books, 1970).

Amis, Kingsley, *Lucky Jim* (Harmondsworth: Penguin, 1961).

—— 'Definition of culture', *New Statesman*, 2 June 1961.

—— 'Martians bearing bursaries: review of *Communications* by Raymond Williams', *The Spectator*, 27 April 1962.

—— *The Alteration* (London: Jonathan Cape, 1976).

—— *The Old Devils* (London: Hutchinson, 1986).

Anderson, Benedict, *Imagined Communities: Reflections on the Origin and Spread of Nationalism*, 2nd edn (London: Verso, 1991).

Barrell, John, 'Sir Joshua Reynolds and the Englishness of English art', in Homi K. Bhabha (ed.), *Nation and Narration* (London: Routledge, 1990).

Bell, Ian A. (ed.), *Peripheral Visions: Images of Nationhood in Contemporary British Fiction* (Cardiff: University of Wales Press, 1995).

Benjamin, Walter, *Illuminations*, trans. Harry Zohn (New York: Fontana, 1992).

Bennett, Tony, *Formalism and Marxism* (London: Methuen, 1986).

Bevan, David (ed.), *University Fiction* (Atlanta, GA: Rodopi Press, 1990).

Bhabha, Homi K. (ed.), *Nation and Narration* (London: Routledge, 1990).

—— 'The other question: the stereotype and colonial discourse', in John Caughie and Annette Kuhn (eds), *The Sexual Subject: A* Screen *Reader in Sexuality* (London: Routledge, 1992).

—— *The Location of Culture* (London: Routledge, 1994).

Bianchi, Tony, 'Aztecs in Troedrhiwgwair: recent fictions in Wales', in Ian A. Bell (ed.), *Peripheral Visions: Images of Nationhood in Contemporary British Fiction* (Cardiff: University of Wales Press, 1995).

Bilan, R. P., 'Raymond Williams: from Leavis to Marx', *Queens Quarterly*, 87 (1980).

Binding, Wyn, 'Some observations on the novels of Raymond Williams', *The Anglo-Welsh Review*, 16, 1967.

Blandford, Steve, *Film, Drama and the Break-Up of Britain* (Pontypridd: University of Glamorgan, 2005).

Bourdieu, Pierre, *Outline of a Theory of Practice*, trans. Richard Nice (Cambridge: Cambridge University Press, 1977).

—— *Reproduction in Education, Society and Culture*, trans. Richard Nice (London: Sage, 1977).

—— *Distinction: A Social Critique of the Judgement of Taste*, trans. Richard Nice (London: Routledge, 1986).

—— *The Field of Cultural Production*, trans. Randal Johnson (Cambridge: Polity Press, 1993).

Bowen, John, 'Active-passive readers: Williams and "English"', in Tony Pinkney (ed.), *Raymond Williams: Third Generation* (Oxford: Oxford English Limited, 1989).

Bradbury, Malcolm, 'Campus fictions', in David Bevan (ed.), *University Fiction* (Atlanta: Rodopi University Press, 1990).

Brannigan, John, *New Historicism and Cultural Materialism* (London: Macmillan, 1998).

Brantlinger, Patrick, *Crusoe's Footprints: Cultural Studies in Britain and America* (London: Routledge, 1990).

—— *The Reading Lesson: The Threat of Mass Literacy in Nineteenth-Century British Fiction* (Bloomington: Indiana University Press, 1998).

—— 'Raymond Williams: culture is ordinary', *Ariel*, 22(2), 1991.

Brenkman, John, 'Raymond Williams and Marxism', in Christopher Prendergast (ed.), *Cultural Materialism: On Raymond Williams* (Minneapolis: University of Minnesota Press, 1995).

Byatt, A. S., *The Virgin in the Garden* (Harmondsworth: Penguin, 1981).

—— *Still Life* (London: Vintage, 1995).

Carey, John, *The Intellectuals and the Masses* (London: Faber and Faber, 1992).

Caughie, John and Kuhn, Annette (eds), *The Sexual Subject: A Screen Reader in Sexuality* (London: Routledge, 1992).

Chrisman, Laura and Williams, Patrick (eds), *Colonial Discourse and Post-Colonial Theory: A Reader* (Hemel Hempstead: Harvester, 1993).

Colley, Linda, *Britons: Forging the Nation 1707–1837* (London: Yale University Press, 2005).

Connery, Brian, 'Inside jokes: familiarity and contempt in academic satire', in David Bevan (ed.), *University Fiction* (Atlanta: Rodopi Press, 1990).

Connor, Steven, 'Raymond Williams's time', in Jeff Wallace, Rod Jones and Sophie Nield (eds), *Raymond Williams Now: Knowledge, Limits and the Future* (London: Macmillan, 1997).

Conran, Tony, *The Cost of Strangeness: Essays on the English Poets of Wales* (Llandysul: Gomer Press, 1982).

Crawford, Robert, *Devolving English Literature* (Edinburgh: Edinburgh University Press, 2000).

Crowley, Tony, 'Language in history: that full field', in Tony Pinkney (ed.), *Raymond Williams: Third Generation* (Oxford: Oxford English Limited, 1989).

Curtis, Tony (ed.), *Wales: The Imagined Nation. Essays in Cultural and National Identity* (Bridgend: Poetry Wales Press, 1986).

Davey, Kevin, 'Fictions of familial socialism', in Tony Pinkney (ed.), *Raymond Williams: Third Generation* (Oxford: Oxford English Limited, 1989).

Davie, Donald, 'Towards a new aestheticism', *Guardian*, 21 July 1961.

Davies, Rhys, *Honey and Bread* (London: Putnam, 1935).

—— *A Time to Laugh* (London: Heinemann, 1937).

—— *Jubilee Blues* (London: Heinemann, 1938).

De Bolla, Peter, 'Antipictorialism in the English landscape tradition: a second look at *The Country and the City*', in Christopher Prendergast (ed.), *Cultural Materialism: On Raymond Williams* (Minneapolis: University of Minnesota Press, 1995).

Di Michele, Laura, 'Autobiography and the "Structure of Feeling" in *Border Country*' in Dennis L. Dworkin and Leslie G. Roman (eds), *Views Beyond the Border Country: Raymond Williams and Cultural Politics* (New York: Routledge, 1993).

Doane, Mary Ann, 'Film and the masquerade: theorizing the female spectator', in John Caughie and Annette Kuhn (eds), *The Sexual Subject: A Screen Reader in Sexuality* (London: Routledge, 1992).

Dollimore, Jonathan, *Radical Tragedy: Religion, Ideology and Power in the Drama of Shakespeare and his Contemporaries* (Brighton: Harvester, 1984).
—— and Sinfield, Alan (eds), *Political Shakespeare: Essays in Cultural Materialism* 2nd edn (Manchester: Manchester University Press, 1994).
Donahaye, Jasmine, 'Is there anybody out there?', *New Welsh Review*, 77, autumn 2007.
Dworkin, Dennis L. and Roman, Leslie G. (eds), *Views Beyond the Border Country: Raymond Williams and Cultural Politics* (New York: Routledge, 1993).
Eagleton, Terry, *Literary Theory* (Oxford: Blackwell, 1985).
—— (ed.), *Raymond Williams: Critical Perspectives* (Cambridge: Polity Press, 1989).
Easthope, Anthony, *Literary into Cultural Studies* (London: Routledge, 1991).
Eldridge, John and Eldridge, Lizzie, *Raymond Williams: Making Connections* (London: Routledge, 1994).
Eldridge, Lizzie, 'Drama in a dramaturgical society', in Jeff Wallace, Rod Jones and Sophie Nield (eds), *Raymond Williams Now: Knowledge, Limits and the Future* (London: Macmillan, 1997).
Eliot, T. S., *The Sacred Wood: Essays in Poetry and Criticism* (London: Faber and Faber, 1997).
Enright, D. J., *Academic Year* (Oxford: Oxford Twentieth-Century Classics, 1985).
Esty, Jed, *A Shrinking Island: Modernism and National Culture in England* (Princeton: Princeton University Press, 2004).
Flew, Terry, 'Cultural materialism and cultural policy', *Social Semiotics*, 7(1), 1997.
Fox, Ralph, *The Novel and the People* (London: Lawrence and Wishart, 1979).
Freire, Paulo, *The Paulo Freire Reader*, ed. Ana Maria Araújo Freire and Donaldo Macedo (New York: Continuum, 2000).
Gallie, Menna, *The Small Mine* (Dinas Powys: Honno, 2000).
Gilroy, Paul, *After Empire: Melancholia or Convivial Culture* (London: Routledge, 2004).
Gramich, Katie, 'Both in and out of the game: Welsh writers and the British dimension' in M. Wynn Thomas (ed.), *Welsh Writing in English* (Cardiff: University of Wales Press, 2003).
Gray, Alasdair, *Poor Things* (London: Bloomsbury, 1992).
Habermas, Jürgen, *The Theory of Communicative Action*, Vol. 1: *Reason and the Rationalization of Society*, trans. Thomas McCarthy (London: Heinemann, 1984).
—— *The Theory of Communicative Action*, Vol. 2: *Lifeworld and System – The Critique of Functionalist Reason*, trans. Thomas McCarthy (Cambridge: Polity Press, 1987).

Hall, Stuart, 'Politics and letters', in Terry Eagleton (ed.), *Raymond Williams: Critical Perspectives* (Cambridge: Polity Press, 1989).

Hassan, Ihab, *The Postmodern Turn: Essays in Postmodern Theory and Culture* (Columbus: Ohio State University Press, 1987).

Heath, Stephen, 'Difference', in John Caughie and Annette Kuhn (eds), *The Sexual Subject: A* Screen *Reader in Sexuality* (London: Routledge, 1992).

—— 'Raymond Williams: a tribute', *New Welsh Review*, 1(2), 1988.

Heath, Stephen and Skirrow, Gillian, 'Interview with Raymond Williams', in Christopher Prendergast (ed.), *Cultural Materialism: On Raymond Williams* (Minneapolis: University of Minnesota Press, 1995).

Hewison, Robert, *In Anger: Culture in the Cold War, 1945–60* (London: Weidenfeld and Nicolson, 1981).

—— *Future Tense: A New Art for the 90s* (London: Methuen, 1990).

Higgins, John, 'Forgetting Williams', in Christopher Prendergast (ed.), *Cultural Materialism: On Raymond Williams* (Minneapolis: University of Minnesota Press, 1995).

—— *Raymond Williams: Literature, Marxism and Cultural Materialism* (London: Routledge, 1999).

Higgins, Michael, 'The migrant's return: a personal reflection on the importance of Raymond Williams', *Critical Quarterly*, 39(4), 1997.

Hirschkop, Ken, 'A complex populism: the political thought of Raymond Williams', in Tony Pinkney (ed.), *Raymond Williams: Third Generation* (Oxford: Oxford English Limited, 1989).

Hobsbawm, Eric, *The Invention of Tradition* (Cambridge: Cambridge University Press, 1984).

Humphreys, Emyr, *The Taliesin Tradition: A Quest for the Welsh Identity* (London: Black Raven Press, 1983).

Hutcheon, Linda, *The Politics of Postmodernism* (London: Routledge, 2002).

Inglis, Fred, *Raymond Williams* (London: Routledge, 1995).

Ishiguro, Kazuo, *When We Were Orphans* (London: Faber and Faber, 2000).

Jameson, Fredric, *The Prison House of Language: A Critical Account of Structuralism and Russian Formalism* (Princeton: Princeton University Press, 1972).

—— *Postmodernism, Or, The Cultural Logic of Late Capitalism* (London: Verso, 1991).

—— *Late Marxism* (London: Verso, 1996).

—— *The Political Unconscious* (London: Routledge Classics, 2002).

Jardine, Lisa and Swindells, Julia, 'Homage to Orwell: the dream of a common culture, and other minefields', in Terry Eagleton (ed.), *Raymond Williams: Critical Perspectives* (Cambridge: Polity Press, 1989).

Jencks, Charles, *What is Post-Modernism?* (London: Academy Editions, 1996).

Jones, Jack, *Rhondda Roundabout* (London: Hamish Hamilton, 1949; first published 1934).

—— *Black Parade* (London: Faber and Faber, 1935).

—— *Bidden to the Feast* (London: Pan Books, 1979; first published 1938).

—— *Off to Philadelphia in the Morning* (Harmondsworth: Penguin, 1951; first published 1947).

—— *River Out of Eden* (London: Corgi, 1970; first published 1951).

Jones, Lewis, *Cwmardy* (London: Lawrence and Wishart, 1978; first published 1937).

—— *We Live* (London: Lawrence and Wishart, 1980; first published 1939).

Jones, Paul, 'The technology is not the cultural form? Raymond Williams's sociological critique', *Journal of Australian and Canadian Studies*, 16(2), 1998.

Kaplan, Cora, '"What we have again to say": Williams, feminism, and the 1840s', in Christopher Prendergast (ed.), *Cultural Materialism: On Raymond Williams* (Minneapolis: University of Minnesota Press, 1995).

Kavanagh, Kevin, 'Against the new conformists: Williams, Jameson, and the challenge of postmodernity', in Jeff Wallace, Rod Jones and Sophie Nield (eds), *Raymond Williams Now: Knowledge, Limits and the Future* (London: Macmillan, 1997).

Kenyon, J. P., 'The business of university novels', *Encounter*, June 1980.

King, Noel, '"How Welsh are my eyes?" *So That You Can Live:* textual analysis and political cinema in the 80s', in David Lusted (ed.), *Raymond Williams: Film, TV, Culture* (London: British Film Institute, 1989).

Klaus, H. Gustav (ed.), *The Socialist Novel in Britain* (Brighton: Harvester, 1982).

Knight, Stephen, 'Regional crime squads: location and dislocation in the British mystery', in Ian A. Bell (ed.), *Peripheral Visions: Images of Nationhood in Contemporary British Fiction* (Cardiff: University of Wales Press, 1995).

—— 'A new enormous music: industrial fiction in Wales', in M. Wynn Thomas (ed.), *Welsh Writing in English* (Cardiff: University of Wales Press, 2003).

Kristeva, Julia, *Desire in Language: A Semiotic Approach to Literature and Art*, trans. Thomas Gora, Alice Jardine and Leon S. Roudiez (Oxford: Blackwell, 1980).

—— *Revolution in Poetic Language*, trans. Margaret Waller (New York: Columbia University Press, 1984).

Kruger, Loren, 'Placing the occasion: Raymond Williams and performing culture', in Dennis L. Dworkin and Leslie G. Roman (eds), *Views Beyond the Border Country: Raymond Williams and Cultural Politics* (New York: Routledge, 1993).

Kuhn, Annette and Caughie, John (eds), *The Sexual Subject: A Screen Reader in Sexuality* (London: Routledge, 1992).

Lacan, Jacques, *Écrits*, trans. Alan Sheridan (London: Tavistock Publications, 1977).

—— *The Four Fundamental Concepts of Pyscho-Analysis*, trans. Alan Sheridan (Harmondsworth: Penguin, 1979).

Laing, Stuart, 'Raymond Williams and the cultural analysis of television'. *Media, Culture and Society*, 13(2), 1991.

Larkin, Philip, *Jill* (London: Faber and Faber, 1985).

Lea, Daniel and Schoene, Berthold (eds), *Posting the Male: Masculinities in Post-War and Contemporary British Literature* (Amsterdam: Rodopi Press, 2000).

Leavis, F. R., *The Great Tradition* (London: Chatto and Windus, 1979).

—— *The Common Pursuit* (Harmondsworth: Peregrine, 1969).

Lewis, Barry, *Kazuo Ishiguro* (Manchester: Manchester University Press, 2000).

Llewellyn, Richard, *How Green Was My Valley?* (London: New English Library, 1976).

Lloyd, David and Thomas, Paul, '*Culture and Society* or "Culture and the State"', in Christopher Prendergast (ed.), *Cultural Materialism: On Raymond Williams* (Minneapolis: University of Minnesota Press, 1995).

Lobb, Edward, 'The dead father: notes on literary influence', *Studies in the Humanities*, 13(2), 1986.

Loomba, Ania and Okrin, Martin (eds), *Post-Colonial Shakespeares* (London: Methuen, 1998).

Lukács, Georg, *The Meaning of Contemporary Realism*, trans. John and Necke Mander (London: Merlin, 1963).

—— *The Historical Novel*, trans. Hannah and Stanley Mitchell (Harmondsworth: Penguin, 1969).

—— *Writer and Critic*, trans. Arthur Kahn (London: Merlin Press, 1978).

Lusted, David (ed.), *Raymond Williams: Film, TV, Culture* (London: British Film Institute, 1989).

Marx, Karl and Engels, Friedrich, *The Marx–Engels Reader*, ed. Robert C. Tucker (London: Norton, 1978).

Matthews, Sean, 'Change and theory in Raymond Williams's structure of feeling', *Pretexts*, 10(2), 2001.

McEachern, Claire, *The Poetics of English Nationhood, 1590–1612* (Cambridge: Cambridge University Press, 1996).

McGuigan, Jim, '"A Slow Reach Again for Control": Raymond Williams and the vicissitudes of cultural policy', in Jeff Wallace, Rod Jones and Sophie Nield (eds), *Raymond Williams Now: Knowledge, Limits and the Future* (London: Macmillan, 1997).

McIlroy, John and Westwood, Sallie (eds), *Border Country: Raymond Williams in Adult Education* (Leicester: National Institute of Adult Continuing Education, 1993).

McMillan, Dorothy, 'Constructed out of bewilderment: stories of Scotland', in Ian A. Bell (ed.), *Peripheral Visions: Images of Nationhood in Contemporary British Fiction* (Cardiff: University of Wales Press, 1995).

McMillan, Neil, 'Heroes and zeroes: monologism and masculinism in Scottish men's writing of the 1970s and beyond', in Daniel Lea and Berthold Schoene (eds), *Posting the Male: Masculinities in Post-War and Contemporary British Literature* (Amsterdam: Rodopi Press, 2000).

Middleton, Peter, 'Why Structure Feeling?', in Tony Pinkney (ed.), *Raymond Williams: Third Generation* (Oxford: Oxford English Limited, 1989).

Miklitsch, Robert, 'New from somewhere: reading Williams's readers', in Christopher Prendergast (ed.), *Cultural Materialism: On Raymond Williams* (Minneapolis: University of Minnesota Press, 1995).

Milner, Andrew, 'Cultural materialism, culturalism and postculturalism', *Theory, Culture and Society*, 11(1), 1994.

—— *Literature, Culture and Society* (London: University College Press, 1996).

Morgan, Prys, 'From a death to a view: the hunt for the Welsh past in the Romantic period', in Eric Hobsbawm (ed.), *The Invention of Tradition* (Cambridge: Cambridge University Press, 1983).

Morgan, W. John and Preston, Peter (eds), *Raymond Williams: Education, Politics, Letters* (London: MacMillan, 1993).

Moores, Shaun, 'Television, geography, and "mobile" privatisation', *European Journal of Communication*, 8(3), 1993.

Moriarty, Michael, '"The longest cultural journey": Raymond Williams and French theory', in Christopher Prendergast (ed.), *Cultural Materialism: On Raymond Williams* (Minneapolis: University of Minnesota Press, 1995).

Mulhern, Francis, 'English reading', in Homi K. Bhabha (ed.), *Nation and Narration* (London: Routledge, 1990).

—— 'Towards 2000, or news from you-know-where', in Terry Eagleton (ed.), *Raymond Williams: Critical Perspectives* (Cambridge Polity Press, 1989).

Mulvey, Laura, 'Visual pleasure and narrative cinema' in John Caughie and Annette Kuhn (eds), *The Sexual Subject: A* Screen *Reader in Sexuality* (London: Routledge, 1992).

Murphy, Terry, 'The determinations of cultural materialism', in Tony Pinkney (ed.), *Raymond Williams: Third Generation* (Oxford: Oxford English Limited, 1989).

Nairn, Tom, *The Break-Up of Britain: Crisis and Neo-Nationalism* (London: Verso, 1981).

— *After Britain: New Labour and the Return of Scotland* (London: Granta, 2001).

Neale, Steve, 'Masculinity as spectacle', in John Caughie and Annette Kuhn (eds), *The Sexual Subject: A* Screen *Reader in Sexuality* (London: Routledge, 1992).

Ngugi Wa Thiong'o, *Moving the Centre: The Struggle for Cultural Freedoms* (London: Heinemann, 1993).

—— *Decolonising the Mind: The Politics of Language in African Literature* (London: Heinemann, 1994).

Niranjana, Tejaswini, *Siting Translation: History, Post-Structuralism, and the Colonial Context* (Berkeley: University of California Press, 1992).

Norris, Christopher, '*Keywords*, ideology and critical theory', in Jeff Wallace, Rod Jones and Sophie Nield (eds), *Raymond Williams Now: Knowledge, Limits and the Future* (London: Macmillan, 1997).

O'Connor, Alan, *Raymond Williams: Writing, Culture, Politicsm* (Oxford: Blackwell, 1989).

—— 'Introduction', in Raymond Williams, *Raymond Williams on Television* (London: Routledge, 1989).

Pinkney, Tony, 'Raymond Williams and the two faces of modernism', in Terry Eagleton (ed.), *Raymond Williams: Critical Perspectives* (Cambridge: Polity Press, 1989).

— 'Introduction', in Raymond Williams, *The Politics of Modernism* (London: Verso, 1990).

— *Raymond Williams* (Bridgend: Seren, 1991).

— (ed.), *News From Nowhere. Raymond Williams: Third Generation* (Oxford: Oxford English Limited, 1989).

Plain, Gill, 'Hard nuts to crack: devolving masculinities in contemporary Scottish fiction', in Daniel Lea and Berthold Schoene (eds), *Posting the Male: Masculinities in Post-War and Contemporary British Literature* (Amsterdam: Rodopi Press, 2000).

Prendergast, Christopher (ed.), *Cultural Materialism: On Raymond Williams* (Minneapolis: University of Minnesota Press, 1995).

—— 'Raymond Williams and the Culture of Nations.' *Pretexts*, 1–2, 1995.

Pryce, Malcolm. *Aberystwyth Mon Amour* (London: Bloomsbury, 2002).

—— *Last Tango in Aberystwyth* (London: Bloomsbury, 2004).

Radhakrishnan, R., 'Cultural theory and the politics of location' in Dennis L. Dworkin and Leslie G. Roman (eds), *Views Beyond the Border Country: Raymond Williams and Cultural Politics* (New York: Routledge, 1993).

Readings, Bill, *The University in Ruins* (Cambridge: Harvard University Press, 1996).

Rees, John (ed.), *Essays on Historical Materialism* (London: Bookmarks, 1998).

Richards, I. A., *Principles of Literary Criticism* (London: Routledge, 1989).

Rizvi, Fazal, 'Williams on democracy and the governance of education', in Dennis L. Dworkin and Leslie G. Roman (eds), *Views Beyond the Border Country: Raymond Williams and Cultural Politics* (New York: Routledge, 1993).

Robbins, Derek, 'Ways of knowing cultures: Williams and Bourdieu', in Jeff Wallace, Rod Jones and Sophie Nield (eds), *Raymond Williams Now: Knowledge, Limits and the Future* (London: Macmillan, 1997).

Roberts, Gwyneth, 'The cost of community: women in Raymond Williams's fiction', in Jane Aaron, Teresa Rees, Sandra Betts and Moira Vincentelli (eds), *Our Sisters' Land: The Changing Identity of Women in Wales* (Cardiff: University of Wales Press, 1994).

Rushdie, Salman, *The Satanic Verses* (London: Vintage, 1998).

Said, Edward, 'Jane Austen and empire', in Terry Eagleton (ed.), *Raymond Williams: Critical Perspectives* (Cambridge: Polity Press, 1989).

—— *The World, The Text and The Critic* (London: Vintage, 1991).

—— *Musical Elaborations* (New York: Columbia University Press, 1991).

—— *Culture and Imperialism* (London: Vintage, 1994).

—— *Representations of the Intellectual* (New York: Vintage, 1996).

—— *Beginnings: Intention and Method* (London: Granta, 1997).

San-Juan, E., 'Raymond Williams and the idea of cultural revolution', *College Literature*, 26(2), 1999.

Schoene, Berthold and Lea, Daniel (eds), *Posting the Male: Masculinities in Post-War and Contemporary British Literature* (Amsterdam: Rodopi Press, 2000).

Sharrat, Bernard, 'In whose voice? The drama of Raymond Williams', in Terry Eagleton (ed.), *Raymond Williams: Critical Perspectives* (Cambridge: Polity Press, 1989).

Sheppard, Richard. 'From Narragonia to Elysium: some preliminary reflections on the fictional image of the academic', in David Bevan (ed.), *University Fiction* (Atlanta: Rodopi Press, 1990).

Shiach, Morag, 'A gendered history of cultural categories', in Christopher Prendergast (ed.), *Cultural Materialism: On Raymond Williams* (Minneapolis: University of Minnesota Press, 1995).

Simpson, David. 'Raymond Williams: feeling for structures, voicing "History"', in Christopher Prendergast (ed.), *Cultural Materialism: On Raymond Williams* (Minneapolis: University of Minnesota Press, 1995).

Sinfield, Alan, 'Four ways with a reactionary text', *Journal of Literature Teaching Politics*, 2, 1983 (6).

—— *Faultlines: Cultural Materialism and the Politics of Dissident Reading* (Oxford: Clarendon Press, 1992).

—— *Literature, Politics and Culture in Post-War Britain* (London: Athlone Press, 1997).

—— and Dollimore, Jonathan (eds), *Political Shakespeare: Essays in Cultural Materialism*. 2nd edn (Manchester: Manchester University Press, 1994).

Skirrow, Gillian and Heath, Stephen, 'Interview with Raymond Williams', in Christopher Prendergast (ed.), *Cultural Materialism: On Raymond Williams* (Minneapolis: University of Minnesota Press, 1995).

Smith, Dai, 'Relating to Wales', in Terry Eagleton (ed.), *Raymond Williams: Critical Perspectives* (Cambridge: Polity Press, 1989).

—— 'Miss Rhymney Valley 1985', in David Lusted (ed.), *Raymond Williams: Film, TV, Culture* (London: British Film Institute, 1989).

Soja, Edward, *Postmodern Geographies* (London: Verso, 1997).

Spivak, Gayatri, 'Three women's texts and a critique of imperialism', in Henry Louis Gates (ed.), *Race, Writing and Difference* (Chicago: University of Chicago Press, 1985).

—— *In Other Worlds: Essays in Cultural Politics* (London: Routledge, 1988).

—— *Death of a Discipline* (Chichester: University of Columbia Press, 2003).

Stern, Lesley, 'The body as evidence', in John Caughie and Annette Kuhn (eds), *The Sexual Subject: A* Screen *Reader in Sexuality* (London: Routledge, 1992).

Stevenson, Nick, 'Rethinking human nature and human needs: Raymond Williams and mass communications', in Jeff Wallace, Rod Jones and Sophie Nield (eds), *Raymond Williams Now: Knowledge, Limits and the Future* (London: Macmillan, 1997).

Surin, Kenneth, 'Raymond Williams on tragedy and revolution', in Christopher Prendergast (ed.), *Cultural Materialism: On Raymond Williams* (Minneapolis: University of Minnesota Press, 1995).

Swindells, Julia and Jardine, Lisa, 'Homage to Orwell: the dream of a common culture and other minefields', in Terry Eagleton (ed.), *Raymond Williams: Critical Perspectives* (Cambridge: Polity Press, 1989).

Tanner, Tony, *The Reign of Wonder: Naivety and Reality in American Literature* (Cambridge: Cambridge University Press, 1977).

Thomas, Gwyn, *All Things Betray Thee* (London: Lawrence and Wishart, 1986; first published 1949).

Thomas, M. Wynn (ed.), *Welsh Writing in English* (Cardiff: University of Wales Press, 2003).

Thomas, Paul and Lloyd, David, '*Culture and Society* or "Culture and the State"', in Christopher Prendergast (ed.), *Cultural Materialism: On Raymond Williams* (Minneapolis: University of Minnesota Press, 1995).

Thompson, Jon, 'Realisms and modernisms: Raymond Williams and popular fiction', in Dennis L. Dworkin and Leslie G. Roman (eds), *Views Beyond the Border Country: Raymond Williams and Cultural Politics* (New York: Routledge, 1993).

Tillyard, E. M. W., *The Elizabethan World Picture* (London: Pimlico, 1998).

—— *Shakespeare's History Plays* (Harmondsworth: Penguin, 1991).

Tredell, Nicholas, *Uncancelled Challenge: The Work of Raymond Williams* (Nottingham: Paupers' Press, 1990).

Viswanathan, Gauri, *Masks of Conquest: Literary Study and British Rule in India* (London: Faber and Faber, 1990).

—— 'Raymond Williams and British colonialism', in Christopher Prendergast (ed.), *Cultural Materialism: On Raymond Williams* (Minneapolis: University of Minnesota Press, 1995).

Volosinov, V. N./ Bakhtin, M. M., *Marxism and the Philosophy of Language,* trans. L. Matejka and I. R. Titunik (Cambridge: Harvard University Press, 1986).

Wain, John, *Hurry On Down* (Harmondsworth: Penguin, 1960).

—— *The Contenders* (Harmondsworth: Penguin, 1962).

—— *A Winter in the Hills* (London: MacMillan, 1970).

—— 'The coronation of the novel', *The Listener*, 4 June 1970.

Wallace, Jeff, 'Language, nature and the politics of materialism', in Peter Preston and W. John Morgan (eds), *Raymond Williams: Education, Politics, Letters* (London: Macmillan, 1993).

—— 'Driven to abstraction? Raymond Williams and the road', *Welsh Writing in English*, 5, 1999.

—— Wallace, Jeff, Jones, Rod and Nield, Sophie (eds), *Raymond Williams Now: Knowledge, Limits and the Future*. London: Macmillan, 1997.

Ward, J. P., *Raymond Williams* (Cardiff: University of Wales Press, 1981).

Watts, Carol, 'Reclaiming the border country: feminism and Raymond Williams', in Tony Pinkney (ed.), *Raymond Williams: Third Generation* (Oxford: Oxford English Limited, 1989).

Willemen, Paul, 'Letter to John', in John Caughie and Annette Kuhn (eds), *The Sexual Subject: A* Screen *Reader in Sexuality* (London: Routledge, 1992).

Williams, Patrick and Chrisman, Laura (eds), *Colonial Discourse and Post-Colonial Theory: A Reader* (Hemel Hempstead: Harvester, 1993).

Williams, Raymond, 'Soviet literary controversy in retrospect', *Politics and Letters*, 1, 1947.

—— 'Dali, corruption and his critics', *Politics and Letters*, 2–3, 1947.

—— *Reading and Criticism* (London: Frederick Muller, 1950).

—— *Drama from Ibsen to Eliot* (London: Chatto and Windus, 1952).

—— 'Film as a tutorial subject', in John McIlroy and Sallie Westwood (eds), *Border Country: Raymond Williams in Adult Education* (Leicester: National Institute of Adult Continuing Education, 1993; first published in *Rewley House Papers* 3, no. 2, summer 1953).

—— 'Figures and Shadows', *The Highway*, February 1954.

—— 'Science Fiction', *The Highway*, December 1956.

—— *Culture and Society*, (Harmondsworth: Penguin, 1966; first published 1958).

—— *Border Country* (Harmondsworth: Penguin, 1964; first published 1960).

—— *The Long Revolution* (London: Chatto and Windus, 1961).

—— *Communications*. 3rd edn (Harmondsworth: Penguin, 1976; first published 1962).

—— *Second Generation* (London: Chatto and Windus, 1964).

—— *Modern Tragedy* (London: Chatto and Windus, 1966).

—— 'Oxbridge, their Oxbridge', *Tribune*, June 1966, 6.

—— *A Letter from the Country* (BBC Television, April, 1966; *Stand*, 12, 1971).

—— *Public Inquiry* (BBC Television, 15 March 1967; *Stand*, 9, 1967).

—— *The May Day Manifesto* (Harmondsworth: Penguin, 1968).

—— *Drama from Ibsen to Brecht* (London: Hogarth Press, 1987; first published 1968).

—— *The English Novel From Dickens to Lawrence* (London: Hogarth, 1984; first published 1970).

—— *Orwell* (Glasgow: Fontana, 1971).

—— *The Country and the City* (London: Hogarth, 1985; first published 1973).

—— *Television: Technology and Cultural Form*, 3rd edn, ed. Ederyn Williams (London: Routledge, 2003; first published 1974).

—— 'Communication as cultural science', *Journal of Communication*, 24, 1974.

—— 'Variations on a Welsh theme', *The Listener*, 94, 1975.

—— 'The referendum choice', *New Statesman*, 89, May 1975.

—— *Marxism and Literature* (Oxford: Oxford University Press, 1977).

—— *Politics and Letters* (London: New Left Books, 1979).

—— *The Fight for Manod* (London: Chatto and Windus, 1979).

—— *The Volunteers* (London: Hogarth, 1985; first published 1978).

—— 'Pierre Bourdieu and the sociology of culture', *Media, Culture and Society*, 2, 1980.

—— *Problems in Materialism and Culture* (London: Verso, 1980).

—— *Culture* (Glasgow: Fontana, 1981).

—— 'Working-class, proletarian, socialist: problems in some Welsh novels', in H. Gustav Klaus (ed.), *The Socialist Novel in Britain* (Brighton: Harvester, 1982).

—— *Cobbett* (Oxford: Oxford Past Masters, 1983).

—— *Keywords*, 2nd edn (Glasgow: Fontana, 1983).

—— *Towards 2000* (London: Chatto and Windus, 1983).

—— *Writing in Society* (London: Verso, 1984).

—— *Loyalties* (London: Hogarth, 1989; first published 1985).

—— 'Signs of the time: review of *The Grain of the Voice* by Roland Barthes', *New Society*, 11 (October 1985).

—— *Resources of Hope*, ed. Robin Gable (London: Verso, 1988).

—— *People of the Black Mountains. 1: The Beginning* (London: Paladin, 1989).

—— *The Politics of Modernism*, ed. Tony Pinkney (London: Verso, 1989).

—— *Raymond Williams on Television*, ed. Alan O'Connor (London: Routledge, 1989).

—— *People of the Black Mountains. 2: The Eggs of the Eagle* (London: Paladin, 1990).

—— *What I Came to Say*, ed. Neil Belton, Francis Mulhern and Jenny Taylor (London: Radius, 1990).

—— *Who Speaks for Wales?*, ed. Daniel Williams (Cardiff: University of Wales Press, 2003).

Williams, Raymond and Orrom, Michael, *Preface to Film* (London: Film Drama Limited, 1954).

Wilson, Keith, 'Academic Fictions and the Place of Liberal Studies: A Leavis Inheritance' in David Bevan (ed.), *University Fiction* (Atlanta: Rodopi Press, 1990.

Wilson, Scott, *Cultural Materialism* (Oxford: Blackwell, 1995).

Wortham, Simon, *Rethinking the University: Leverage and Deconstruction* (Manchester: Manchester University Press, 1999).

Wotton, George, 'Writing from the Margins', in Ian A. Bell (ed.), *Peripheral Visions: Images of Nationhood in Contemporary British Fiction* (Cardiff: University Of Wales Press, 1995).

SUPPLEMENTARY BIBLIOGRAPHY
TO THE NEW EDITION

Aaron, Jane and Williams, Chris (eds), *Postcolonial Wales* (Cardiff: University of Wales Press, 2005).

Ashcroft, Bill, Griffiths, Gareth and Tiffin, Helen, *The Empire Writes Back: Theory and Practice in Post-Colonial Literatures* (London: Routledge, 1989).

Aughey, Arthur, *Nationalism, Devolution and the Challenge to the United Kingdom State* (London: Pluto Press, 2001).

Bohata, Kirsti, *Postcolonialism Revisited* (Cardiff: University of Wales Press, 2004).

Carey, Peter, *Jack Maggs* (London: Faber, 1997).

Davies, R. R., *The First English Empire: Power and Identity in the British Isles, 1093–1343* (Oxford: Oxford University Press, 2002).

Gardiner, Michael, *The Cultural Roots of British Devolution* (Edinburgh: Edinburgh University Press, 2004).

Green, Diane, *Emyr Humphreys: A Postcolonial Novelist* (Cardiff: University of Wales Press, 2009).

Hewison, Robert, *The Heritage Industry: Britain in a Climate of Decline* (London: Methuen, 1987).

Humphreys, Emyr, *The Taliesin Tradition* (Bridgend: Seren, 1989; first published 1983).

Kent, Alan, *Proper Job, Charlie Curnow!* (Tiverton: Halsgrove, 2005).

Kerrigan, John, *Archipelagic English: Literature, History, and Politics, 1603–1707* (Oxford: Oxford University Press, 2008).

Knight, Stephen, *A Hundred Years of Fiction: From Colony to Independence* (Cardiff: University of Wales Press, 2004).

Morris, Marc, *A Great and Terrible King: Edward I and the Forging of Britain* (London: Windmill, 2009).

Rhys, Jean, *Wide Sargasso Sea* (Harmondsworth: Penguin, 2000; first published 1966).

Smith, Dai, *Raymond Williams: A Warrior's Tale* (Cardigan: Parthian, 2008).

Spivak, Gayatri, *Death of a Discipline* (Chichester: University of Columbia Press, 2003).

Swift, Graham, *Last Orders* (London: Picador, 1996).

Walcott, Derek, *Omeros* (London: Faber, 1990).

Williams, Daniel (ed.), 'Introduction: the return of the native', in *Who Speaks for Wales?: Nation, Culture Identity* (Cardiff: University of Wales Press, 2003).

Williams, Gwyn Alf, *When Was Wales?* (Harmondsworth: Penguin, 1985).

INDEX